Enochian Vision Magick

An Introduction and Practical Guide to the Magick of Dr. John Dee and Edward Kelley

LON MILO DUQUETTE

FOREWORD BY CLAY HOLDEN

WEISERBOOKS
San Francisco, CA / Newburyport, MA

THE AUTHOR DEDICATES THIS WORK TO
THE MEMORY OF DAVID P. WILSON, THE MOST
TALENTED SCRYER I HAVE EVER MET.

*Thy Name be mighty, O God, which canst open the veil whereby
Thy All-Powerful Will may be opened unto men. Power,
Glory, and Honour be unto Thee, For Thou art the same
God of all things, and art life eternal.*

—PRAYER OF NALVAGE, APRIL 10, 1584

First published in 2008 by
Red Wheel/Weiser, LLC
With offices at:
500 Third Street, Suite 230
San Francisco, CA 94107
www.redwheelweiser.com

ISBN: 978-1-57863-382-1
Library of Congress Cataloging-in-Publication Data available upon request.

Cover and interior design by Maija Tollefson
Cover photograph © Michael Knight/iStockphoto
Interior painting, *Dr. John Dee,* oil on canvas © 2008 Zefxis The Elder

Printed in Canada
TCP
10 9 8 7 6 5 4 3 2 1

Contents

List of Illustrations

Acknowledgments

This book could not have been written without the inspiration and generous assistance of the following friends, scholars, and master Enochian magicians: David P. Wilson (S. Jason Black), Clay Holden, Christeos Pir, David R. Jones, Robin Cousins, Josh Norton (Benjamin Rowe), James Wasserman, Judith Hawkins-Tillirson, Rick Potter, I.Z. Gilford, Poke Runyon, Christopher S. Hyatt, and Robert Powell—and to the regular members of the Monday Night Magick Class of Heru-ra-ha Lodge O.T.O., I give my most heartfelt thanks; Constance DuQuette, who co-hosts this 30-year on-going class (and is my most ruthless heckler); Jonathan Taylor; Mike Strader; Jill Belanger; Olver Althoen; Carlos Casadas; and Sandy, Arto, Cobra, Vanessa, Bret, Michael, Patricia, Coleen, Mary, Evgeniy, Jane, Alan, Danny, and scores of others who throughout the years have brought Life, Love, and Liberty into our home each week.

I would also like to thank Glacier Nitz-Mercaeant, of The Enochian's Keep in Indiana, for his beautiful gifts of my gold Enochian Ring and Lamen; and the late Cecil Eugene Burns (a.k.a. Frater White Haired Bull) who built and donated the true and faithful replica of the Holy Table that now adorns our Enochian Temple space.

My thanks also go to Brothers Michael Strader, for his rendering of the Ensigns of Creation in the angelic script, and Robert Powell for his beautiful images of the Tablet of Union and the four Elemental Tablets. They are perhaps the clearest black and white renderings of these complex figures ever published.

Finally I offer my heartfelt gratitude to Clay Holden for his encouragement and support of this project. I am also deeply indebted to him for allowing me to use his magnificent recreations of the original angelic alphabet and his images of the Forty-nine Good Angels, the Holy Table, the Sigillum Dei Aemeth, and Golden Talisman.

I also draw the reader's attention to Brother Holden's original image of John Dee's Monas Hieroglyphica that adorns the cover page of each of the five books that make up *Enochian Vision Magick*. This image is in itself a most profound and historic element in the entire book for it represents a solution of a geometric puzzle going back to ancient Greek mathematical texts—that is, the production of a regular heptagon in a circle using only a compass and ruler. Please pay special attention to Clay's foreword to discover more.

Finally I offer very special thanks to Jan Johnson, Brenda Knight, and Amber Guetebier of Weiser Books who patiently (and graciously) forgave several deadline breaches.

Foreword

This is the book I would have given my eyeteeth for twenty-five years ago. It is the first work to systematically lay out the whole corpus of Dee and Kelley's magickal system, and the only one to provide a useful path through the dense and multilayered labyrinth of what has come down to us as "Enochian Magick," based almost entirely on their original manuscripts.

When Lon asked me to consider writing a foreword to his book, I think he knew that I had not been deeply involved in Enochian research for a number of years, but asked me to at least consider looking at what he was writing. It took only about fifteen minutes of reading to reignite my enthusiasm for the material which at one time was an all-consuming passion, and to realize that what he was in the process of writing would become a landmark text on the subject. Now that the book is finished, I am even more deeply honored to be able to write a few words of introduction to his remarkable work.

What particularly impresses me with Lon's book is not only the sheer volume of material covered or the clarity with which it is presented, but its immense readability and the fact that he has struck an elegant balance between classical scholarship, practical magickal instruction, and anecdotal events.

One never loses the sense that there is a real person at work here, questioning, organizing, and reporting his conclusions together with his experiences along the path. The self-important tone of many so-called "Enochian Magick" texts is entirely absent, replaced by clear and well-organized content.

When I first encountered Enochian magick, the only available published materials were Regardie's *Golden Dawn* and Crowley's *Gems from the Equinox,* fascinating but largely incomprehensible to me. Next was the first of several largely incoherent books on Enochian Magick by Gerald Shueler, which elaborated on the Golden Dawn material and added much of his own invention, most of it of dubious value. In hindsight, they seem more suitable for Dungeons and Dragons than serious magickal work (though to be fair, as David Jones once pointed out to me, D&D is probably an excellent introductory discipline for magickal ritual work).

Then came Geoffrey James's *The Enochian Evocation of John Dee*, a completely different matter altogether. Still more of a synopsis of a system than a workable guidebook (based largely on Sloane MS. 3191, Dee's precis of the materials received between 1582 and 1587), it gathered together the bulk of Dee and Kelley's work, and gave a sense of where it all came from. Still incredibly useful many years later, when coupled with an examination of the original scrying sessions that produced the material, it still does not serve as a proper guidebook through the system. The heart is there, but the how and why are largely absent.

When looking at what the Golden Dawn and Crowley and their successors put together as "Enochian Magick," it seems clear that they were missing huge chunks of this "how and why," along with many critical pieces to understanding what they were dealing with, and their attempts to graft basically everything else in their magickal system onto it produce a cumbersome thing that Dee and Kelley would not recognize as what they pulled through.

I have likened their resulting patchwork as similar to what happens when one attempts to open a Word document or a highly formatted database file in a text editor: one can read and even extract a good bit of raw data, but the formatting and links to other programs are entirely unreadable and bear little resemblance to the original document.

Without an understanding of Dee and Kelley's early material, mostly presented in Sloane MS. 3188, what comes later on, while workable on its own, will be largely incomprehensible. And while in many ways it can be convincingly argued that the later system, centered on the four Elemental Tablets, and the Tablet of Union are independent of the earlier material, Dee's diaries demonstrate that he went back and added marginal notes to even the earliest diaries to refer to events and communications that transpire several years later, as well as referencing the earlier communications in the later entries.

Fortunately for the reader, Lon's book gives full treatment, background, and application of both the early and the later materials, and provides in spades both the how and why that are missing from so many other books that purport to be guides to the system.

For me, not until David Jones's Center for Enochian Studies, based out of Thelema Lodge OTO in Oakland, began their annotated transcriptions of the first of Dee's spirit diaries, did I get a real sense for the background story of Enochian magick. All of a sudden, it was like reading a Philip K. Dick novel, with the tables and diagrams coming to life, populated by spirits, angels, and demons of all sorts, each with his or her own personality. And notably, John Dee and Edward Kelley for the first time became real people, questioning and struggling to understand and document what was being communicated to them.

I was finally able to borrow microfilms of the spirit diaries from the always truly generous and helpful Bill Heidrick, and I spent countless days printing them out on microfilm reader printers. When I finally had a set of Sloane MS. 3188 (*Quinti Libri Mysteriorum*) printed out and bound in front of me, the real magick began to take place for me. It was as if one discovered that Jules Verne's Captain Nemo was a real person, and could read his own words and step back 400-plus years into the past, to share his thoughts and experiences. To this day, it is the closest thing to real time travel I have ever felt.

Dee's handwriting presented some difficulty at first, as did his use of many antiquated terms, abbreviations, and frequent recourse to Latin. To my aid came Elias Ashmole's "fair-copy" of the diaries (Sloane MS. 3677), transcribed many decades later, in a beautiful hand which was much easier to read than Dee's. It also has the benefit of being more complete in some cases than Dee's original, as the manuscript was in considerably better shape in the 1600s than it is today, and Ashmole made notes indicating where materials were missing.

Given the difficulty in reading the original texts, it occurred to me to begin transcribing the diaries into electronic texts, laid out exactly as Dee had in the original manuscripts, and this was the birth of the John Dee Publication Project. The idea, which I tested in reading circles at Thelema Lodge, was that once one could get past the difficulties of Dee's sixteenth-century italic and secretarial handwriting, the actual English was not so different from that of Shakespeare, and that the modern reader would more easily be able to approach the work. Producing small batches of texts, with my transcription facing pages of the actual manuscript, it proved a fairly simple matter for people to actually read and understand the material.

While the world has changed immensely over the past two decades, and it is now possible to download electronic copies of all of Dee and Kelley's spirit diaries off the Net, it is still valuable to have the reconstructed electronic texts. And while I have never completed the transcriptions of the *Quinti Libri Mysteriorum*, it both taught me many valuable computer skills that ultimately changed my life and demonstrated that the text could be reproduced as written in an easily readable form. I am pleased that it still provides many readers with a place to begin in reading the spirit diaries.

It was suggested to me early on by David Jones that rather than attempting to comprehend the whole system, I should concentrate on a particular section and work to understand the mechanism of that piece of the system. In my case, that piece of the puzzle was the Sigillum Dei Aemeth.

While Lon in this book suggests that, rather than trying to reproduce Dee and Kelley's work, one ought to use the system they transmitted, I found it of inestimable value to read through the text of *Mysteriorum Liber Secundus*, where the layout and working of the Sigillum is systematically laid out, and fill in each of the squares in a blank Sigillum as I went through it. By so doing, this impressive talisman became a truly living being for me, and it was possible also to rectify certain errors which exist in Dee's diagram of the Sigillum.

Case in point: at the bottom of the Sigillum Dei Aemeth, both in Dee's original illustration at the end of *Mysteriorum Liber Secundus* and in virtually every version published since, one finds the character "y" with a "14" under it. The text however clearly gives this number as "15." Replacing this number, and applying the method of backwards and forwards rotation around the outer circle, one utilizes the remaining unused squares, and two additional names are produced, neither of which is mentioned in the text. This exercise is left to the reader.

It further demonstrated that Dr. Dee, in fact, *lies* in certain places in the record, indicating that there is material hidden even there that he did not want to be visible to an unthinking reader.

One of my favorite quotes from the beginning of *Mysteriorum Liber Secundus* is Dee's interchange with the archangel Michael:

Mi. [...] Thow shalt sweare by the Living God, the strength of his Mercy, and his Medicinall vertue, powred into man's soule never to disclose these Mysteries

D. Yf no man, by no means, shall perceyve any thing hereof, by me, I wold think that I shold not do well.

Mi. Nothing is cut from the churche of God. We in his Saincts are blessed for ever.

We separate the, from fyled and wycked persons: We move the to God.

D. I vow, as you require: God be my help, and Gwyde, now and ever, amen.

MIC. This is a Mystery, skarse worthy for us, ourselves, to know, muche lesse to Reveale. Art thow, then, so Contented?

D. I am: God be my strength.

Keeping this in mind, one may begin to understand why Dee occasionally misdirects the reader in his diaries. As with Aleister Crowley's works several hundred years later, if one is paying attention to what one is reading, the erroneous data should just about jump out from the page, and provide a pointer to the actual information.

Investigating such parts of the magickal furniture can provide further unknown or undocumented information, such as the following:

If one adds and subtracts the numbers at the top and bottom of the letters around the outer ring of the Sigillum (having corrected the "y/15"), one arrives at a total number of 440. Adding the "1" in the concentric circles that is given at the end of the instructions on the outer ring (accompanied by the statement "Omnia unum est"), the total comes to 441, the gematric value of the Hebrew "Aemeth," or Truth. Without the correction of the "y/15" square, the total remains 440, the gematric value for "Meth," or Dead. Thus, the Sigillum may be considered as a Golem, and the published version an inactive and unworkable "dead" talisman.

There is also an additional Table to be generated from the instructions given for the characters around the outer ring, as they are described in the text:

D. Note: All the Cumpanies of these 40, stode, five togither, and five togither, and so in eight Cumpanyes; each, of five

Thus one can lay out the characters in eight rows of five, and in so doing, can produce symmetrical character sigils similar to the ones found on the Elemental Tablets for the angels of the outer ring.

In attempting to find a simple way to generate a regular heptagram in a circle for the purposes of reproducing the Sigillum on paper, I further discovered an interesting connection between the spirit diaries and Dee's earlier Monas Hieroglyphica.

While one cannot in fact produce a regular heptagon in a circle using only a compass and ruler (a geometric puzzle going back to ancient Greek mathematical texts), one can approximate it. There are several classical solutions, each of them rather close, but also involving complex methodology. Laying out the Monas Hieroglyphica in its 4 x 9 grid, as given in Dee's book, using a compass from the mid-point to trace a circle, and rotating the Monas so its "horns" touch on the circle from the top of the grid, one finishes with a *very* close approximation of a heptagon, in fact, as close or closer than any known classical solution.

Finally, it is perhaps fitting to suggest that one can read and consider Dee and Kelley's spirit diaries in a number of different ways, some of them mutually exclusive, but all of them perhaps of interest and value.

First, they can be considered as authentic records of spirit communication. Over the years I have worked closely with practicing Enochian magicians, including at least one incredibly talented scryer, who can both see and hear through the crystal ball, a very rare combination. Most scryers can do one or the other, but not both. In Edward Kelley, Dee found a rare man, however difficult he may have been to work with, and clearly knew it. Dee could only rarely see or hear anything himself, but with his amazing mathematical and classically trained mind, was perhaps the only man in the world capable of understanding and organizing the instructions that were presented to him. He was also skeptic enough to question and reject transmitted material that appeared to come from lying spirits, as Kelley periodically pulled through "illuding divils" that specialized in disinformation. The internal consistency of the bulk of the spirit diaries, as well as the coherent interrelationship of its many parts, speaks convincingly to its being a genuine record of actual events over a period of years.

Second, one can consider the material as an exercise in cryptographic method, intended as a means of communicating secret information back from the continent to Dee's colleagues and superiors in Elizabeth's court. Clearly, as one reads through *Liber Mysteriorum Quartus*, and to a certain extent Secundus, one can see similarities to the methodology of Trithemius's *Steganographia,* a work with which Dee was quite familiar, and which has now been demonstrated to be entirely a cryptographic treatise.

The arrays of "dignified" and "undignified" spirits can be seen as referring to encryption methods involving "nulls," and Dee and Kelley's discussion of "transposition of letters" in *Quinti Libri Mysteriorum* Appendix is at the very least suggestive again of the same. Then there are the tables in *Liber Loagaeth,* at the end of which (Sloane MS. 3189) Dee has appended eight tables from "Aldaraia Sive Soyga," the mathematical methods of which have been demonstrated by Jim Reeds. They appear even on the surface to be cryptographic tables, though no one to date has made a systematic study of their content, nor provided any translation or decryption or methodology. They remain the most hermetically sealed of all Dee and Kelley's documents.

In a similar way, one may usefully compare this "cryptography" theme with the Kabbalistic method of transposition of letters along with numeric values as a strictly spiritual exercise (e.g., the "Sepher Yetzirah"), and arrive at the conclusion that the Enochian system might be considered "sacred cryptography" in the same sense as the classical Kabbalistic method, unrelated to the mundane world of secret transmission of political secrets.

Lastly, and perhaps most amusingly, I have entertained the idea that Dee was the author of the first science fiction novel over a period of years, and indeed the first to give thought to the idea of "cyberspace," an interdimensional world where communication takes place through a portal, giving thought to the twentieth-century works of H. P. Lovecraft, Philip K. Dick, and William O. Gibson.

In this view, while Edward Kelley is still a historic personage (he appears in Dee's private diaries as well as being clearly documented both in England and in Prague, usually in conjunction purely as an alchemist), the "Edward Talbot" and "Edward Kelley" presented in the Spirit Diaries, his frequent turns from devout scryer to blaspheming conjurer and back again, along with all the mischievous and light-hearted spirits who are trotted on and off the stage, can be seen as an immense work of fiction. Whether written purely for Dee's amusement or as a secret means of documenting a different sort of spiritual transmission remains hidden today.

Of course, as anyone who has spent any time actually working with the system(s) presented in the Spirit Diaries can attest, when you put them to work *as if* true, stuff happens. Once invoked (or evoked), the spirits do in fact seem to appear and go to work, whether one believes in them or not.

Which leads to the one piece of advice I would give to anyone starting out in working Enochian Magick: Be very clear of what you ask for, as you are certain to get as much of it as you can handle, and once started, it is much more difficult to get it to stop.

In closing, I would like to quote a passage from W. Wynn Westcott's translation of the "Chaldean Oracles" (quoting Proclus), which I have always found incredibly useful to keep in mind when working Enochian Magick, or indeed, any ritual work:

> As the Oracle therefore saith: God is never so turned away from man, and never so much sendeth him new paths, as when he maketh ascent to divine speculations or works in a confused or disordered manner, and as it adds, with unhallowed lips, or unwashed feet. For of those who are thus negligent, the progress is imperfect, the impulses are vain, and the paths are dark.

Lon's wonderful book provides the reader—for the first time—with a clearly lit and well-ordered guide through the maze of Dee and Kelley's Enochian system. The hallowed lips and well-washed feet are up to the reader.

Keep an open mind, a pure heart, and a clean temple, and you will surely hear their angels and spirits speaking to you.

Clay Holden
The John Dee Publication Project
www.john-dee.org

A Note Regarding Original Source Material and Footnote References

The original Enochian magick material is a labyrinth of manuscripts. In preparing this book, I was fortunate to have at my disposal electronic files containing the photographic images of original material currently housed at the British Library, London. The manuscripts are numbered and designated by the name of past owners. The ones I used for the present work are designated: Sloane 3188, 3189, 3191; and Cotton Appendix XLVI parts I and II.

Within these numbered manuscripts are various "books," or "Libers" bearing separate titles. Some of these Libers were copied by Kelley or others and reproduced in subsequent manuscripts (sometimes renamed) and have found their way to London's British Library and the Bodleian and Ashmolean libraries at Oxford University. For my purposes the material from the British Library's Sloane 3188, 3189, 3191; and Cotton Appendix XLVI parts I and II proved to be quite sufficient. Digital scans of the Enochian manuscripts can be accessed electronically at: *http://www.themagickalreview.org/enochian/mss/*.

Enochian scholar Geoffrey James prepared a concise summary breakdown of Dee and Kelley manuscripts for the bibliography of his excellent book, *Enochian Magick of Dr. John Dee*.[1] He has graciously allowed me to reproduce his entries for the material that relates directly or indirectly to *Enochian Vision Magick*. The reader who wishes to explore the source material in greater detail (or who simply wishes to track the book's footnotes and references) should find this list very helpful.

SLOANE MS. 3188.

This manuscript contains Dee's earliest scrying sessions. It contains six individual 'books', which are:—

Mysteriorum Liber Primus covering December 22, 1581 to March 15, 1582, and containing a ceremony with Saul (Dee's first scryer) and the first ceremonies with Edward Talbot, in which the table and Solomon's ring are described.

Mysteriorum Liber Secondus covering March 6, 1582 to March 21, 1582, and containing the first elements of the Heptarchic system, the spirits of the Sigil of Æmeth, and the first suggestion that an antediluvian language would be delivered to Dee. This title page is missing, but can be inferred from textual references in SLOANE MS. 3677.

Mysteriorum Liber Tertius covering April 28, 1582 to May 4, 1582, and containing numerous sigils related but apparently not essential to the Heptarchic system, as well as the names of the 49 good angels.

Quartus Liber Liber Mysteriorum covering November 15, 1583 to November 21, 1583, and containing the remainder of the Heptarchic system; this book is the first to record the name of Edward Kelly[2] as the scryer.

Liber Mysteriorum Quintus covering March 23, 1583 to April 18, 1583, and containing the tables later transcribed by Kelly into SLOANE MS. 3189.

Quinti Libri Mysteriorum Appendix covering April 20, 1583 to May 23, 1583, and containing the famous *Enochian* letters, as well as information concerning the construction of the Great Table.

SLOANE MS. 3189.

Liber Mysteriorum Sextus and Sanctus or *The Book of Enoch revealed to John Dee by the Angels* which contains 49 double-sided tables of (apparently) random letters. It is in Edward Kelly's handwriting.

SLOANE MS. 3191.

This manuscript is the only book of ceremonial magic extant in Dee's handwriting. It consists of three separate 'books,' each dealing with a different aspect of Dee's angelic magickal system. The books are:—

49 Claves Angelicæ Anno 1584 Cracoviæ (Liber 18) which contains Dee's transcription of the Angelical Keys (often called the Enochian Keys or Enochian Calls.)

Liber Scientiæ Auxillii et Victoriæ Terrestris which contains a complex system of magic based upon the Great Table (often called The Table of Watchtowers). It is entirely in Latin, and related to the Call of the Thirty Aires.

De Heptarchia Mystica which describes a complete system of planetary magic, along with excerpts from the various scrying sessions.

COTTON APPENDIX XLVI, PARTS 1 & 2.

This manuscript is occasionally referred to as Royal Appendix XLVI, or SLOANE MS. 5007. It contains thirteen 'books,' which are:—

Liber Mysteriorum (et Sancti) parallelus Novalisque covering May 28, 1583 to July 4, 1583, and containing the tail end of the Heptarchic system and the only recorded incident of Kelly speaking Greek.

Liber Pergrinatonis Prime Videlicet A Mortlaco Angeliæ Ad Craconiam Poloniæ covering September 21, 1583 to March 13, 1584, and containing the journey from Mortlake to Cracow, Poland and various political speculations.

Mensis Mysticus Saobaticus Pars primus ejusdem covering April 10, 1584 to April 30, 1584, and containing the dictations of the first calls (backwards).

Libri Mystici Apertorii Cravoviensis Sabbatici covering May 7, 1584 to May 22, 1584, and containing the remainder of the calls (except for the call of the Thirty aires, in the Angelical tongue, and the spirits of the Thirty aires.

Libri Septimi Cracoviensis Mystici Sabbatici covering May 23, 1584 to July 12, 1584, and containing the geographic locations of the spirits of the Thirty aires, the *Great Table or Watchtowers,* and the first third of the *Call of the Thirty Aires,* as well as the names of the Thirty aires.

Libri Cracoviensis Mysticus Apertorius Præterea Præmium Madimianum covering July 12, 1584 to August 15, 1584, and containing the remainder of the *Call of the Thirty Aires,* as well as the names of the Thirty aires.

Mysteriorum Pragensium Liber Primus Cæsarusque covering August 15, 1584 to October 8, 1584, and containing an attempt to convince the Holy Roman Emperor of the canonical nature of the visions.

Mysteriorum Pragensium Confirmatio covering December 20, 1584 to March 20, 1585, and containing mostly political speculation.

Mysteriorum Cracoveinsium Stephanicorum Mysteria Stephanica covering April 12, 1585 to June 6, 1585, and containing an alchemical formula and a letter from Dee's wife to the spirits.

Unica Action, quæ Pucciana vocetor covering August 6, 1585 to September 6, 1585, and containing religious visions obviously meant to impress the Papal Nuncio who was then attending the ceremonies.

Liber Resurrectionis Pragæ, Pactum sev Fædus Sabbatismi covering fragments from April 30, 1586 to January 21, 1587, and containing further ceremonies with the Papal Nuncio.

Actio Tertia Trebonæ Generalis covering April 4, 1587 to May 23, 1587, and containing a complex series of corrections to the *Watchtowers* and the infamous wife-swapping episode.

Jesus, Omnipoten sempiterne & une Deus covering March 20, 1607 to September 7, 1607 and containing the last records of Dee's magickal experiment.

———

Some of this material has been published in more modern times in books that are still readily available. Foremost of these are *A True & Faithful Relation of What Passed for Many Yeers Between Dr. John Dee and Some Spirits,*[3] and *John Dee's Five Books of Mystery.*[4]

To make things a bit easier for the reader to access more readily available source material, I will, wherever possible, try to make references with the text and in notes to passages in these modern works.

Prologue to the Prologue

Something Secret

Vyasa: There's something secret about a beginning. I don't know how to start.

Ganesha: As you claim to be the author of the poem, how about beginning with yourself?

—The Mahabharata[5]

There is indeed something secret about a beginning, secret and invisible like the soul of infinite potential that broods in the heart of every living seed. My tongue is tied. I stare at the blank screen of my monitor. I don't know how to start. For the writer it is the most difficult moment—a million things to say, but where to begin? My eyes search the walls and ceiling of my little office and fall upon the mask of the Hindu god Ganesha. His bright, pleasant face reminds me of the opening scene of Jean-Claude Carrière's play, *The Mahabharata,*[6] where Vyasa, the author of the epic poem is faced with his own writer's block as he strives to begin his monumental story. Unable to read or write himself, Vyasa is blessed by the arrival of Ganesha, the beloved elephant-headed god, who offers to serve as Vyasa's scribe and take down his story from dictation. He also gives Vyasa some advice about how to start.

"How about beginning with yourself?"

And so, in pale imitation of the poet Vyasa, I will heed the wise counsel of my elephant-headed lord, the remover of obstacles. I shall begin this work of magick by telling you something about myself. Don't worry, I won't tell you much. Just enough to get us started.

I am a man. I am what they call in the East a householder—that is, I am married and have for my entire adult life endeavored with varying degrees of success to provide a loving and stable environment for my family. I am also an exceedingly lucky man, for in truth, throughout the years it has been my sainted wife and beloved son who have provided *me* with a loving and stable environment.

Fate (coupled with a conspicuous lack of ambition) has conspired to make our lifestyle one of genteel poverty (well, not always so genteel). We've never owned a house, a new car, or a credit card. On the other hand, we've always lived in moderately affluent communities and safe neighborhoods. We've always owned old cars that usually get us where we're going. Our bills consist primarily of the rent, the utilities, health insurance, and our groceries. We have no debts.

Some people say that's a miracle. I agree. Miracles are part of my job, for I am a magician. I'm not the type of magician who creates illusions to entertain audiences, but the type of who seeks to *dispel* the myriad illusions that hinder my own spiritual growth and enlightenment.

Aleister Crowley (1875–1947), the great twentieth-century magician, defined magick as the "science and art of causing change to occur in conformity with Will."[7] This is obviously a very broad definition of the term. In my opinion, however, it is the only one that is entirely accurate. You are, of course, free to interpret this definition any way you wish. Personally, I've come to the realization that the only real changes I can effect with magick are changes in myself. By changing myself, I change the world around me, hopefully for the better.

Naturally, I haven't always considered myself a magician, but for as long as I can remember I've been a seeker. Please don't project any undue piety upon this statement. I'm as wicked as anyone who seldom breaks any criminal or civil statutes can be. But even as I wallow in my dark and lazy wickedness, I find myself again and again stumbling inadvertently toward the Light.

As a magician I have also been extraordinarily lucky. Early in my career I was befriended (and many times guided) by some very wonderful, and in their own ways masterful, magicians to whom I owe an immeasurable debt: Israel Regardie, Phyllis Seckler, Helen Parsons Smith, and Grady L. McMurtry. I have also collaborated with others who have enlarged and enriched my magickal life. Foremost among these is my wife, Constance, who is the greatest natural magician I have ever known. There are many others as well: Karen James, whose profound sense of beauty and passion for the art of dramatic ritual keeps alive the mysteries of Eleusis; Douglas James, William Breeze, James Wasserman, Steven Abbott, LeRoy Lauer, David P. Wilson, Rick Potter, Dewey Warth, Nathan Sanders, Christopher S. Hyatt, Poke Runyon, Michael Strader, Sandra Brautigam, and Jonathan Taylor; and, for the last twenty-eight years, the assembled magi of my weekly magick class.

On my fortieth birthday I began to write professionally. In this vocation I have also been exceedingly fortunate. Readers who are familiar with the body of my work know that I am occasionally taken to task by knowledgeable critics who accuse me of writing for beginners and who chide me for diluting or oversimplifying complex and esoteric concepts. Against these charges I can say very little in my defense except to confess that I am indeed a simple man who, by conventional academic standards, is a lazy and undisciplined student. I have to learn anecdotally. I need to put things in a personal context. I need to appreciate and understand the general before I can be thrilled and inspired by the specifics.

Yes, I'm proud to write for beginning students of magick. But first and foremost I write to explain things to myself. I write to find out what I know. I write the books that I wish I could have studied during the first five years of my magickal studies—books that might have saved me years of frustration, blind alleys, and wheel-spinning. I also like to think that I write for more advanced students who may find themselves entangled in the elegance of magickal minutiae or else have become so entranced and self-impressed with their encyclopedic memories that they've lost sight of why they are doing magick in the first place.

I write about things with which I'm familiar and have had hands-on experience. One of those things is Enochian magick. I began my study of this most curious of quaint and curious subjects in late 1979 and began practicing it in earnest in autumn of 1980. Back then there was very little published information available. The only person I actually knew who had any significant hands-on experience with the system was Dr. Francis (Israel) Regardie,[8] who cautioned me in no uncertain terms that I probably shouldn't be dabbling in such things.

Nevertheless, armed with my copy of Aleister Crowley's *Gems from the Equinox*[9] and the two-volume set of Regardie's *The Golden*

Dawn,[10] I naïvely plunged into what I thought was the deep end of the Enochian magick swimming pool. A year or so later a friend would present me with a huge stack of photocopied[11] documents from the British Museum. This material represented several significant portions of surviving diaries and magickal notebooks of Elizabethan magus Dr. John Dee (1527–1608 or 1609) and his clairvoyant partner Edward Kelley[12] (1555–1595).

Only then did I begin to realize how dreadfully deep the waters of Enochiana really are. By then, however, it was too late for me to get out of the pool. What little of the system I had mastered had already yielded breathtaking results. My life was becoming very magickal.

Those primitive photocopies eventually yellowed, then browned, then charcoal-blackened into illegibility, but my interest didn't fade. Neither did the interest of others in the magickal community. Today clear copies of the museum manuscripts are readily available to the serious student, and there are no less than thirty books currently in print with the word "Enochian" in the title. I confess a few of those are my doing. In 1991 Dr. Christopher S. Hyatt and I wrote a commentary on Aleister Crowley's little Enochian masterpiece, *Liber Chanokh*.[13] A year latter Herman Slater of Magickal Childe Publishing asked me to pen the introduction to the new facsimile edition of the 1659 *A True & Faithful Relation of What Passed for Many Yeers Between John Dee . . . and Some Spirits*. In 1995, my wife, Constance, and I created a deck of tarot cards[14] that incorporates a large number of images relating to the Enochian Elemental Tablets. In the book that accompanies the cards,[15] I elucidate on how they can be used for practical Enochian magick operations.

But writing (and reading) about Enochian magick is one thing; actually using it in a practical way to advance one's own spiritual evolution is another. With few exceptions, the thirty odd books mentioned above are very long on theory and history and very short on straightforward suggestions on how to actually sit down and perform Enochian magick, or reasons why one would want to do such a thing in the first place. I hope to remedy this, at least in small measure, by writing this book. I feel qualified to do this not because I have any illusions that I am the world's most knowledgeable scholar on the subject (I assure you I am not). I offer simply the credentials of nearly thirty years of applied experience with several aspects of Enochian magick. I have come to some very fundamental conclusions that I believe might be of significant and practical value to both the speculative student and the operative practitioner of this elegant and complex magickal system.

Before I plunge us directly into those waters, however, I need to briefly address the question of why a relatively sane and rational twenty-first-century adult would wish to seriously embark upon the path of magick. I will do this with a device that will most assuredly irritate my publisher—a second prologue. And once again, to please my Lord Ganesha,[16] I will begin by talking about myself.

Prologue

Why Magick?

Magick is as mysterious as mathematics, as empirical as poetry, as uncertain as golf, and as dependent on the personal equations as Love.

—ALEISTER CROWLEY[17]

I'm a magician. I practice the art of ceremonial magick. I adore and *invoke* the essence of highest Deity and hold congress with divine angels. I also *evoke* and command spirits and demons.[18] Ceremonial magick is the path I have chosen to give expression to the spiritual yearnings I believe are inherent in every human being. It is my Tao, my Way, my religion, my philosophy, my psychology. But ceremonial magick isn't my life. I already have a life, thank you. But I use magick to help make my life magick.

I have closets and chests full of bizarre and colorful robes and crowns and wands and daggers and chalices and swords and lances and thuribles and banners and veils and rings and incense and candles and oils and tablets and talismans and mirrors and crystals. I have books—strange books (some very old and rare), books that would scare the daylights out of most of my neighbors. I use these magickal tools; I study these books in order to perform the rites of ceremonial magick. These things are not my life. But I use them to make my life magick.

On the surface one might think it reasonable and fair to ask, "Why are you a magician, Lon? Why do you believe in this stuff? Why do you do these crazy things?"

It might surprise you to know I don't have a proper answer to these questions. It is impossible for me to adequately explain or justify why

I celebrate my spiritual life through the vehicle of magick, for the same reasons it is impossible for any artist to properly explain why he or she has taken up the brush or the chisel or the violin or ballet slippers. If reasonableness were the sole criterion for the existence of art, there would be no music, no dance, no magick.

Make no mistake about it, magick is an art form, and every true magician is an artist. Just like the musician and dancer, the magician must practice, create, and perform. Just like the painter or sculptor, he or she must be armed with proper tools, skills, knowledge, and, most of all, inspiration. But what about people who've never learned to play a musical instrument, never learned to dance or paint or sculpt, yet who find themselves spiritually touched by listening to music, watching ballet, and visiting galleries? Are they not artists too?

In a very important way, I believe they are. As quantum physicists tell us, both the observer and that which is observed are changed by the act of observation itself. By appreciating the artist's handiwork, we are fundamentally affecting the reality and life of that creation. More importantly, when we expose ourselves to the artist's creation, we enjoy the passive luxury of allowing our consciousness to be altered, elevated, and enriched in unique and personal ways the artist might have never imagined.

The art of ceremonial magick, however, is a little different. There is no painted canvas to display, no audience to applaud. Regardless of how altruistic the magician's motives may be, magick is spiritual *performance art* that must ultimately be executed and appreciated by the magician alone. He or she is at once the teacher, the student, the medium, the conductor, the performer, the venue, the audience, and the critic. The magician touches the broader audience of humanity only by affecting changes in the *magician*, and success can be weighed only in the silent Holy of Holies of his or her own soul.

So, here and now and for the duration of this book, I shall lay aside the question of "why magick?" If my magickal efforts seem to propel me closer to self-realization, if my work brings me a measure of health or happiness or wisdom or a sense of fulfillment, good. But none of these things, nor indeed any *thing*, can be the goal of my art. Instead of asking, "why magick?" I suggest all who would fancy themselves magicians seek answers to the following questions, questions I struggle to answer every day of my life:

Am I really an artist? Am I drawn to this strange and irrational art form because of my mad passion to enrich my art and fulfill my creative life purpose? Or am I doing all this to *avoid* fulfilling my destiny? Am I running away from myself? When I don my magickal robes and enter the temple, do I do so as a radiant artist-magician, armed and ready to storm the gates of heaven and hell to do battle for the triumph of my soul, poised to take the next step in my spiritual evolution? Or am I merely a foolish man in an exotic costume, a mystic poseur in serious need of a life?

BOOK I

Don't Try to Duplicate the Magick Dee and Kelley Did to Receive the System—Just Use the System They Received!

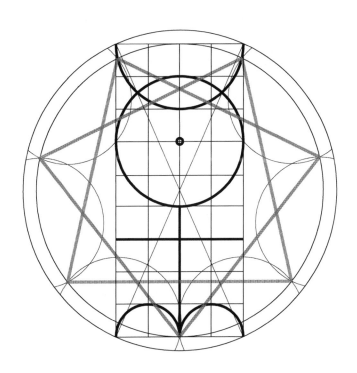

CHAPTER ONE

In the Middle of the Night

Teach me (O creator of all things) to have correct knowledge and understanding, for your wisdom is all that I desire. Speak your word in my ear (O creator of all things) and set your wisdom in my heart.

—JOHN DEE[19]

It's 3:43 a.m. I've been up for about a half an hour bathing, dressing, and preparing myself to operate. Constance is asleep in the bedroom, and I'm trying to be as quiet as I can. In just a few minutes I will turn off the computer here in my office, take up my almond wand, and go into the darkened living room. There I will quietly perform a Lesser Banishing Ritual of the Pentagram, light two tapered candles, and sit down before the Holy Table.

Once comfortably seated I will close my eyes and pray:

Teach me (O creator of all things) to have correct knowledge and understanding, for your wisdom is all that I desire. Speak your word in my ear (O creator of all things) and set your wisdom in my heart. Amen.

I will then open my eyes, take the golden Ring, and quietly recite the Prayer of the Ring:

Behold the Ring. Lo, this it is. This is it, wherewith all miracles, and divine works and wonders were wrought by Solomon: this is it, which the Archangel Michael has revealed to me. This is it, which Philosophy dreameth of. This is it, which the Angels scarce know. This is it, and blessed be his name: yea, his Name be blessed forever. Without this I shall do nothing. Blessed be his name, that encompasses all things: Wonders are in him, and his name is WONDERFUL: PELE. His Name works wonders from generation to generation. Amen.

I will put on the Ring and then take up the golden Lamen that is attached to a black ribbon. Before putting it around my neck I will again pray:

Behold the Lamen. As the Holy Table conciliates Heaven and Earth, let this Lamen which I place over my heart conciliate me to the Holy Table. Amen.

I will then take up my almond wand, reach across the Holy Table, tap the upper right-hand corner, and begin to chant. As I do so, I will move the tip of the wand from right to left along the far edge of the table and chant:

Pa Med Fam Med Drux Fam Fam Ur Ged Graph Drux Med Graph Graph Med Med Or Med Gal Ged Ged Drux.

Then, moving the tip of the wand down the left edge of the table, I will continue to chant:

Pa Drux Un Tal Fam Don Ur Graph Don Or Gisg Gon Med Un Ged Med Graph Van Ur Don Don Un.

Then, moving from left to right along the bottom edge:

Pa Drux Ur Ur Don Ur Drux Un Med Graph Graph Med Med Graph Ceph Ged Ged Ur Mals Mals Fam Un.

Then up the right-hand edge to finish where I started:

Pa Gon Med Un Graph Fam Mals Tal Ur Pa Pa Drux Un Un Van Un Med Un Gon Drux Drux Ur.

I will repeat this entire procedure six more times, each time increasing the intensity of my focus on the words and movements. When I've completed the seventh round of chanting, I will hold the wand over the center of the table and chant seven rounds of the following:

Med Gon Gisg, Don Ur Van, Ur Don Ur, Med Med Graph.
Med Don Ur Med, Gon Ur Don Med, Gisg Van Ur Graph.

Then I will trace a circle over the center of the table and say:

Seven, rest in Seven: and the Seven, live by Seven: The Seven, govern the Seven: And by Seven all Government is.

Galas Gethog Thaoth Horlwn Innon Aaoth Galethog,

Zaphkiel Zedekiel Cumael Raphael Haniel Michael Gabriel,

E(l) Me Ese Iana Akele Azdobon Stimcul,

I Ih Ilr Dmal Heeoa Beigia Stimcul,

S Ab Ath Izad Ekiei Madimi Esemeli,

E An Ave Liba Rocle Hagonel Ilemes,

Sabathiel Zadkiel Madimiel Semeliel Nogahel Corabiel Lavanael.

Finally, I will place the tip of my wand upon the center of my forehead and whisper:

luah lang sach urch

Iad moz zir—iad bab zna—iad sor gru—iad ser osf.

The chanting will take about eighteen minutes. By then I will have chanted myself into an altered state of consciousness. In fact, I'll be high as a kite and struggling to avoid drifting into a directionless rapture. I will no longer be the overweight knot of worries and vices that haunts the daylight world of bills and phone calls and deadlines—vampires of time. I will be a magician, a key player in the business of creation, a spiritual being occupying my own indispensable rung on a hierarchical ladder of spiritual beings: gods, archangels and angels, spirits, and demons—spiritual entities who personify in metaphoric Technicolor every natural force, every monad of energy, every atom of matter, every concept and principle, potentiality, and tendency in the visible and invisible cosmos.

My living room will disappear, and in its place will tower the Temple of the Universe, holy ground demarcated by a consecrated carpet of red silk, upon which rests the Holy Table, the center of the universe, the Holy of Holies where heaven touches earth.

The table is completely veiled by a red silk cloth, with its gold tassels that hang from each corner. The cloth conceals an elaborately painted and engraved tabletop, the perimeter of which is carved with eighty-four squares containing letters from a sacred angelic alphabet—letters whose names I chanted in the angelic tongue during my seven rounds of chanting. A large carved hexagram spans the entire inner surface of the tabletop. And in the center of the hexagram broods a large rectangle made up of twelve squares, each containing an oversized angelic letter—the same letters whose names I chanted during the second round of chanting—artfully carved into the surface of the table. Seven talismans, Ensigns of Creation, are arrayed around the central rectangle. They are made of purified tin and are peculiarly lettered in the angelic script.

The centerpiece of the Holy Table is the *Sigillum Dei Aemeth*, a wax disk approximately nine inches in diameter and one and one-half inches thick, bearing the carved image of a complex diagram consisting of an interlocked heptagram, two heptagons, a pentagram, and an array of numbers and letters, which, when decoded, spell the names of seven sets of seven divine beings: *Seven who rest in seven, seven who live by seven, the seven who govern the seven, and seven by whom all government is.* Four smaller waxed versions of this Sigillum (wrapped in red silk bags) rest under the legs of the Holy Table, insulating it from distracting geocurrents.

The chanting completed, I will unveil a circular black mirror made of highly polished obsidian. I have it placed in a stand directly upon the covered Sigillum Dei Aemeth, and I will carefully angle it so I see my dimly lit face reflected in its pool of deep blackness. After only a few moments the reflection of my face will disappear, and I will see with magick eyes and hear with magick ears.

Now, the vision magick begins.

In the middle of the night I will call upon the angels.

I will call upon the angels, and they will answer.

CHAPTER TWO

The Magick of Dr. John Dee

If Merlin is an inner resonator who generated the literature which gathered about his name, then Dr. John Dee must be considered almost his outer manifestation in the real world.
He is probably the single most influential aspect of the magician ever to have lived and a worthy successor to the Arthurian mage.

—JOHN AND CAITLIN MATTHEWS[20]

The little ceremony I described in chapter one cannot be found in any other book of magick. I composed it in the spring of 2006 for the benefit of the members of my weekly magick class. It is designed as a ritual of preparation—a ceremonial "drug," as it were, to safely induce an altered state of consciousness, a trance in which specific techniques of magick may be practiced and visions can occur.

The components of the ritual are not, however, a modern invention. The magical implements and furniture were fabricated as faithfully as possible from descriptions found in sixteenth-century manuscripts and items currently housed at the Bodleian Library of Oxford University, the British Library, and the King's Library wing of the British Museum.

The prayers and the chants were drawn from those same ancient texts. In a group magical working, the prayers are recited in unison and the chants intoned Tibetan style, in a deep monotone chorus of two or four groups of voices. The hypnotic effect on the participants is tangible and powerful. (I have yet to discover what it does to our eavesdropping neighbors.)

The ancient manuscripts I refer to are the diaries and magical records of Dr. John Dee[21] and his partner Edward Kelley, and these texts represent the source material for the system of magick known and practiced today as *Enochian magick*.

It is not my intention, nor is it within the scope of the present work, to present a proper biography of Dee. That has been handled nicely in Peter French's brilliant biography[22] and other texts that I've itemized in the bibliography. I cannot, however, escape the necessity of providing a brief outline of his life and work, because it will have a direct bearing on our understanding of Enochian vision magick and why I think my little ritual of preparation is so important for those who wish to pursue this path.

Son of a gentleman server to Henry VIII, John Dee was a true Renaissance magus and one of the most extraordinary individuals of his time. Historian John Aubrey called him "one of the ornaments of his Age."[23] That is saying a lot, for his age was peopled with some of the brightest lights in the history of western civilization: Queen Elizabeth I, Charles V, Francis Bacon, Ben Johnson, Edmund Spenser, Giordano Bruno, Christopher Marlowe, and William Shakespeare.

Dee's unique genius blossomed at Cambridge University, and his fame as a published mathematician propelled him as a young man to academic rock-star status throughout Europe. It also brought him to the attention of the rulers of his world, including the future Queen Elizabeth.

He was the master of scores of disciplines. He was a physician, an engineer, a theologian, an astronomer, and cartographer. He invented the nautical instruments and developed the advanced navigational charts that helped make Britannia ruler of the waves. He even coined the term *Britannia*. A master astrologer, he was allowed to choose the date of Elizabeth's coronation, and throughout her reign he remained her friend and counselor.

Because he was fluent in many languages and lectured often on the continent, Elizabeth enlisted his services as a spy. Dee enjoyed this role very much. As a matter of fact, I believe he remained in this position until the day she died. He was fascinated with cryptography and loved word and letter puzzles. Dee was secretly known as "the queen's eyes," and he signed his dispatches to her with the stylized image of a hand shading two eyes.

ōōī

Yes, John Dee, on "her majesty's secret service," was the first agent 007.[24] Dee possessed the largest private library in England and was constantly enlarging it. He was perhaps the most educated man of his day. Part of his education included esoteric philosophy, Qabalah, alchemy, and magick—not illogical pursuits for a Renaissance magus. Magick, in particular, was a science to be explored and exploited. Dee wanted to talk to angels (as did the biblical patriarch Enoch) not only to discover the wisdom of the past and the secrets of the universe, but also, more immediately, to discover the secrets of Elizabeth's enemies and brandish the power to magically manipulate the spiritual forces that control them. Dee wanted to be a magical spy.

His approach to magick (at least at first) was pretty standard procedure for the day. After bathing and dressing in clean clothes (extraordinary measures for the times—unless, of course, it was May, when many people of the day took their annual bath), he would enter a room set aside for the purpose. There he would drop to his knees before a consecrated table/altar and for a half hour or so pray fervently to God and His good angels, alternately reciting a litany of self-abasing confessions of his unworthiness to enter into the divine presence and boasting of his God-given right to do that very thing. With his consciousness duly exalted by prayer, he would then gaze into a crystal or a black mirror (a process known as scrying[25]) and wait to receive a vision.

In theory that's how it was supposed to work. However, even though Dee was skilled at composing long and eloquent prayers, he was not very good at scrying. In 1581 he started to advertise for someone who was. He had a small measure of success with a handful of rented seers until March of 1582, when he made the acquaintance of one Edward Talbot. Talbot (who would soon confess that his name was actually Kelley) was an unemployed alchemist's assistant and convicted forger. Kelley's questionable character notwithstanding, his skills as a scryer immediately impressed Dee, who hired him on the spot at a salary of fifty pounds a year, a handsome figure for the day.

The partnership of Dr. John Dee and Edward Kelley would last until 1587. Their angelic-magick workings for the most part concluded in 1584. During their time together they engaged in hundreds of scrying sessions of varying lengths, in which Kelley gazed into a crystal ball or a black obsidian mirror and reported everything he saw and heard during a variety of angelic communications. Dee, sitting at a nearby table with pen and ink, led the questioning and recorded everything in anal-retentive detail.

Not all of the sessions yielded profound revelations. Indeed, many appear to be attempts by the communicating intelligences to simply keep the conversation going. There were numerous instances when information received in earlier sessions was amended (sometimes radically) in subsequent sessions. There were even times when the magicians were informed that they had been deceived in earlier communications by evil spirits. Nevertheless, the consistency of the bulk of the material is staggeringly impressive, and the double-/triple-blind nature in which it was delivered, especially the angelic language, calls, and magical tablets, boggles the imagination.

The Dee and Kelley years can be viewed as having occurred in three major phases, resulting in what appears on the surface to be three separate and unique magical systems. I will discuss these in more detail shortly. Here at the beginning it is enough to simply point out it is the third and last phase of their angelic workings (the three-month period between April 10 and July 13, 1584) that yielded the material for the system of vision magick that can be properly called Enochian.

The Enochian period was highly productive and bore much promise. In fewer than a hundred days Dee and Kelley received an angelic language, tablets containing the names of elemental and celestial beings, and calls in the angelic tongue that promised to unlock the secrets of heaven and earth. With sad, almost Faustian irony, however, once the Enochian material was in their hands, Dee and Kelley did not proceed to actually operate the system in subsequent workings.

They would go on to other magical adventures, attempting to impress (with little success) the crown heads of Europe with their supernatural counsel. Finally, after nearly five years of working together, years of exhausting magical sessions, and years of traipsing their families around Europe (not to mention a notorious wife-swapping incident), familiarity finally bred contempt, and the two magicians parted company without ever getting into the driver's seat of Enochian magick and turning the key.

Dee's complicated life would draw him back to the English court and the distracting world of political intrigue and survival. In 1588, as the Spanish armada set sail to annihilate England's much smaller fleet (an event Dee predicted years earlier), Elizabeth called again upon her Merlin. Dee shocked her courtiers by urging the queen to not engage the Spanish armada and keep her ships at bay, prophesizing that a mighty storm would scatter and destroy the Spaniards. Elizabeth wisely heeded Dee's words. The storm manifested right on cue, and in the chaos that followed, the Spanish armada went down to defeat. In many circles Dee was credited with magically raising the tempest that saved England. The story of this event became instant legend. William Shakespeare, writing only twenty-three years later, would use Dee as the model for Prospero, the storm-raising magician in his play, *The Tempest*.

Kelley's post-Enochian years would not earn him such renown. His ambitions kept him on the continent, where he peddled the promise of alchemical treasures to the crown heads of Europe. He was knighted by Emperor Rudolph II of Bohemia but was shortly thereafter imprisoned by his royal patron for failing to manufacture alchemical gold. With fairy-tale panache, Sir Edward Kelley plunged to an untimely death in November of 1595 while attempting to escape from the turret of Emperor Rudolph's prison tower.

Dee's end was not so colorful. Elizabeth appointed him warden of Christ's College in Manchester, but it was not a happy tenure. His wife (and, it is believed, several of his children) died there during the plague in 1605. Dee returned to his home at Mortlake, where his daughter Katherine cared for him until his death in late 1608 or early 1609.

How so many of Dee's manuscripts survived to see the light of the twenty-first century is a magical wonder story in and of itself. Several of the most important documents Dee had hidden in the false bottom of a cedar chest (can we get much more romantic?), where they lay undiscovered for over fifty years after his death. Through a curious chain of events (that tragically saw a portion of the manuscripts baked as pie wrappings), the surviving material came to the attention of the illustrious antiquary, politician, astrologer, chemist, and Freemason, Alias Ashmole (1617–1692), one of the few people in the world capable of recognizing the importance of the discovery. Thanks to Ashmole, the material was catalogued and finally housed safely in his own museum at Oxford, the British Museum, and the British Library, where, over three hundred years after its reception, it captured the attention of S. L. MacGregor Mathers, Wynn Wescott, and the adepts of the Hermetic Order of the Golden Dawn, then Aleister Crowley—and now you.

CHAPTER THREE

Dee and Kelley vs. the Golden Dawn
and Aleister Crowley

*Now hath it pleased God to deliver this Doctrine again out of dark-
nesse: and to fulfill his promise with thee, for the books of Enoch:To
whom he sayeth as he said unto Enoch. Let those that are worthy
understand this, by thee, that it may be one witness of my promise
toward thee.*

—THE ANGEL AVE, MONDAY, JUNE 25, 1584[26]

Modern Enochian magick (as first developed in the late nineteenth century by S. L. MacGregor Mathers and the adepts of the Hermetic Order
of the Golden Dawn and later adapted and augmented by Aleister
Crowley and others) is a remarkable and tidy self-referential system of
visionary magick. It is based upon a small portion of sixteenth-century
manuscripts of Dr. John Dee and Edward Kelley, and the mystique of
its colorful origins make it initially alluring to magical dilettantes and
dabblers. However, the complexity of the system, as outlined by Golden
Dawn/Crowley texts, continues to effectively guard the mysteries of
this marvelous magical art form from all but the most serious, coura-
geous, tenacious, foolish, or naïve.[27]

For most of us who cut our Enochian-magick teeth during the latter half of the twentieth century, the Golden Dawn (GD) and Crowley books were at the time the only source material readily available to us. By following the intricate procedures outlined in these texts, we proceeded with our visionary quests along the two avenues of experimentation offered us by the GD/Crowley model: one branch of the system dealing with the elemental (manifest) universe, the other dealing with the aethyric (celestial). I'll discuss these branches in more detail in book IV.

Both of these magical environments are populated by spiritual beings whose names are drawn from five grids of lettered squares received by Dee and Kelley during a series of angelic communications during the third (or Enochian) period of their magical operations. Both the elemental and the celestial magical environments (and their spirit inhabitants) are accessed by intoning one or more of nineteen calls, which are chanted in an angelic language that was given to the Elizabethan magicians under breathtaking and extraordinary circumstances during the last months of their angelic magick workings. Theoretically, these calls induce very specific trances, whereby the magician can pinpoint particular spiritual entities or environments he or she wishes to contact or visit. As you can imagine, this is a very attractive prospect to the magical explorer.

The visionary labor of many post-modern Enochian explorers was well repaid, for we soon discovered that despite our very limited access to the original texts (not to mention our inexperience and ineptitude) this kind of magick actually worked. With surprisingly few exceptions, when we followed the GD/Crowley procedures and techniques, even the most insensitive and skeptical among us received visions we deemed appropriate to the particular regions we were exploring.

The technique used to receive visions such as these is called scrying. The Golden Dawn and Crowley often referred to the practice as "traveling in the spirit vision." Scrying is, quite simply, the ability to put oneself in touch with one's own psychic senses. In magical operations the scrying session is usually preceded by a formal ceremony designed to put the magician in an altered state of consciousness. It is, for all intents and purposes, a shamanistic experience. The thoughts, mental images, and impressions that flood the magician's mind during this altered state are subsequently recorded in the magician's journal and analyzed.

Naturally, some of us proved more talented than others. Art lovers and movie fans make particularly good candidates for Enochian vision magick, for they see with the romantic's eye and already possess a vast memory bank of evocative landscapes, archetypal characters, and supernatural beings. They are by nature dreamers skilled at communicating through a vocabulary of images and visual metaphors. But even the least imaginative of us, in short order, learned to develop our own visionary skills that became increasingly honed by our repeated work with the system.

There is no question (in my mind, at least) that the Enochian magick procedures and techniques developed by the Golden Dawn and Crowley embody a highly effective system of magical working that, if properly applied, can become an integral component in the modern magician's program of personal self-development. This is especially true for those of us whose magical careers have led us to the Qabalah-based disciplines referred to today in specialized circles as *hermetic* or *ceremonial* magick.

To modern ceremonial magicians, Enochian magick appears at first glance to enjoy a comfortable compatibility with our world of pentagram rituals, hexagram rituals, tarot cards, trees of life, qabalistic path workings, chakra work, invocations, god-forms, and spirit evocations. This compatibility, however, has been, for the most part, contrived and jerry-rigged. For as efficacious as the GD/Crowley applications and techniques are, they bear little resemblance to anything Dee and Kelley practiced or were instructed to engage in by their angelic contacts. With all due respect to Mathers, it is clear that he and his Golden Dawn adepts chose to limit their attention to only those portions of source texts that offered material that they could fit easily into the qabalistic/hermetic schema to which they were so passionately committed. Furthermore, it is clear that in many instances, when the original material didn't fit the schema, they found a way to make it fit.

This fact should not diminish in our respect for the wonderfully effective system the Golden Dawn and Crowley have bequeathed to us. But it has prompted many of us (who obviously have an inordinate amount of time on our hands) to examine in greater detail the surviving Dee and Kelley material that has now become more readily available to the serious student. What we discovered is an overwhelmingly large body of work—books, notebooks, and diaries—the most interesting of which span the better part of three years of intense magical operations.

Most of this material appears to have nothing whatsoever to do with Enochian magick as practiced today.

As I mentioned earlier, Dee and Kelley's magical workings took place in three distinct phases that yielded three unique magical systems. For convenience, I will refer to these as (1) *Heptarchia Mystica* (or simply *Heptarchia*), (2) *Loagaeth* (which includes an angelic alphabet), and (3) *Enochian*.

One could argue quite convincingly that the revelations Dee and Kelley received during the Enochian period represent the crème de la crème of their magical workings and that it is unnecessary to waste our time on the painfully complex details of the Heptarchia and Loagaeth working periods. After all, the GD/Crowley system and techniques were developed from this *plus ultra* Enochian material, and everything seems to work just fine, thank you. In fact, for the better part of twenty years I was one of the most vocal apologists for the Enochian school whose motto is, "Don't try to duplicate the magick Dee and Kelley did to receive the system—just use the system they received!" Then, starting in 1999, a couple of things happened that caused me to rethink the wisdom of this attitude.

First, I became enthralled with the work of Clay Holden and the John Dee Publication Project, which brought the glories of *Quinti Libri Mysteriorum* to life on the World Wide Web. Then, in 2003, my O.T.O.[28] Brother and Enochian magick adept Christeos Pir sent me a computer disk of material from a marvelous Enochian seminar he presented in Pittston, Pennsylvania. Along with the seminar material, he sent me a collection of photographic files of surviving Dee manuscripts from the British Library and other materials that were of great interest to me. I assure you, I could not have written this book without these materials and the profound insights of this great modern magician.

Around the same time, my publisher sent me a copy of Joseph H. Peterson's book *John Dee's Five Books of Mystery: Original Sourcebook of Enochian Magic*. I had years earlier examined much of this material enlarged from microfilm, but now I had the luxury of comfortably reviewing it in clearer formats (with Latin translations) on my home computer and from Peterson's marvelously well-organized book.

I must confess that even with this information stacked conveniently and legibly under my nose, I was overwhelmed by the sheer immensity of it all. I'm interested in the magical adventures of Dee and Kelley as much as the next fellow, but I also have a life. Did I need to sacrifice three years of my own life in order to eavesdrop on every detail of three years of theirs? More than ever I saw the wisdom of simply using the magical system Dee and Kelley received and of not wasting precious time trying to recreate the magick they practiced to receive the system. After all, can't I drive a car without first having to build it myself?

But we're not talking about driving cars; we're talking about the art of magick. In the final analysis, no matter what system the magician chooses, in order to make it work most effectively he or she must first become attuned to that system's particular way of viewing of the universe. This concept is so important to the understanding of what will follow in this book that I will pause to illustrate with an example.

The ceremonial magician who practices qabalistic magick acquiesces (at least for the duration of the working) to see all things in heaven and earth in terms of a hierarchy of spiritual personages expressed by the various god names, archangels, angels, spirits, intelligences, and demons of the system. In Qabalah-based magic, such spiritual beings are conveniently organized and arranged according to fourfold formulas dictated by the Hebrew letters that make up the great Name of God, *Yod Heh Vav Heh*, and by the familiar schema of the Tree of Life, with its ten sephiroth and the twenty-two paths that connect them. Before the magician is ready to operate within the laws and peculiarities of this qabalistic worldview, he or she must first become a fit component of that universe—a harmonious and integral part of this great divine machine, a vital step on this hierarchical stairway of consciousness.

Like the ballerina whose ninety minutes on stage is the product of years of practice and thousands of hours of rehearsal, the magical artist must also be first transformed into a proper instrument of his or her craft. Magicians achieve this transformation with preliminary meditations and rituals, by which we adjust our focus step-by-step until we become comfortable citizens of the specific magical world in which we intend to operate. For the western ceremonial magician, the well-worn curriculum of the Golden Dawn provides perfect examples of this step-by-step adjustment process.

First the magician becomes master of the pentagram and a full citizen of the world of the five elements of the microcosmic universe. By repeated performances of the pentagram rituals and meditations, the magician's psyche becomes balanced and accustomed to the world of the four directional winds, the four elements, and the corresponding magical weapons: the wand, cup, sword, and disk.

Once the elemental (microcosmic) universe is mastered, the magician then moves on to the next step in the attunement process by mastering rituals of the hexagram. Here the magician's point of reference is enlarged as his or her consciousness and identity is obliged to expand from the microcosmic world of the elements to the macrocosmic greater world—the world characterized by the sun orbited by the planets and surrounded by the belt of the zodiac.

This is very basic stuff, but it illustrates how rituals enable the ceremonial magician to externalize internal processes and undergo self-transformation. Would-be magicians who attempt more advanced work without being adjusted by these early attunements are ill prepared to understand or properly absorb what is happening to them within the context of the progressively higher magical environments in which they presumptuously wish to operate. It is true that some magicians may receive seemingly dramatic and noteworthy effects from such premature efforts, but seeds of promise cannot long take root in soil that is not properly prepared or that is too shallow.

Late in 2005, while gathering material for yet another workshop series on Enochian magick for my Monday night magick class, I poured over the records of Dee and Kelley's pre-Enochian workings in hopes of finding the key to their preparatory processes. What exactly did the angels *do* to Dee and Kelley during the years prior to the final Enochian revelations? Dee and Kelley received some pretty interesting things during those earlier workings, including instructions for the creation of an array of magical implements that the Golden Dawn and Crowley all but ignored:

- a Ring;[29]
- a Lamen, which was to be worn by the magician as a breastplate and which connects him or her to the Holy Table;
- the Holy Table itself, inscribed with letters from an angelic alphabet and upon which would rest the Sigillium Dei Aemeth;
- the Sigillium Dei Aemeth, an intricately carved disk made of purified beeswax (an artifact so stunning and historically

intriguing that it is prominently displayed today in the King's Library wing of the British Museum);

- seven talismans (five squares and two circles), called Ensigns of Creation, which surround the Sigillium on the Holy Table.

All of these items were linked to one another and to the magicians by an overwhelmingly complex process that distilled, shuffled, and organized thousands of letters from numerous and varied alphanumeric grids. These grids had been painstakingly received in vision, one letter at a time, by Kelley and duly transcribed by Dee. The letters spelled the names of great angels, which, in turn, when manipulated, yielded the names of subordinate angels, which produced still more names.

Now, before we get too excited about dusting off and playing with all these pre-Enochian magical tools and furniture, I have to make myself clear on one very important point. These items were received during the first phase of Dee and Kelley's workings.

This period yielded a unique system of planetary magick they referred to as Heptarchia Mystica (see book II). To all appearances, heptarchic magick has little or no direct relationship to the Enochian magick system they received during their final days of practice. Also, it is demonstrably clear (in my mind at least) that Enochian magick can be performed quite effectively without using the Ring, the Lamen, the Holy Table, and so on. However, it is equally clear to me that, as Dee and Kelley were receiving and working with the items and concepts of heptarchic magick, their minds and psychic bodies were, day by day, undergoing subtle yet profound evolutionary changes.

Could the reason the practical Enochian material came so very late in the game be that Dee and Kelley had to first complete their transformation into magicians who could appreciate and handle the advanced work? After all, isn't that what magick is really about—changes in the magician? Could these changes have been brought about by the mere act of meticulously following the angels' complex directions, which filtered and distilled these magical concepts into material manifestation? If so, this would be a vital preparatory step that modern Enochian magicians are omitting entirely.

I grew intrigued with this idea. Given the fact that the GD/Crowley methods of Enochian magick already work so well right out of the box, how much better might these same techniques work if the magician were first prepared and attuned in a manner similar to the way Dee and Kelley had been prepared and attuned. A magician so equipped would be picking up, as it were, where the two Elizabethans left off in 1584.[30]

I was at first uneasy with this theory because it came dangerously near to destroying my comfortable philosophy of "Don't try to duplicate the magick Dee and Kelley did to receive the system—just use the system they received!" However, my inherent laziness was rewarded, and I eventually took comfort in the realization that in order to ceremonially prepare oneself to perform Enochian magick, one might not need to torturously repeat everything Dee and Kelley did to receive the Ring, the Holy Table, the Lamen, the seven Ensigns of Creation, and the Sigillum Dei Aemeth. Instead, one must simply understand and use (in a way that mirrors the preparation process) the Ring, the Holy Table, the Lamen, the seven Ensigns of Creation, and the Sigillum Dei Aemeth that they received!

This book was written to show the practicing Enochian magician how to do precisely that, and the little ritual in chapter one (and outlined in greater detail in appendix I) is the ceremony that embodies this preparation process. Like the rituals of the pentagram that prepare us for elemental magick, like the rituals of the hexagram that prepare us for planetary magick, I believe this little ceremony captures the essence of the step-by-step processes of personal alchemy that prepared and attuned Dee and Kelley.

The material is based on two series of classes that Constance and I held in our home in 2005 and 2006—visionary workings that spanned a period of just over seven months. While the class spent a considerable amount of time discussing and analyzing the magical theories that underlie these methods of preparation, most of our time was spent actually applying the techniques in a formal and ceremonial manner prior to group and individual Enochian scrying sessions.

My biggest challenge, for both the class series and writing this book, has been how best to communicate the essence of the breathtakingly intricate procedures that occupied Dee and Kelley during their years of preparation without enmeshing the reader in a time-devouring web of details. It is somewhat like trying to convey the profundity of a great cathedral without dwelling minutely on every action of every stonemason who fashioned each perfect stone. I have resolved, there-fore, to stay focused on the big picture and allow the reader to wrap his or her mind around the major themes, secure in the knowledge that he or she can proceed to dissect the method of the madness—and discover further revelations—by referring to the now readily available source texts. It is very important for the reader to understand that this book was not written as a substitute for the source material but simply as a guide to the practical, self-transformational applications of this magi-cal art. I advise those of you who may be committed to in-depth acad-emic research of this subject *not* to view my book as an authoritative replacement for the original texts. Dee and Kelley's records are liberally peppered with irregularities, conflicting instructions, missing pieces, and typos. I've done my best to wade through these and be as consis-tent and accurate as possible. But when I say I'm going to stay focused on the big picture, that is exactly what I mean.

Are you ready to begin? If so, we need to first talk briefly about the mind of Dr. John Dee and explore the reasons why the secrets of heaven and earth were communicated to him in alphanumeric ciphers, tables, and squares.

CHAPTER FOUR

The Mind of a Cryptographer

Now first I understand what he, the sage, has said: "The world of spirits is not shut away; Thy sense is closed, thy heart is dead!"

—*Faust*, Act I, Scene I[31]

Are angels, spirits, and demons real? Do they have an existence apart from and outside the mind? Ever since human beings could frame thoughts into words, we have asked ourselves that question. It is an eternal debate among magicians and mystics and one that likely will never be resolved to anyone's complete satisfaction. Personally, I agree with the venerable Rabbi Lamed Ben Clifford who said, "It's all in your head. You just have no idea how big your head is."[32] Certainly every outside impression we receive is ultimately processed inside our own minds. Just keeping that fact in mind we might conclude that, where objective reality is concerned, there is no outside-of-ourselves.

In either case, in the art of magick, the magician must behave (at least for the duration of the operation) as if the spirits are independent intelligences and have an objective existence in a dimension outside his or her own mind. Dee and Kelley (who believed most fervently in a tangible heaven, hell, and the characters and events of the Bible) certainly assumed that the communicating spirits and angels were real and enjoyed an independent existence. This gave the Elizabethan partners a decided psychological edge over modern magicians, who must overcome a smug mountain of logic, rationality, and spiritual cynicism in order to even begin to operate this most naïvely romantic of spiritual art forms.

For practical purposes, it does not matter whether the magician is making contact with "spirit" intelligences from a "spirit world" or merely tapping into currently unexplainable levels in his or her own mind. If the magician is properly prepared (and operating under the right circumstance), it is indeed possible for him or her to make contact with intelligences that for all intents and purposes could be characterized (objectively or metaphorically) as angels, spirits, and demons.

No two individuals are alike, and the art of preparing oneself and arranging the right circumstances for spirit contact is unique for every magician. For us to understand the elements of Enochian magick, we will need to get a basic idea of how the spirits went about reaching the minds of Dee and Kelley—especially Dee, who was, after all, the operating magician. In fact, there are instances where the communicating intelligences indicated that they viewed the two magicians as a single entity with Kelley acting as an extension of Dee's mind. On April 28, 1582, Dee asks of the archangel Michael, "You mean us two (Dee and Kelley) to be joined so, and in mind united, as if we were one man?" and Michael answered, "Thou understandest."

As I mentioned earlier, Dee was not a particularly talented scryer. Although his diaries record several instances when he saw certain spirits and phenomena, he relied almost entirely on the visionary skills of others. This makes perfect sense to me. Dee's immense intellect was actually a magical handicap. His magnificent brain was too engaged to surrender its analytical control. His mind worked too fast, and his thoughts were too loud to hear the subtle messages from the spirits. This is not good for mystical experiences. In order for the communicating intelligences to get past Dee's constantly churning mind, they had to force him to *use* his mind to *overcome* his mind. They had to beat his brain at its own game.

And what were the favorite games of Dr. John Dee's brain? Ciphers, codes, puzzles, magick squares—these were the arts that touched Dee's sense of wonder. Had he been obsessed with music, the spirits might have communicated to him through melodies or harmonies or rhythm. Had he been a dancer, they would have communicated through elements of body movement; had he been a military man, they would have through the metaphors of battle. But he wasn't a musician or a dancer or a soldier. Dee was, at heart, a cryptographer—perhaps the best in the world—and whether he consciously realized it or not, this was how he could make contact with his subconscious mind. This is how he expected the cosmos to unveil her secrets to him. For Dr. John Dee, the secrets of the universe were codes that could be broken. Divine revelation was a matter of decipherment, and he was willing to work for it. Indeed, by working for it, he would prepare himself to receive it. *Give me the raw data, and I will decode the mind of God.*

Dee was already looking for that raw data the day Edward Kelley first knocked on his door. He was looking for it in the *Book of Soyga.*

CHAPTER FIVE

The Book of Soyga

Dee: Is my book of Soyga of any excellency?

Uriel: That book was revealed to Adam in Paradise by God's good angels . . .

Dee: . . .Oh, my great and long desire hath been to be able to read those tables of Soyga.

—JOHN DEE AND THE ARCHANGEL URIEL, MARCH 10, 1582[33]

Even before Dee met Kelley he was immersed in the study of a magical treatise written in Latin called *Aldaraia sive Soyga: Tractatus Astrologico magicus* or, more simply, the *Book of Soyga*.[34] We know that Dee was intrigued by the *Book of Soyga* because his diary records that it was the subject of one of the very first questions he asked of the archangel Uriel during Edward Kelley's inaugural scrying session on March 10, 1582. In later diary entries he laments that he has misplaced his *Book of Soyga*, and still-later entries indicate that he eventually found it.

The book is an anonymous, late-medieval grimoire of planetary, angelic, and demonic magick that is in many ways not too dissimilar from other magical treatises of the period. However, there are several things that distinguish *Soyga*—things that obviously made it particularly attractive to Dee. For one thing, a great deal of the text concerns itself with alphanumeric exercises and puzzles; letters with numerical, astrological, and elemental values, which are combined, recombined and reduced to form magick words (spelled forwards and backwards), all of which contain increasingly complex values and magical virtues. As we will see, this magical letter distillation process is characteristic of Enochian magick.

Perhaps most intriguing to Dee were the last eighteen leaves of *Soyga*. These pages contain thirty-six tables, each comprising a grid of 1,296 squares, arranged in 36 x 36 grids. Each of the tables' 1,296 squares is filled with a Latin letter. Together the tables could form a cube comprising 46,656 squares. Each of the thirty-six tables is identified by an astrological or elemental symbol; the first twenty-four are attributed (in pairs) to signs of the zodiac, the next seven to the planets, the next four to the elements (Fire, Water, Air, and Earth), and one simply to "Magistri."[35,36]

For our purposes, I impress upon the reader's mind the profound importance of alphanumerics and how much information can be encoded within a grid of a magick table. I will try to demonstrate this with a very simple illustration, shown in figure 1.

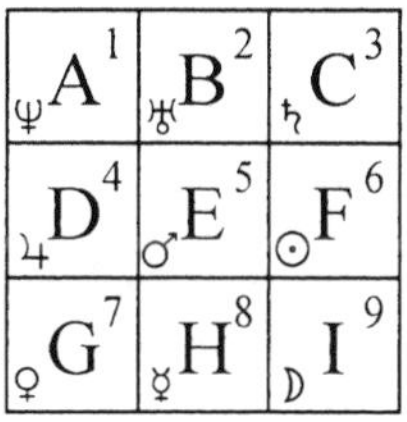

Figure 1: A simple alphanumeric magick table

This table is made up of nine squares. Each square contains one of nine letters, and these letters can be considered by themselves or in combination with the others to spell magical words. Each individual letter has many traditional meanings attached to it. To keep things simple, I've arbitrarily assigned just two correspondences (numerical and planetary) to each of the letters; these are shown in the corners of each lettered square. Theoretically, the number of correspondences each square can represent is nearly infinite.

For example, in this particular table, c not only represents the letter c but also the number three and all things threeish. What do I mean by threeish? One very big example is all things in the universe that *exist* in *time* and have *movement*, and all things that have a *beginning*, a *middle*, and an *end*. In this example c also represents Saturn and everything Saturnian (from wisdom and restriction to darkness, old age, and lead).

Like DNA, alphanumeric squares carry an unimaginably vast amount of information in a deceptively small package. As a resident of our 3 x 3 table, the c square also carries information drawn from its position relative to the other letters and their correspondences. Can you begin to see how much information is contained in that one little square alone? Imagine, then, the mass of complex data that could be tightly stored in a 36 x 36 x 36 square cube represented by the *Book of Soyga*.

I've discovered no evidence of a direct connection between the *Book of Soyga* and any of the magical workings that led ultimately to the reception of Enochian magick. Nevertheless, the fact remains that even before Dee met Kelley, the mechanics of the alphanumeric cipher system, as presented in *Soyga*, captured Dee's analytical imagination and had become part of the way he expected to receive divine information. Indeed, at every phase of Dee and Kelley's workings, alphanumeric squares and codes would play a major role.

We know Dee held the *Book of Soyga* in high regard and was particularly preoccupied with learning the secrets of the thirty-six tables. The magical process of the *Book of Soyga* (shuffling and distilling immense numbers of letters and squares into smaller and smaller bits of concentrated information) would become the modus operandi by which the spirits would ultimately communicate the secrets of Enochian magick to Dee and Kelley. It would be the method by which they received the Holy Table, the Lamen, the Ensigns of Creation, the Sigillum Dei Aemeth, the Table of Nalvage, the Elemental Tablets, and, most dramatically, the angelic language and the forty-eight calls. In a way, this process is a metaphor of the mechanics of creation itself. As Carl Sagan[37] said, "If you wish to make an apple pie from scratch, you must first create the universe." In this case, our apple pie is the manifest universe—the world as it presently exists—the world Dee and Kelley wished to understand and magically affect.

This world is the end product of a progression of cosmic events that physicists believe began with an immeasurably dense singularity (containing all the potential information that would eventually become the universe) that burst open and set into motion the phases of creation. The immensely packed assembly of thirty-six 36 x 36 alphanumeric squares found in the *Book of Soyga* is a crude but appropriate model for such a singularity. The intricate process of combining, shuffling, and distilling information-packed squares magically mimics the astronomical processes by which atoms and elements to stars and planets were formed in the creation cycle from seemingly chaotic units of a potential universe.

The *Book of Soyga* did not play a direct role in the magical operations of Dee and Kelley, but the patterns and formulae it embodied would remain the methodology of their angelic communications until the end of their association. I believe that the two magicians, by taking part in this incremental process of creation, became personally *attuned* to the magical universe as it presently exists, and thus prepared themselves to receive and engage in Enochian magick. In the chapters that follow, I will present only the briefest snapshots of the step-by-step process that I believe was the *attunement program* that prepared Dee and Kelley to receive the Enochian magick system. Hopefully, by your participation in the process, you also will undergo (however vicariously) a similar transformational experience and become fully prepared to actually practice Enochian vision magick.

But first, let us pray.

CHAPTER SIX

Let Us Pray

No man should ever undertake any great or important undertaking without first invoking the blessing of God.

—Master's admonition, California Free and Accepted Masons

The whole secret may be summarized in these four words: "Inflame thyself in praying."

—ALEISTER CROWLEY[38]

One of the most fundamental and important magical tools Dee used throughout his life was prayer. So, before we begin to examine magick rings and protective breastplates and holy tables and other such wizardly items, we need to first get something straight about prayer.

It's okay to pray. Even if you think you don't believe in the same God that Dee and Kelley believed in, it's okay to pray. I realize for many twenty-first-century magicians the word *prayer* carries with it unpleasant memories of childhood church and Sunday school traumas, and bedtime fears that "if I die before I wake" somebody was going to take my soul to God knows where.

In magick, prayer has nothing to do with religion. It does, however, have everything to do with the magician's grasp of facts of life in the magical world in which he or she intends to operate. Part of that reality is the mystical fact that existence itself is an expression of consciousness, and there are levels of consciousness higher and lower than the one we are currently attuned to.

By the simple act of uttering a prayer, our apparently limited consciousness reaches out and makes contact with a higher level of consciousness, and by doing so, we insert ourselves into the divine circuitry of the cosmos. As we do, part of us (a part that we might not be aware of) wakes up, as it were, and recognizes our rightful place in this circuitry.

In my book *The Key to Solomon's Key*,[39] I illustrate this concept using the legend of King Solomon as my example. In the excerpt below, I discuss prayer in the context of spirit evocation, but the same thoughts hold true to all forms of magick, including Enochian.

> The third chapter of the book of Kings[40] tells us that at the beginning of his reign the Lord appeared to Solomon in a vision by night and said, "Ask that which I should give you." Solomon answered:
>
> *"Give therefore to thy servant an understanding heart to judge thy people and to discern between good and bad; for who is able to judge this thy so great a people?" And it pleased the Lord because Solomon had asked this thing. And the Lord said to Solomon, "Because you have asked this thing and have not asked for yourself riches, neither have you asked the lives of your enemies nor have you asked for yourself long life, but have asked for yourself wisdom to discern judgment; Behold, I have done according to your words; lo, I have given you a wise and understanding heart, so that there has been none like you before you, neither shall any arise after you like you."[41]*
>
> Before undertaking the task of ruling his people and building the Temple, Solomon doesn't begin by consulting with his inferiors (his ministers, his generals, his architects, his building-supply contractors, or labor leaders). He doesn't immediately enmesh himself in the energy-draining details of micromanaging

such a huge and important project. Instead he turns his attention upward to the highest level of the hierarchical scale of consciousness. He makes direct contact with Deity and, instead of behaving like a helpless youngster asking a parent for pocket money, he boldly makes himself available to serve as a conduit through which the Deity's infinite wisdom and understanding can pass.

This profoundly mature and uncomplicated request is instantly granted, *as if Deity had no choice but to acquiesce.* A unique[42] spiritual hierarchy is created, with Solomon enthroned midway between heaven and hell—poised to work in cosmic harmony with the divine consciousness above him, poised to compel the infernal spirits to do the same.

This is the primary secret of Solomonic magic. As long as the magician remains plugged in to *that which is above*, he or she is simultaneously plugged into (and must begin to master) *that which is below*.[43]

Dee's prayers, both in English and Latin, fill page after page of his diaries and magical records. I confess I am neither inclined nor devotionally equipped to follow his exhausting example. I do, however, recognize the efficacy of prayer as an indispensable preliminary to magical operations. And, while I do not personally believe that the biblical Solomon ever existed as such in empirical history, as a magical artist I embrace his myth and happily adopt him as a patron saint of magick.

How appropriate, then, that the first magical tool Dee and Kelley would receive from their angelic contacts was the Ring of Solomon, and that before putting on that ring, the magician must first pray.

BOOK II

De Heptarchia Mystica

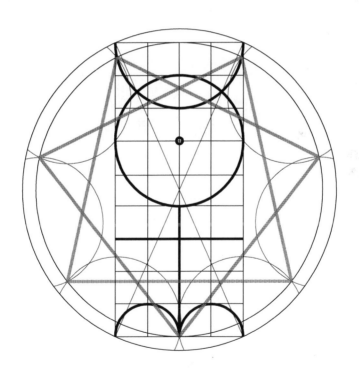

CHAPTER SEVEN

The Ring

Lo, this it is. This is it, wherewith all Miracles, and divine works and wonders were wrowght by Salomon.

—THE ARCHANGEL MICHAEL, MARCH 14, 1582

The first system of magick Dee and Kelley received from their angelic contacts was a form of planetary magick referred to as De Heptarchia Mystica. It was delivered mostly in late 1582 and amended somewhat the following year. The details of how it was painstakingly received are recorded in Dee's *Quinti Libri Mysteriorum*[44] and edited for purposes of practical working in his "De Heptarchia Mystica."[45] Unfortunately, we don't know exactly how, or even if, the magicians actually operated this particular form of magick. What we do know is that besides receiving the names and symbols for forty-nine planetary "good angels" Dee and Kelley were instructed to create a number of magical items—items that were almost entirely ignored by the Golden Dawn and Crowley. These items, I believe, can be extremely important tools for the modern Enochian magician; these are the Ring, the Holy Table, the Ensigns of Creation, the Lamen, and the Sigillum Dei Aemeth.

First we need to examine the Ring, for without the Ring the magicians were told they could "do nothing." Unlike most other things they would receive from their angelic contacts, the Ring was delivered in a relatively straightforward manner.

I will not quote long passages from Dee's records, but his description of the circumstances surrounding the reception of the magic Ring are so colorfully dramatic that I cannot resist quoting a brief passage. The date is Wednesday, March 14, 1582. Dee and Kelley were engaged in their fourth action[46] and experiencing a close encounter with the archangels Michael and Uriel. (The following excerpt retains the inconsistent spelling and punctuation of Elizabethan English. The Greek delta, Δ, is Dee, "Mi" the archangel Michael.)

Δ: Now Michael thrust out his right arme, with the sword: and bad the skryer to loke. Then his sword did seame to cleave in two: and a great fyre, flamed out of it, vehemently. Then he toke a ring out of the flame of his sworde: and gave it, to Uriel: and sayd, thus:

Mi: The strength of God, is unspeakable. Praysed be god for ever and ever.

Δ: Then Uriel did make cursy unto him.

Mi: After this sort, must thy ring be: Note it.

Δ: Then he rose, or disapeared, out of the chayre, and by and by, cam again, and sayde, as followeth.

Mi: I will reveale thee this ring: which was never revealed since the death of Salomon: with whom I was present. I was present with him in strength, and mercy.

Lo, this it is. This is it, wherewith all Miracles, and divine works and wonders were wrowght by Salomon: This is it, which I have revealed unto thee. This is it, which Philosophie dreameth of. This is it, which the Angels skarse know. This is it, and blessed be his Name: yea, his Name be blessed for ever.

Δ: Then he layd the Ring down uppon the Table: and sayd, Note.

Δ: It shewed to be a Ring of Gold: with a seale graved in it: and had a rownd thing in the myddle of the seale and a thing like an **V**, throwgh the top of the circle: and an **L**, in the bottome: and a barr cleane throwgh it: And had these fowre letters in it, P E L E. After that, he threw the ring on the borde, or Table: and it semed to fall throwgh the Table and then he sayde, thus,

Mi: So shall it do, at thy commanndement. Without this, thow shalt do nothing. Blessed be his name, that cumpasseth all things: Wonders are in him, and his Name is WONDERFULL: His Name worketh wonders from generation, to generation.[47]

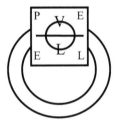

Figure 2: The Ring

Solomon was, and remains, the archetypal magician, and his legendary exploits as a master of spirits fill the pages of traditional Jewish, Islamic, and Ethiopian religious literature. In many of the stories, his magical ring played an important role as the source of his power to control demons. I can imagine Dee and Kelley were very impressed to be given the Ring of Solomon by none other than the archangel Michael himself.

Although the ring's design is unique, the word PELE (wonder worker) is found in two books which Dee already had in his library: *De Verbo Mirifico* by German humanist and Hebrew scholar Johann Reuchlin and Cornelius Agrippa's *Occult Philosophy*. (Agrippa apparently took the term from Reuchlin.)

Dee was told the Ring should be made of pure gold. If he indeed had one made, it has not survived the centuries. Realistically, few of us today have the skill to fashion or the resources to have a golden ring custom made.[48] Nevertheless, Michael seemed adamant, "Without this, thow shalt do nothing." And so I've come to the conclusion if I'm to practice this particular art of magick, then before I do *anything*, I'm going to wear the Ring.

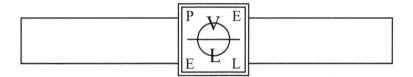

Figure 3: Pattern for a paper Ring

Here is the pattern for a Ring that can be made out of colored paper or poster board. I realize such material is not as impressive or romantic as pure gold. You might even think that a true magick Ring cannot be made from a scrap of paper. You might tell me you'd feel silly wearing a paper ring. If you feel this way, then I hope you won't be offended when I tell you that if you can't make a real magick Ring out of paper, then you'll not be able to make one out of gold. The same goes for the other magical items I am going to discuss in the next few chapters.

Before I practice any aspect of Enochian magick, I recite two short prayers. The first is a prayer John Dee used regularly throughout the years of his magical workings:[49]

> Teach me (O creator of all things) to have correct knowledge and understanding, for your wisdom is all that I desire. Speak your word in my ear (O creator of all things) and set your wisdom in my heart.

The second is a prayer I fashioned from the words the archangel Michael spoke to Dee and Kelley during their March 14, 1582, action:

> Behold the Ring. Lo, this it is. This is it, wherewith all miracles, and divine works and wonders were wrought by Solomon: this is it, which the Archangel Michael has revealed to

me. This is it, which Philosophy dreameth of. This is it, which the Angels scarce know. This is it, and blessed be his name: yea, his Name be blessed forever. Without this I shall do nothing. Blessed be his name, that encompasses all things: Wonders are in him, and his name is WONDERFUL: PELE. His Name works wonders from generation to generation. Amen.

After reciting these prayers and putting on the Ring, I then position myself at the Holy Table and prepare to put on the Lamen.

CHAPTER EIGHT

The Lamen

Beware of wavering. Blot out suspicion of us, for we are God's crea-
tures that have reigned, do reign, and shall reign forever. All our
Mysteries shall be known unto you.

—THE ANGEL BRALGES, ONE OF THE ANGELIC PRINCES
NAMED ON THE LAMEN, NOVEMBER 16, 1582, *PRINCE*
BRALGES, NOVEMBER 16, 1582[50]

The Lamen and the Holy Table are inextricably linked. By wearing the
Lamen over the heart, the magician becomes linked to the Holy Table.
I cannot say it any plainer than that. But putting on the Lamen and sitting at the Holy Table are empty gestures unless the magician has some
idea of what these items represent and how they are connected.

The designs for both the Lamen and the Holy Table were distilled
from tables composed of letters of the names of planetary angels of the
Heptarchia. Even though the chronology of their reception is a bit tan-
gled, it is probably easiest to discuss the Lamen first.

Traditionally a Lamen is a breastplate that is hung from the neck
by a chain or ribbon. The breastplate of the high priest of Israel is the
biblical archetype for this most important piece of magical adornment.
It was a square plate, a 3 x 4 grid embedded with twelve precious
stones representing, among other twelveish concepts, the tribes of Israel

and the signs of the zodiac. The Lamen that the angels delivered to Dee and Kelley contained no precious stones but displayed eighty-four angelic letters arranged in a most curious and exacting manner.

Two versions of the Lamen were received by Dee and Kelley. The first, delivered in 1582, was a rather odd assortment of lines, squiggles, and letters reminiscent of Solomonic or Goetic sigils. This Lamen, they were told, was to be made in gold and worn as a protective device. After receiving it, the magicians spent the rest of the year and part of 1583 receiving material relating to the forty-nine planetary good angels of the Heptarchia (see figure 5).

The seven-letter names of these angels were received (much to Dee's cryptographic delight, I'm sure) by the complex manipulation and distillation of letters from a cross-shaped table composed of seven 7 x 7 tables (343 squares in all, each containing a number and a letter). This process was dictated by the archangel Michael during a grueling three-hour session. Just to give you an idea of the shape and size of this table, I've included a rough image without the letters and numbers.

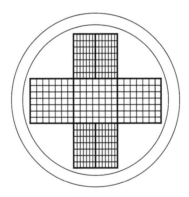

Figure 4: Cross of 343 letters and numbers

The magicians were then instructed how to organize and arrange these 343 letters to reveal the hierarchy of planetary good angels. Each of the seven planetary spheres was assigned a king, a prince, and five ministers. Figure 5 shows how the 343 letters form the names of the forty-nine good angels and how they are arranged according to planet (starting at the top of the wheel and working counterclockwise: Venus, Luna, Saturn, Mercury, Jupiter, Mars, Sol). Note also that only the names of the kings and princes are in all capital letters.

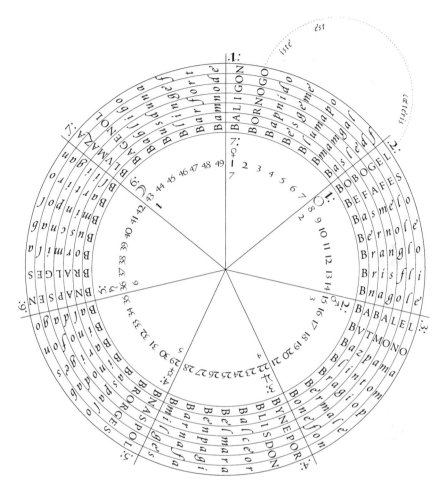

Figure 5: The forty-nine good angels (seven kings, seven princes, thirty-five ministers)

Venus

1. King BALIGON
2. Prince BORNOGO
3. Minister Bapnido
4. Minister Besgeme
5. Minister Blumapo
6. Minister Bmamgal
7. Minister Basledf

Sol

8. King BOBOGEL
9. Prince BEFAFES
10. Minister Basmelo
11. Minister Bernole
12. Minister Branglo
13. Minister Brisfli
14. Minister Bnagole

Mars

15. King BABALEL
16. Prince BVTMONO
17. Minister Bazpama
18. Minister Blintom
19. Minister Bragiop
20. Minister Bermale
21. Minister Bonefon

Mercury

29. King BNASPOL
30. Prince BRORGES
31. Ministers Baspalo
32. Minister Binodab
33. Minister Bariges
34. Minister Binofon
35. Minister Baldago

Luna

43. King BLVMAZA
44. Prince BAGENOL
45. Minister Bablibo
46. Minister Busduna
47. Minister Blingef
48. Minister Barfort
49. Minister Bamnode

Jupiter

22. King BYNEPOR
23. Prince BLISDON
24. Minister Balceor
25. Minister Belmara
26. Minister Benpagi
27. Minister Barnafa
28. Minister Bmilges

Saturn

36. King BNAPSEN
37. Prince BRALGES
38. Minister Bormila
39. Minister Buscnab
40. Minister Bminpol
41. Minister Bartiro
42. Minister Bliigan

It is obvious from the surviving material that some technique of practical magic was intended to call forth the heptarchic kings, princes, and ministers. Illustrations of flat wooden disks containing the names of the kings and other unexplained characters tantalize us with glimpses of an organized magical system. But the sad fact remains that important source material that could shed light on this has not survived the centuries.

However, just as amber encapsulates and preserves the essence of a prehistoric insect (right down to the DNA), so too the Lamen and the Holy Table capture the distilled essence of the heptarchic hierarchy and system.

After receiving the names, sigils, and hierarchical structures of the forty-nine good angels, the magicians were informed that the first Lamen they received during their actions the previous year was a false one, delivered to them by an "illuding spirit." They were given instructions how to create a new one, which was to be worn not for protection per se, but in order to "dignify" the magicians as worthy practitioners of this form of magick.

I'm going to try to illustrate (as painlessly as possible) how both the Lamen and the Holy Table were created and why I believe their use in Enochian magick is important. Now, the reader might be tempted to skim over the following material, invoking my slogan, "Don't try to duplicate the magick Dee and Kelley did to receive the system—just use the system they received." But I beg you to resist that temptation. By following through (even halfheartedly) the methods by which these magical tools were constructed, you will slip, however subtly, into the divine creative stream that produced them. You will become part of the same process that programmed and prepared Dee and Kelley.

The key to the construction of the Lamen was a 12 x 7 table containing the letters of the names (minus the initial b[51]) of the seven planetary heptarchic kings and their princes (see figure 6).

Mimicking the cooling phases of Big Bang creation, this 12 x 7 table was condensed from the 343 lettered squares of the much larger cross-shaped table (see figure 4).

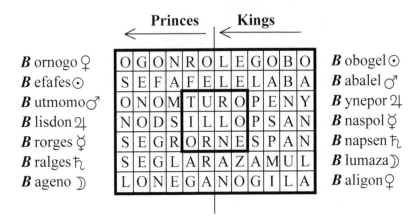

Figure 6: The 12 x 7 table of the Lamen

As you can see, the names of the kings are found on the right half of the table, the names of the princes on the left half. The names in *this* table are read from right to left. You will immediately notice that the kings of one planet are not matched on the same line as the prince of the same planet (e.g., the sun ☉ king, Bobogel, is set on the same line with the Venus ♀ prince, Bornogo, instead of on the line of the sun ☉ prince, Befafes).[52] This odd juxtaposition of planetary king and prince puts a certain strain on the sensitivities of those of us who like the order of our universe nice and symmetrical. However, this is the arrangement the angels insisted upon for the 12 x 7 table from which the Lamen was to be formed. As we will soon see in the following chapter, they will rectify the imbalance in the 12 x 7 table in order to create the Holy Table. But first let's continue to see how the Lamen is built.

The basic form of the Lamen is a table of twenty-four squares (arranged from top to bottom: 2—4—6—6—4—2) enclosed within diamond square, enclosed by a square, enclosed by a larger square.

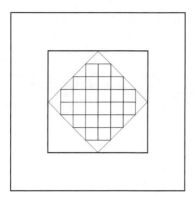

Figure 7: Blank Lamen form

The letters of the 12 x 7 table were applied to the Lamen by means of an exercise that first divided the table into three sections, described as flesh, heart, and skin. The letters were then transferred to the blank Lamen in three steps.

Step One: The letters of the *flesh* were added to the perimeter of the Lamen in their same relative positions to the 12 x 7 table.

Figure 8: Letters of the flesh

Figure 9: Letters of the flesh on the Lamen

Step Two: The letters of the *heart* were added to the corners of the next inner square of the Lamen in a curiously inconsistent manner. (I've added arrows indicating how the letters are applied.)

Figure 10: Letters of the heart

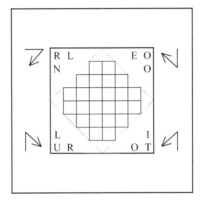

Figure 11: Letters of the heart on the Lamen

Step Three: First, the corners of the *skin* letters were added to the corners of the innermost diamond square of the Lamen in a manner consistent with their relative positions on the 12 x 7 table. Second, the remaining twenty-four letters of the 12 x 7 table were then braided into the remaining squares in the center of the Lamen.

O	G		B	O
S	E		B	A
O	N		N	Y
N	O		A	N
S	E		A	N
S	E		U	L
L	O		L	A

Figure 12: Letters of the skin

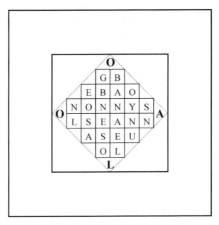

Figure 13: Letters of the skin on the Lamen

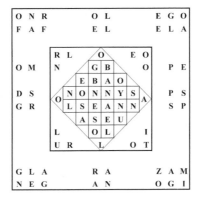

Figure 14: Completed Lamen (Latin letters)

Dee was told that the Latin letters of the finished Lamen should be translated into the angelic script. (I'll discuss the angelic alphabet a bit later.) Figure 15 shows the completed Lamen with angelic letters.

As with the Ring, gold was the material suggested for the Lamen, but it can be made from paper or poster board. The Lamen I first used was printed on both sides (Latin letters on one side, angelic script on the other) and laminated in plastic. In the area just above the top center I punched a hole through which I threaded a black ribbon.

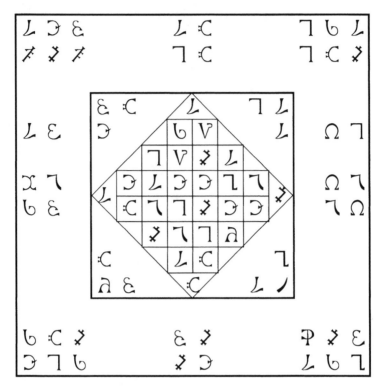

Figure 15: Completed Lamen (angelic letters)

As I put on the Lamen I utter the prayer:[53]

Behold the Lamen. As the Holy Table conciliates Heaven and Earth, let this Lamen which I place over my heart conciliate me to the Holy Table. Amen.

To understand what I mean by that prayer, we'll next need to turn our attention to the Holy Table.

CHAPTER NINE

The Holy Table

Every one of those sides must have 21 Characters: But first, at every corner make a great B.

—THE ANGEL IL, APRIL 28, 1583[54]

Magick tables were nothing new to Renaissance magicians. Unlike the protective circle and triangle spirit-trap apparatus used by Solomonic magicians, a properly consecrated magick table in a room transforms the entire chamber into holy ground. The table itself becomes the Holy of Holies, the place whereupon earth and heaven touch. Drawings of the period show the magician on his knees, his arms stretched in supplication, before a magick table sheltered by a conical tent.

Dee was already using a table of practice before Edward Kelley entered the picture, but afterwards, as the elements of the heptarchic magick developed, it became clear that the communicating spirits wanted Dee to customize his table in a most specific manner. The angels wanted the Holy Table to be an "instrument of conciliation," made of "sweet wood,"[55] and built two cubits square and two cubits high.[56] The table was to stand upon a carpet of red silk that was large enough to accommodate the scryer's chair. Once the Sigillum Dei Aemeth and the seven Ensigns of Creation were in position, the Holy Table was covered by a red silk cloth with gold tassels that hung from the corners.

The scrying stone or black mirror was then placed upon the covered Sigillum.

The public's first view of the Holy Table (sometimes referred to as the Table of Covenant or Table of Practice) was published in 1659 by Meric Casaubon in his *A True & Faithful Relation . . . .*[57] It was Casaubon's image that was reproduced in 1912 in Aleister Crowley's magazine *The Equinox*[58] and numerous books since then.

It may come as a surprise to many (and be highly amusing to others) that Casaubon's impressively printed image of the Holy Table is perhaps the greatest flaw in his liberally flawed and ill-titled *A True & Faithful Relation*. One look at the description and drawing in Dee's *Quinti Libri Mysteriorum: Appendix*[59] reveals the eighty-four letters that form the border of the Holy Table and the twelve letters that fill the 3 x 4 center square of Casaubon's image are printed in backward order. Figures 16 and 19 illustrate the correct arrangement of the letters on the Holy Table.

Figure 16: The Holy Table with Ensigns of Creation

The Holy Table and the Lamen are inextricably linked. By wearing the Lamen, the magician is linked, or conciliated, to the Holy Table. The object that forms this magical link and serves as the common denominator between the Holy Table and Lamen is the same 12 x 7 table that was used to construct the Lamen—the same table that bore the names of the seven planetary kings and the seven planetary princes of the heptarchic hierarchy.

Did I say the *same* 12 x 7 table? That's not entirely accurate.

Recall that when we were discussing the 12 x 7 table in the previous chapter, something appeared out of whack. The names of the planetary kings did not share the same lines as their planetary counterpart prince (e.g., the sun ⊙ king, Bobogel, is set on the same line with the Venus ♀ prince, Bornogo, instead of his sun ⊙ prince, Befafes). This planetary mismatch in the 12 x 7 table's construction did not appear to bother the angels, and indeed the "flaw" seemed to be a vital characteristic of the Lamen.

As you can see in Figure 17, the version of the 12 x 7 table that is the key to the Holy Table "corrects" this imbalance by rearranging the names of the planetary kings to match those of the princes of the same planet. Furthermore, the table is reversed, so that the kings now occupy the left side of the table and princes the right, and the direction in which the names are read is reversed to read from left to right.

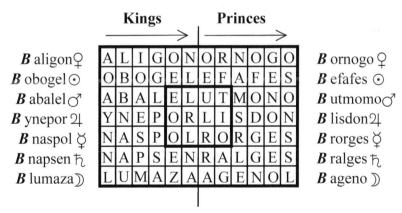

Figure 17: The 12 x 7 table adjusted to create the Holy Table

In my mind, the differences between the two 12 x 7 tables demonstrate a fundamental fact of life—the fact that even though human beings are an integral part of the hierarchy of spiritual beings, we currently find ourselves "on earth," trapped in a tomb of matter and to all appearances separated from the greater realities of the spiritual "heavens."

Qabalists tell us that we are created in the image of Deity—that we are, in the truest sense, a little reflection (a microcosm) of the great intelligence and creative force that creates, sustains, and destroys all things in the universe (the macrocosm). As Hermes Trismegistus said, "As above, so below."

That's all fine and good, and I go about my magical business as if it were true. But honestly, even though I'm composed of the same material that makes up the sun and moon and stars and angels and archangels and the supreme Deity, even though I am striving for self-awareness and do my best to be a divinely creative individual, still I don't feel much like the macrocosmic Deity. Compared to the macrocosm, my microcosm is way out of whack. My life is one of stress and imbalance. From where I stand, there is a very big break between Deity's above and Lon Milo DuQuette's below. I'm like the 12 x 7 table from which the Lamen is created: I've got all the condensed components of a perfectly tuned universe in me, but they are out of sync just enough to keep me from actually being the perfect reflection of the big "way things are."

I can really identify with the way the Lamen is constructed. Like it, my hierarchy of planets is mismatched and unbalanced. (Take one look at my astrological chart if you don't believe it!) Like the curious inconsistencies that characterize how the individual letters are transferred from the 12 x 7 table to the Lamen, my individual components are a litany of curious inconsistencies.

The 12 x 7 table that makes the Holy Table, on the other hand, sets this all straight. It is like the macrocosm showing the microcosm how it's done. As I sit before the Holy Table with the Lamen over my heart, I can almost feel the Holy Table's order and perfection pulling magnetically at my heart through the Lamen, connecting me by an almost tangible electric current to the Holy of Holies, pulling my heart and my attention toward the sacred spot in my living-room temple where heaven touches earth. The Holy Table is indeed an *instrument of conciliation*, an instrument of reunion.[60]

The letters of the 12 x 7 table are transferred to the Holy Table in the following manner. First, to make things a little easier to see let's turn the 12 x 7 table on its end.

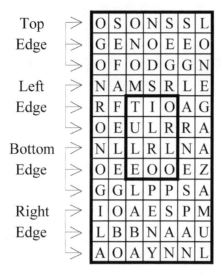

Top	⇢	O	S	O	N	S	S	L

Top ⇢ | O | S | O | N | S | S | L |
Edge ⇢ | G | E | N | O | E | E | O |
⇢ | O | F | O | D | G | G | N |
Left ⇢ | N | A | M | S | R | L | E |
Edge ⇢ | R | F | T | I | O | A | G |
⇢ | O | E | U | L | R | R | A |
Bottom ⇢ | N | L | L | R | L | N | A |
Edge ⇢ | O | E | E | O | O | E | Z |
⇢ | G | G | L | P | P | S | A |
Right ⇢ | I | O | A | E | S | P | M |
Edge ⇢ | L | B | B | N | A | A | U |
⇢ | A | O | A | Y | N | N | L |

Figure 18: The Holy Table's 12 x 7 table turned on its end

The border of the Holy Table is first segmented into twenty-one cells per side. Per angelic instructions, the sacred letter *B* is placed in the four corners, and then the letters of the 12 x 7 table are inserted in the remaining cells as indicated by the four sets of arrows on figure 18. The 3 x 4 square in the center of the Holy Table is extracted from the central heart of the 12 x 7 table, as highlighted in figure 18.

The arrows around the edges of figure 19 (see page 54) show that the letters are arranged to generate a counterclockwise whirl. In the Ritual of Preparation of chapter one, I chant seven rounds of the perimeter letters in this order using the angelic pronunciation. I also do the same for the twelve letters of the center square. By doing so, I effectively activate the Holy Table and the objects that sit upon it (including the Sigillum Dei Aemeth, the Ensigns of Creation, and the skrying mirror). The chant affects a powerful shift in consciousness unlike anything I have experienced before in magical practice.

As the manifest universe is the evolving end product of the dynamic forces that created it, so too the Holy Table manifests on earth as the perfect miniature working model of the heavenly matrix. It is a magical machine with many moving parts, all in perpetual motion.

Picture in your artist/magician's mind how, like the stars in the rotating arms of a spiral galaxy, the eighty-four *angelic letters* that form

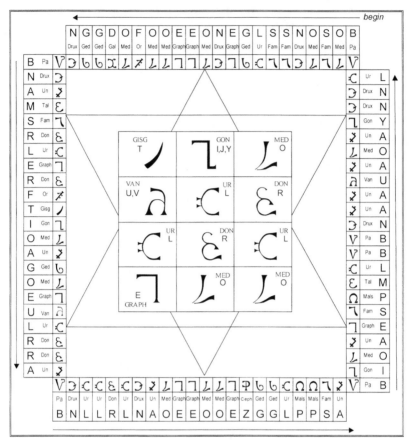

Figure 19: Master key to the Holy Table

the border of the Holy Table circumscribe the other objects on the table-top with an eternal counterclockwise movement around the *outside* of the table's *hexagram* (symbol of the macrocosm).

Within, the twelve *angelic letters* in the *3 x 4 square* in the center of the Holy Table's hexagram churn with the dynamics of the up-down/right-left movement suggested by its four rows of three letters networked with its three columns of four letters.

The Lamen is born of the same alphanumeric codes as the Holy Table, but its construction is flawed by a slight imbalance. So too the magician, in his or her present state, is the seemingly flawed *microcosmic* reflection of Deity. By wearing the Lamen, the imperfect magician is linked to the perfection of the Holy Table, and while in this exalted state may become privy to the secrets of the *macrocosmic* universe.

CHAPTER TEN

The Sigillum Dei Aemeth

Seven, rest in 7: and the 7, live by 7: The 7, govern the 7: And by 7 all Government is.

—The archangel Michael, March 20, 1582[61]

Figure 20: The Sigillum Dei Aemeth

The design of Dee's Sigillum Dei Aemeth ("the seal of God's truth") is perhaps the most recognizable image of Enochian magick. It is a powerful magical device, alive with the angelic forces of an ordered universe in which "Seven, rest in Seven: and the Seven, live by Seven: The Seven, govern the Seven: And by Seven all Government is."

Unlike the hierarchies of the Lamen and the Holy Table, the Sigillum's hierarchy of angels was not condensed, distilled, or otherwise generated from the seven 12 x 7 tables from which the names of the forty-nine good angels were drawn. Nevertheless, the Sigillum is the centerpiece of heptarchic magick and is the object through which all heptarchic energy (if we dare call it that) is focused.

The Sigillum itself was a disk nine inches in diameter and approximately an inch and a half thick. It was made of pure beeswax and placed in the center of the Holy Table. The scrying crystal or black mirror was placed upon it. Four smaller wax versions were placed beneath small boxes, upon which stood the four legs of the Holy Table.

Dee was first told to simply copy the design from a book he already had in his library. But Dee had at least two volumes[62] that contained designs for sigilla. He couldn't make up his mind which one to use, so he asked for further clarification. The angel then gave instructions how to construct an entirely new sigillum based on the format of the others but adding an array of heavenly personages: seven god names enclosing seven sets of angelic names.

It is clear to me that the construction of the Sigillum was a vital step in Dee and Kelley's preparation program and that construction can serve that same important purpose to the modern magician as well. I'm going to walk you through the steps of how it is constructed, because I hope readers who are serious about actually *doing magick*, rather than merely studying it, will want to build their own.

I've provided you with a blank sigillum (figure 21), and I encourage you to make multiple photocopies of it. Enlarge it, if you wish, to nine inches in diameter. Then follow the step-by-step instructions. As you do, you will not only be building this magical device on paper, but you also will be installing it inside yourself. Constructing your own Sigillum Dei Aemeth is the fastest and easiest way I know to meet and connect with the angelic forces resident in the design and make them part of *you*. It may take you several tries to get it all right, but I'm confident when you have completed your Sigillum you will think it worth the effort.

Figure 21: Blank Sigillum Dei Aemeth form

Building the Sigillum

Step One: The Seven God Names

The seven god names were drawn from numbers and letters that appear in the forty cells that make up the perimeter of the Sigillum. The magicians were told to divide the outer perimeter of a blank ring into four sections. Then they were to divide each of the four sections into ten (making forty cells in all). Kelley then had a dramatic and colorful vision, facilitated by the archangel Michael, with the help of Uriel and the angel Semiael. In this vision, forty angels stepped forth, one at a time, and parted their garments to reveal one of three things:

1. a number positioned above a letter,
2. a letter positioned above a number, or
3. a single letter.

Some of the letters were capitalized, but most were lowercase. As they revealed their letters and numbers, each of the forty angels also uttered a different pious declaration in Latin, such as, "O God, God, our God, blessed are you, now and forever" or "And you are true in your works." Then the angel disappeared or was consumed in flashes of fire or other such dramatics. The magicians were then left with a string of numbers and letters, which I've arranged in a table (see figure 22).

Figure 22: Outer perimeter bar code (the lowercase letter l *is italicized so as to not be confused with uppercase* I*)*

First make sure your blank Sigillum is oriented so that the pentagram in the center is pointing toward the top of the page. Then refer to figure 23 and locate the topmost cell of the Sigillum's outer perimeter—the cell that contains the number 4 over the capital letter *T*. Fill in that cell with a 4 over a T. Then, referring to the table (figure 22) and moving clockwise, fill in the remaining thirty-nine cells of the outer perimeter of your blank Sigillum as you see them in figure 23.

From the letters and numbers of the perimeter the seven god names and their sigils are drawn. The starting points for the god names are the cells that contain capital letters. These are also identified in figure 22 with asterisks beneath them.

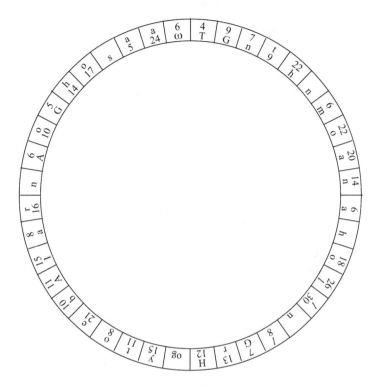

Figure 23: Outer perimeter letters

From those starting points, note the *number* inside the cell and count your way to find the next letter in the god name. You count *clockwise* when the *number* in the cell is positioned above the *letter*, and you count *counterclockwise* when the *letter* is positioned above the *number*. Keep counting until you reach a cell that contains a *letter* but no number. That will be the last letter of that particular god name. It's almost like turning the dial of a combination lock, and, indeed, that's exactly what you're doing.

Confused? Don't be. It's much easier to actually do it than describe it. Just keep figure 23 in front of you as you follow the directions that follow.

Galas

Figure 24: Sigil of Galas

Starting at the cell with 9/G in it (near the top of the circle), count nine cells clockwise (because the *number* is above) to 6/a. From there, count six cells clockwise to *l*/8. Count eight cells *counterclockwise* (because the *letter* is above) to 20/a. Count twenty cells clockwise to 8/a. Count eight cells clockwise to the single letter *s*. Because there is no number assigned to the *s* cell, we know that *s* is the final letter to this god name.

When all the counting is done, we have spelled the god name *Galaas*. The archangel Michael would later advise Dee and Kelley to alter the spelling (an archangel's prerogative) to *Galas*.

Michael assigned Galas a characteristic sigil and a number (see figure 24). He also instructed that the sigil and number of Galas should be placed on the Sigillum, in the area between the perimeter of cells and the outer bar of the heptagon at approximately the eleven o'clock position (see figure 32). Although a connection is not mentioned overtly in the original material, the god name *Galas* and its sigil are generally considered by many modern Enochian magicians to be associated with the qabalistic planetary sphere of Saturn.

Gethog

Figure 25: Sigil of Gethog

Starting with 7/G (near the bottom of the circle), count seven cells clockwise to e/21. Count twenty-one cells counterclockwise to t/9. Count nine cells counterclockwise to h/14. Count fourteen cells counterclockwise to the unnumbered letters *og* to finish the god name *Gethog*.

Michael assigned Gethog the sigil and number shown in figure 25 and instructed that they should be placed on the Sigillum in the area between the perimeter of cells and the outer bar of the heptagon at approximately nine o'clock (see figure 32). Although a connection is not mentioned overtly in the original material, the god name *Gethog* and its sigil are generally considered by many modern Enochian magicians to be associated with the qabalistic planetary sphere of Jupiter.

Thaoth

$_{30}$

Figure 26: Sigil of Thaoth

Starting with 4/T (near the top of the circle), count four cells clockwise to 22/h. Count twenty-two cells clockwise (because the *number* 22 is on top) to 11/A. Count eleven cells clockwise to a/5. Count five cells counterclockwise to o/10. Count ten cells counterclockwise to t/11. Count eleven cells counterclockwise to the cell that contains the single letter *h* to finish the god name *ThAaoth*.

Again using his archangel's prerogative, Michael later advised Dee to slightly alter the spelling to *Thaoth*. He also assigned Thaoth the sigil and number shown in figure 26 and instructed that they should be placed on the Sigillum in the area between the perimeter of cells and the outer bar of the heptagon at approximately seven o'clock (see figure 32). Although a connection is not mentioned overtly in the original material, the god name *Thaoth* and its sigil are generally considered by many modern Enochian magicians to be associated with the qabalistic planetary sphere of Mars.

Horlωn

XE $_{21}$

Figure 27: Sigil of Horlωn

Starting with H/12 (near the bottom of the circle), count twelve cells counterclockwise to 22/o. Count twenty-two cells clockwise to r/16. Count sixteen cells counterclockwise to 26/*l*. Count twenty-six cells clockwise to 6/ω.[63] Count six cells clockwise to single letter *n*, producing the god name *Horlωn*.

Michael assigned Horlωn the sigil and number shown in figure 27 and instructed that they should be placed on the Sigillum in the space between the perimeter of cells and the outer bar of the heptagon at six o'clock (see figure 32). Although a connection is not mentioned overtly in the original material, the god name *Horlωn* and its sigil are generally considered by many modern Enochian magicians to be associated with the qabalistic planetary sphere of Sol.

Innon

Figure 28: Sigil for Innon

Starting with 15/I (near the left-hand side of the circle), count fifteen cells clockwise to 7/n. Count seven cells clockwise to 14/n. Count fourteen cells clockwise to o/8. Count eight cells counterclockwise to the single letter *n*, producing the name *Innon*.

Michael assigned Innon the sigil and number shown in figure 28 and instructed that they should be placed on the Sigillum in the area between the perimeter of cells and the outer bar of the heptagon at approximately four o'clock (see figure 32). Although a connection is not mentioned overtly in the original material, the god name *Innon* and its sigil are generally considered by many modern Enochian magicians to be associated with the qabalistic planetary sphere of Venus.

Aaoth

Figure 29: Sigil for Aaoth

With Aaoth, you have your choice of either (1) starting at 11/A (near the left-hand side of the circle) and counting eleven cells clockwise to a/5 or (2) starting with 6/A (near the left-hand side of the circle) and counting six cells clockwise to a/5.

In either case, once you get to a/5, count five cells counterclockwise to o/10. Count ten cells counterclockwise to t/11. Count eleven cells counterclockwise to finish at *h*, producing the god name *Aaoth*.

Michael assigned Aaoth the sigil and number shown in figure 29 and instructed that they should be placed on the Sigillum in the space between the perimeter of cells and the outer bar of the heptagon at approximately two o'clock (see figure 32). Although a connection is not mentioned overtly in the original material, the god name *Aaoth* and its sigil are generally considered by many modern Enochian magicians to be associated with the qabalistic planetary sphere of Mercury.

Galethog

Figure 30: Sigil of Galethog

Starting at 5/G (near the left-hand side of the circle), count five cells clockwise to a/24. Count twenty-four cells counterclockwise to *l*/30. Count thirty cells counterclockwise to e/21. Count twenty-one cells counterclockwise to t/9. Count nine cells counterclockwise to h/14. Count fourteen cells counterclockwise to the single letters *og*, producing the name *Galethog*.

Michael assigned Galethog the sigil shown in figure 30 and instructed that they should be placed on the Sigillum in the area between the perimeter of cells and the outer bar of the heptagon at approximately one o'clock (see figure 32). Although a connection is not mentioned overtly in the original material, the god name *Galethog* and its sigil are generally considered by many modern Enochian magicians to be associated with the qabalistic planetary sphere of Luna.

These seven god names—*Galas, Gethog, Thaoth, Horlwn, Innon, Aaoth*, and *Galethog*—are distilled into one supreme name. Strangely enough, the great name is also spelled *Galethog*. The code that reveals this distillation can be found on those little numbers that appear beside six of the sigils of the god names. Let's take a look at the supreme god name as it appears with the sigils.

$$\overset{+}{G}_5 \ A\overset{+}{\rfloor}_{24} \ \overset{+}{\Gamma}^{\circ}L_{30} \ XE_{21} \ \overset{+}{\overset{\bullet}{\Phi}}_9 \ \overset{+}{\overset{\boxplus}{\overset{\bullet}{\cdot}}}_{14} \ \overset{+}{\textcircled{\scriptsize{OJ}}}$$

Figure 31: Supreme god name of the Sigillum Dei Aemeth

Obviously, the sigils of the divine names contain the stylized letters *G*, *a*, *l*, *xe*, *t*, and *og*. The little numbers beside the letters point out seven landmarks among the forty cells: 5/*G*, *a*/24, *l*/30, *e*/21, *t*/9. *Og* has no number attached to it, confirming that it is the end of the supreme god name.

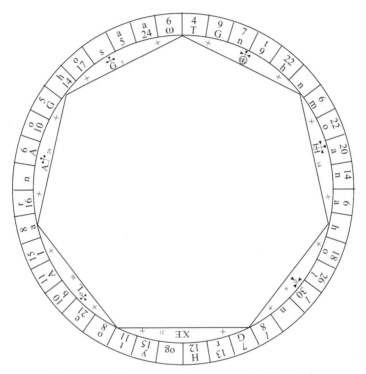

Figure 32: The seven god names and their sigils

Step Two: The Seven God Names of the Outer Heptagon and of the Planetary Archangels

A heptagon (a seven-sided figure) rests just inside the perimeter of the Sigillum. Each of the seven bars that compose the heptagon is divided into seven cells and is filled with the names of the next order of angels in the hierarchy of the Sigillum. These seven names were drawn from a 7 x 7 (sevenfold) table delivered to Dee and Kelley in a series of brief and colorful visions (see figure 33).

Z	l	l	R	H	i	a
a	Z	C	a	a	c	b
p	a	u	p	n	h	r
h	d	m	h	i	a	i
k	k	a	a	e	e	e
i	i	e	e	l	l	l
e	e	l	l	M	G	☩

Figure 33: The first sevenfold table

The names are read horizontally and are inserted in the bars of the outer heptagon as shown in figure 34.

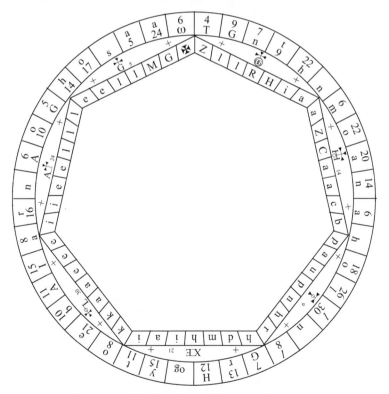

Figure 34: God names of the outer heptagon

When the table is read vertically, however, the names of the seven classic planetary archangels appear:

Zaphkiel (Saturn)   Zadkiel   (Jupiter)
Cumael   (Mars)   Raphael   (Sol)
Haniel   (Venus)   Michael   (Mercury)
Gabriel   (Luna)

These archangels were assigned to these planets many years before Dee and Kelley received them and could have been found in any number of books in Dee's library. However, Dee and Kelley insisted that the table was given to them before they noticed these names were generated by the table. Whether we choose to believe their assertion or not, the fact remains that these particular angels are not unique to the Enochian system.

Zaphkiel (Saturn)

Z	1	1	R	H	I	a
a	Z	C	a	a	c	b
p	a	u	p	n	h	r
h	d	m	h	I	a	I
K	K	a	a	e	e	e
I	I	e	e	1	1	1
e	e	1	1	M	G	✠

Zadkiel (Jupiter)

Z	1	1	R	H	I	a
a	Z	C	a	a	c	b
p	a	u	p	n	h	r
h	d	m	h	I	a	I
K	K	a	a	e	e	e
I	I	e	e	1	1	1
e	e	1	1	M	G	✠

Cumael (Mars)

Z	1	1	R	H	I	a
a	Z	C	a	a	c	b
p	a	u	p	n	h	r
h	d	m	h	I	a	I
K	K	a	a	e	e	e
I	I	e	e	1	1	1
e	e	1	1	M	G	✠

Raphael (Sol)

Z	1	1	R	H	I	a
a	Z	C	a	a	c	b
p	a	u	p	n	h	r
h	d	m	h	I	a	I
K	K	a	a	e	e	e
I	I	e	e	1	1	1
e	e	1	1	M	G	✠

Haniel (Venus)

Z	1	1	R	H	I	a
a	Z	C	a	a	c	b
p	a	u	p	n	h	r
h	d	m	h	I	a	I
K	K	a	a	e	e	e
I	I	e	e	1	1	1
e	e	1	1	M	G	✠

Michael (Mercury)

Z	1	1	R	H	I	a
a	Z	C	a	a	c	b
p	a	u	p	n	h	r
h	d	m	h	I	a	I
K	K	a	a	e	e	e
I	I	e	e	1	1	1
e	e	1	1	M	G	✠

Gabriel (Luna)

Z	1	1	R	H	I	a
a	Z	C	a	a	c	b
p	a	u	p	n	h	r
h	d	m	h	I	a	I
K	K	a	a	e	e	e
I	I	e	e	1	1	1
e	e	1	1	M	G	✠

Figure 35: Planetary archangels from the first sevenfold table

In order to read each archangel's name using the seven god names on the bars of the heptagon, we are obliged to project the letters in progressive layers rising from the surface of the Sigillum itself. I wish I could graphically illustrate this using the modern magick of animation, but you can demonstrate this for yourself. Let's turn to the first table in figure 35 and use the name of the planetary archangel of Saturn, Zaphkiel, as our example.

Start with the capital Z found in the first cell of the name *ZllRHia*, then move to the first cell of the name *aZCaacb* (to pick up the *a*), then move to the first cell of the name *paupnhr* (to pick up the *p*), then move to the first cell of *hdmhIaI* (to pick up the *h*), then move to the first cell of *Kkaaeee* to pick up the *K*, then move to the first cell of *eellMG* (to pick up the *e*). Finally, move to the *second* cell of the *ZllRHia* bar of the heptagon and pick up the final *l* to spell *Zaphkiel*.

I hope you can visualize what happens every time you move to another bar of the heptagon to pick up a letter in the archangel's name. As you move, you are literally shifting the dimensional structure of the Sigillum up another level—in the case of *Zaphkiel*, eight levels in all (see figure 36). (Picture the multilevel chess game played by characters on *Star Trek*.)

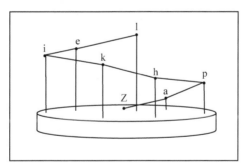

Figure 36: The name of the planetary archangel Zaphkiel spelled in eight layers above the Sigillum

Compound this with the fact that Zaphkiel's name is braided together in these same layers with the names of the six other archangels' names. Viewed this way, the Sigillum is no longer a flat image placed on the flat surface of the Holy Table. It is a multidimensional space hovering over the Holy Table—a magical basket formed of the netting of the entwined letters of the names of the seven planetary archangels. It is within this invisible basket that the scrying stone or black mirror is placed during the magical operation. Is it any wonder visions appear in such an environment?

But we're far from through with the wonders of the Sigillum. Fill the cells of your personal Sigillum's outer heptagon, and then let's move inward another step.

Step Three: The Seven Names of the Planetary Angels Beneath the Bars of the Outer Heptagon

Just inside the bars of the outer heptagon are seven more divine names. These names are drawn from a second 7 x 7 (sevenfold) table given to Dee and Kelley, letter by letter, in vision. These names are read horizontally and placed beneath the bars of the outer heptagon.

S	A	A	I $^{21}_{8}$	E	M	E $_8$
B	T	Z	K	A	S	E $_{30}$
H	E	I	D	E	N	E
D	E	I	M	O	$_{30}$	A
I $_{26}$	M	E	G	C	B	E
I	L	A	O	I $^{21}_{8}$	V	N
I	H	R	L	A	A	$^{21}_{8}$

Figure 37: The second sevenfold table

You will immediately notice some of the squares in this table contain tiny numbers (21 over 8, 8, 26, 30, and so on) and variously placed dots. These are added to indicate the addition of the letter *l* or letters *el* or *al* (angelic suffixes) to the letter in the square, the better to spell out the names of the various angels this table will produce.

These names of these seven great angels are added to the Sigilum as shown in figure 38.

*Figure 38: Names of the seven planetary angels beneath
the bars of the outer heptagon*

Step Four: The Daughters of the Light

Five more sets of planetary angels are drawn from the second sevenfold table. The first set was revealed in vision by seven young women (called "Daughters of Light" or "Women") clad in green silk. Each bore a little blue tablet on her forehead that identified her by name: El, Me, Ese, Iana, Akele, Azdobn, and Stimcul.

The names of the Daughters of Light are drawn from the second sevenfold table by reading the upper right section of the table in a diagonal, downward direction.

Figure 39: Names of the Daughters of Light on the second sevenfold table

Although the angels were not identified with planets in the original material, the manner in which the vision proceeded to reveal these names suggests these seven angels carry the following planetary assignments:

E(l)	Saturn	Me	Jupiter
Ese	Mars	Iana	Sol
Akele	Venus	Azdobn	Mercury
Stimcul	Luna		

The names of the Daughters of Light are placed on the Sigillum in clockwise order in the points created by the interlocking lines of the heptagram (see figure 40).

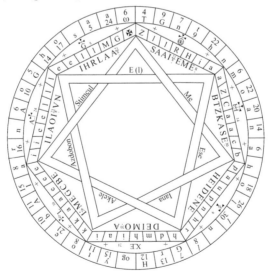

Figure 40: The Daughters of Light on the Sigillum

Step Five: The Sons of the Light

Next came seven young men (called the "Sons of the Light" or "Men") dressed in white, each carrying a metal ball: the first ball was gold, the second silver, the third copper, the fourth tin, the fifth iron, the sixth quicksilver, and the seventh lead. Each had a tablet of gold on his breast that identified him by name: I, Ih, Ilr, Dmal, Heeoa, Beigia, and Stimcul.

The names of the Sons of Light are drawn from the second sevenfold table by reading the lower left section of the table in a diagonal, downward direction.

S	A	A	I $\frac{21}{8}$	E	M	E 8
B	T	Z	K	A	S	E 30
H	E	I	D	E	N	E
D	E	I	M	O	30	A
I 26	M	E	G	E	B	E
I	I	A	O	I $\frac{21}{8}$	V	N
I	H	R	I	A	A	21

Figure 41: Names of the Sons of Light on the second sevenfold table

The metal of the ball carried by each of these characters suggests these seven angels carry the following planetary assignments:

I	Saturn	Ih	Jupiter
Ilr	Mars	Dmal	Sol
Heeoa	Venus	Beigia	Mercury
Stimcul	Luna		

The names of the Sons of Light are placed on the Sigillum in clockwise order on the interlocking bars of the heptagram (see figure 42).

Figure 42: The Sons of Light on the Sigillum

Step Six: The Daughters of Daughters of the Light

Next came seven "little wenches" ("Daughters of Daughters") dressed in white, having tablets, which appeared to be white ivory, on their bosoms, identifying them as S, Ab, Ath, Izad, Ekiei, Madimi, and Esemeli.

The names of the Daughters of Daughters are drawn from the second sevenfold table by reading the upper left section of the table in a diagonal, downward direction.

S	A	A	I	E	M	E
B	T	Z	K	A	S	E 30
H	E	I	D	E	N	E
D	E	I	M	O	30	A
26 M	E	G	C	B	E	
I	E	A	O	I 21/8	V	N
I	H	R	L	A	A	21/8

Figure 43: Names of the Daughters of Daughters of Light
on the second sevenfold table

Although these seven angels are not identified with planets, they are generally believed to carry the following planetary assignments:

S	Saturn	Ab	Jupiter
Ath	Mars	Izad	Sol
Ekiei	Venus	Madimi	Mercury
Esemeli	Luna		

The names of the Daughters of Daughters of Light are placed on the Sigillum in clockwise order beneath the bars of the heptagram (see figure 44).

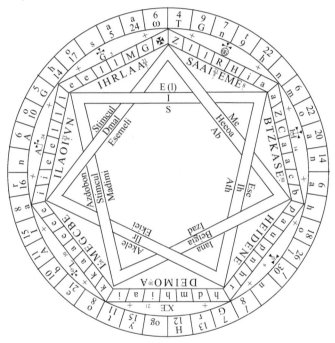

Figure 44: The Daughters of Daughters of Light on the Sigillum

Step Seven: The Sons of Sons of the Light

Next came seven "little children . . . like boys" ("Sons of Sons") dressed in robes of purple silk with long pointed sleeves and hats such as priests or scholars wear. They had triangular green tablets on their breasts identifying them as E, An, Ave, Liba, Rocle, Hagonel, and Ilemese.

The names of the Sons of Sons are drawn from the second sevenfold table by reading the lower right section of the table in an upward, diagonal.

S	A	A	I $^{21}_{8}$	E	M	E
B	T	Z	K	A	8	E
H	E	I	D	E	A	E
D	E	I	M	O		A
I $_{26}$	M	E	G	C	B	E
I	E	A	O	L	V	N
A	H	R	L	A	A	7

Figure 45: Names of the Sons of Sons of Light on the second sevenfold table

The names of the Sons of Sons of Light are placed on the Sigillum in clockwise order on the inner heptagon (see figure 46).

Figure 46: The Sons of Sons of Light on the Sigillum

Step Eight: The Planetary Angels of the Pentagram

Finally, Dee and Kelley were instructed in a relatively straightforward manner how to arrange the names of seven planetary angels—*Sabathiel*

(Saturn), *Zedekiel* (Jupiter), *Madimiel* (Mars), *Semeliel* (Sol), *Nogahel* (Venus), *Corabiel* (Mercury), and *Lavanael* (Luna)—around a pentagram at the very center of the Sigillum. These seven names are also drawn from the second sevenfold table by reading it in a zigzag manner, illustrated in figure 47.

*Figure 47: Names of the pentagram planetary angels
on the second sevenfold table*

Figure 48 shows the how the names of the pentagram planetary angels are arranged on the Sigillum.

Figure 48: The pentagram planetary angels on the Sigillum

Because the original Dee and Kelley material does not confirm the planetary attributions to all the various names on the Sigillum, I will not presume to do so either. I have, however, created a chart (see figure 49) that I currently use to help me in my meditations on the subject. I offer it along with the key to reading the names of planetary archangels from the first sevenfold table.

Figure 49: Possible key to the planetary angels on the Sigillum

Zaphkiel	Saturn ♄ 1–8
Zadkiel	Jupiter ♃ 1–7
Cumael	Mars ♂ 1–6
Raphael	Sol ☉ 1–7
Haniel	Venus ♀ 1–6
Michael	Mercury ☿ 1–7
Gabriel	Luna ☽ 1–7

Step Nine: The Crosses

Once the names of these angels were placed around the central pentagram, a number of tiny crosses were added to the Sigillum in a curiously inconsistent manner (see figure 50).

Figure 50: The completed Sigillum

And now your Sigillum is nearly complete. The only thing left to add is the design on the back. It is a very simple image of a cross dominating a small circle, around which are the letters of the divine word *AGLA* (an acronym for the Hebrew phrase *Ateh Gibor Le-olam Adonai*, "the Lord is mighty forever.")

Years ago, on a Christmas morning, I melted the stubs of scores of candles into a round Christmas cookie tin.[64] After the wax cooled and hardened, I removed the wax disk from the tin and set to work carving

Figure 51: The back of the Sigillum Dei Aemeth

my own Sigillum. Other magicians I know have sealed their drawings of the Sigillum upon wooden disks that they purchased for pennies at a crafts store, or glued the image to foam board. Whatever the medium, I think the presence of the Sigillum is an important factor in creating the magical environment conducive to Enochian vision magick.

There is so much more the angels told Dee and Kelley about the Sigillum, including suggestions for how every letter in each of the names contains a set of angels, and on and on by sevens by sevens. I encourage you to continue your exploration of the Sigillum's mysteries. But now we must move on to the seven Ensigns of Creation, where I promise you a much shorter journey.

CHAPTER ELEVEN

The Ensigns of Creation

Of these seven tables, characters, or scotcheons. Consider the words spoken in the fifth book Anno 1583, April 2nd. How they are proper to every King and prince in their order. They are Instruments of Conciliation.

—JOHN DEE, FOOTNOTE TO *Quinti Libri Mysteriorum: Liber Tertius*

The Ensigns of Creation are seven planetary talismans designed to be positioned on the Holy Table in a circle surrounding the Sigillum Dei Aemeth or laid out in a line along the edge of the table nearest the scryer. They were to be made of purified tin or else painted directly upon the Holy Table. Like the Lamen and the Holy Table, they are "Instruments of Conciliation" connected to the Heptarchia planetary kings and princes in a manner that, I must confess, is not altogether clear to me.

Five of them are square tables containing squares filled with numbers, letters, crosses, and lines. Two ensigns are a circle surrounded by a square. The letter *B* (*Pa* in the angelic language) is by far the most used letter in the ensigns.

The ensigns originally displayed Latin letters. The communicating angel would later insist that the Latin letters be replaced with the corresponding characters of the angelic script (see chapter fourteen). Dee was reluctant to do this and even asked the angel if he really had to. The angel said he must. We don't know if he ever did.

It is clear that the ensigns were to be utilized ritualistically, such as being held in the magician's hand during prayers or invocations. But information on exactly how things were to be done is incomplete, and there are no records whatsoever of Dee and Kelley actually performing rituals of heptarchic magick.

Figure 52 shows the ensigns with their Latin letters and the planet, king, and prince each represents.

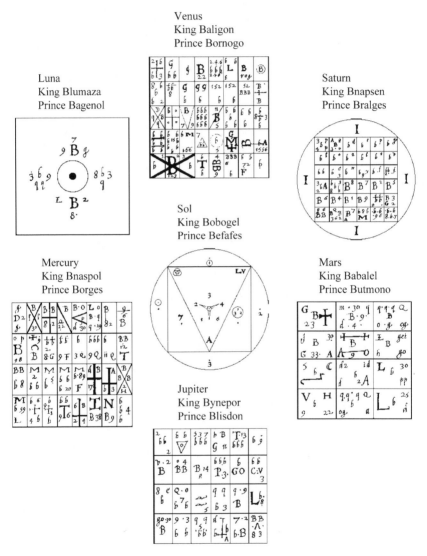

Figure 52: The seven Ensigns of Creation and their kings and princes

However, the ensigns remain part of the Holy Table ensemble, and their subsequent connection to the table and the magician's own Lamen make them, in my opinion, an integral component of the hierarchical current that charges the holy ground of the Enochian magick temple.

Figures 53 and 54 show the ensigns lettered in the angelic script. To my knowledge, this is the first time the ensigns have appeared in print in their correct form.[65] As with the Ring, Holy Table, Lamen, and Sigillum, the ensigns can be reproduced in paper board or whatever material is at the magician's disposal.

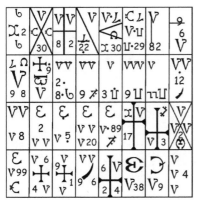

Ensign of Mercury

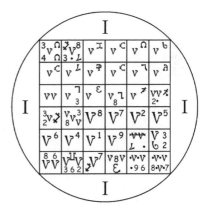

Ensign of Saturn

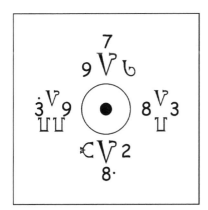

Ensign of Luna

Figure 53: Mercury, Saturn, and Luna Ensigns
of Creation in the angelic script

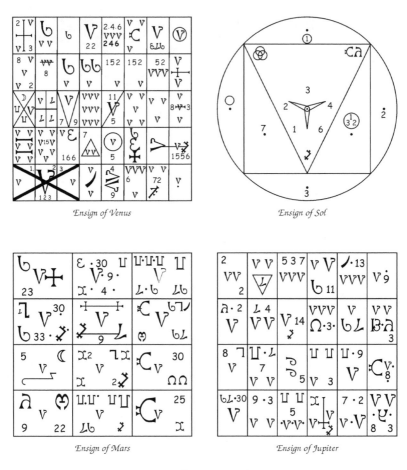

Figure 54: Venus, Sol, Mars, and Jupiter Ensigns
of Creation in the angelic script

Figure 55 shows the positions in which the ensigns are placed on the Holy Table around the Sigillum. Note they are positioned near the points of the Sigillum's heptagram.

The entire assembly is one big magical machine—the Sigillum resting like a sevenfold, multidimensional dynamo in the center of the Holy Table's swirling and churning angels and the circling Ensigns of Creation. The *scrying stone* or *black mirror* is placed upon the Sigillum at the very heart of this magnificent instrument like the monitor screen of a magical computer connected to the ultimate worldwide-web.

Figure 55: Position of the ensigns around the Sigillum

We have made only the tiniest scratch on the surface of Dee and Kelley's material of this period. There is much more information concerning De Heptarchia Mystica available to the serious student, and I encourage the reader who feels drawn to this system to make the effort. I know it is only a matter of time before some bright magician fine-tunes, perfects, and transforms the material into a workable magical system.

The focus of this book, however, is Enochian vision magick, and we must now move on to the second phase of Dee and Kelley's magical operations. Through our understanding of the Ring, the Lamen, the Holy Table, the Sigillum Dei Aemeth, and the Ensigns of Creation and of their construction, we have prepared ourselves to meet with angels on the holy ground of our temple.

CHAPTER TWELVE

Do I Need All This Stuff?

Never since the beginning of the world was this secret delivered, nor this holy mystery set open, before the weaklings of this world.

—THE ANGEL IL, APRIL 29, 1583

The question I'm sure many of you are asking at this point is, "Do I need all this stuff?"

During the classes that I conducted in our home in 2005 and 2006 (with experienced magicians) and subsequent day-long workshops I've conducted around the country with people having little or no prior magical experience) it has become abundantly clear to me that the magical objects and "furniture" Dee and Kelley received during the Heptarchia periods (the Ring, the Holy Table, the Lamen, the Ensigns of Creation, and the Sigillum Dei Aemeth) can and *should* be formally employed in order to create the specific environment of consciousness conducive to the practice of angelic vision magick.

Furthermore, it has been my observation that regular and repeated activation of this magical "temple" by means of the little ritual outlined in chapter one (and laid out more fully in appendix I) can attune the magician to this uniquely ordered universe and serve to progressively strengthen and enhance his or her visionary capabilities.

Most exciting for me was the discovery that once the magician is prepared and the temple activated the angelic forces (especially the good angels resident in the Holy Table, Lamen, Ensigns of Creation, and the planetary angels resident in the Sigillum) can be individually called forth or visited by means of classic evocation techniques or even informal extemporaneous prayers and conjurations. In other words, I believe that even if he or she never went on to practice Enochian magick per se, a resourceful magician, willing to experiment, and armed with a proper understanding of the tools and formulae of the Heptarchic periods would be already prepared to engage in angelic vision magick of a high order.

This is new territory for all of us, but it holds much promise, for it entails the possibility of contacting the same angelic forces that engaged Dee and Kelley throughout most of their day-to-day actions. Obviously, dealing with these angelic forces offers an alluring challenge for today's more intrepid magicians who, when frustrated by gaps and perplexities in the original material, will not be afraid to go straight to the communicating angels for guidance and clarification on how all this should operate. Indeed, I expect to see in the years to come exciting and viable magical systems develop as the result of the magical efforts of gifted practitioners who dare to make such angelic contact.

But do you need all this stuff?

My answer is this: In order to do this particular variety of magick you need all this stuff *inside* you. That's where the real magick takes place. But until such time as you have internalized all this (even in the most cursory and general manner) it is necessary to have some outward, visible, material representation of the magical concepts and forces you are dealing with.

I suggest, if you're serious about engaging in this magical art form, then you should, at the very least, provide yourself with a Ring, a Holy Table, a Lamen, a Sigillum Dei Aemeth, and the seven Ensigns of Creation. Make them out of paper if you have to. Copy them straight out of this book if you have to. But have them. Make them real to you. Consecrate them by using them. Use them to create your Enochian magick temple.

The sense of art for some magicians is stimulated by replicating as much as humanly possible the tools and procedures as outlined in ancient texts. By doing so, they achieve a level of empowerment they believe is necessary to execute the work. Personally, my sense of art is quite happy with paper rings and photocopied Holy Tables. However,

I have over the years been blessed with many talented colleagues who have generously helped me equip my temple so I might better demonstrate these things to others.

Here is as good a place as any for me to pause and describe what I believe the source material suggests would transform a clean uncluttered room into the holy ground of an Enochian magick temple.

The Temple

Upon the floor in the center of the room is a square carpet of red silk cloth large enough to accommodate the Holy Table and the chair of the scryer.

Upon the silken carpet are placed four miniatures of the Sigillum Dei Aemeth, made of wax. They are covered and protected from the table legs by shallow cylindrical boxes.

Upon the box-covered sigilli rest the four legs of the Holy Table.

The Holy Table is made of sweet wood (laurel).

Upon the Holy Table, arranged as we've discussed, are the seven Ensigns of Creation (lettered in the angelic script) and the Sigillum Dei Aemeth, made of purified beeswax, nine inches in diameter and an inch and a half thick.

The Holy Table and all the objects upon it are covered by a red silk cloth with gold tassels that dangle from the corners. This cloth should match in material and color that of the red silk carpet.

Upon the covered Sigillum the scrying stone (a crystal ball) or black mirror is placed.

The scryer's chair is placed on the carpet near the table. His or her feet should touch the carpet.

The Ring and Lamen should be near. The magician should ceremonially put them on at the beginning of each session and remove them at the conclusion.

Renaissance magicians often wore crowns and white linen robes, and on one occasion in preparation for a specific working, Dee and Kelley were instructed to wear white linen robes. In an operation that took place on July 13, 1584 (at the very end of the Enochian communications), the archangel Gabriel told the magicians:

> See that your garments be clean. Herein be not rash: Nor over hasty; For those that are hasty and rash, and are loathsomely appareled, my knock long before they enter.[66]

In practical operations conducted by my Monday night class and my Enochian magick workshops, everyone is shoeless and wears comfortable street clothes. In private sessions, such as the one I described in chapter one, I put on a simple black robe. Not only does it carry with it a certain personal magical virtue, but its color does not distract from the images reflected in the black mirror as I scry.

BOOK III

Liber Loagaeth and the
Angelic Alphabet

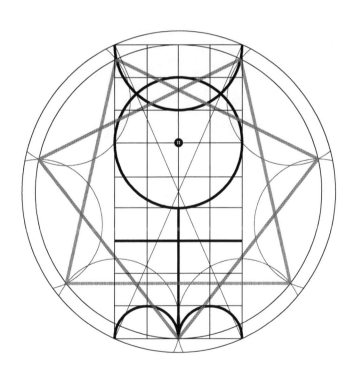

CHAPTER THIRTEEN

Liber Loagaeth

Every element (of the book) hath 49 manner of understandings.
Therein is comprehended so many languages. They are all spoken at
once, and severally, by themselves, by distinction many be spoken.
Until thou come to the City, thou canst not behold the beauty thereof.

—THE ANGEL ME TO JOHN DEE, EASTER DAY, 1583[67]

The second phase of Dee and Kelley's magical operations remains, for the most part, a tantalizing mystery to modern students. Covering most of 1582 and 1583, it is a period characterized by considerable tension between the two magicians, but one that also produced a large body of work in the form of a book referred to at various times as *Liber Mysteriorum Sextus et Sanctus*, the *Book of Enoch*, and *Liber Loagaeth*.[68] While in recent years Enochian scholars have courageously set out to give us a closer examination of this information, it unfortunately has not been enough to allow modern practitioners to develop anything near a workable system from this material.

One of the reasons more attention isn't paid to this period is the nature of the material itself and the nearly complete lack of direction concerning how it is to be applied. Also, the focus of the communications of this period is driven by Dee's very personal fixation on discovering lost books of the Bible, the Apocrypha, and in particular the *Book of Enoch*, which is mentioned in several places in the Bible. The resulting character of *Liber Loagaeth* is rich in apocalyptic imagery and prophetic sounding rhetoric. This has been seized upon in recent years by commentators who would project a patently sectarian interpretation upon the material, even going so far as to suggest sinister (perhaps even Satanic or Lovecraftian) motives behind the "angelic" communications.

We are all, of course, free to our own religious convictions and spiritual worldviews. After all, they are part of the magical artist's pallet of tools. I think it wise, however, to keep in mind that when we study the Dee and Kelley material, we are not only eavesdropping on questions framed in the minds of two sixteenth-century Englishmen and put in the context of biblical literature, but we are also hearing the answers to those questions given in such a manner as these men could understand—that is, framed within the same cultural and Biblical context. I'm sure if Dee had been a Chinese alchemist or an African shaman in these same circumstances, the angels would have communicated the same universal answers unencumbered by the apocalyptic nomenclature familiar to the Jewish or Christian mind.

Joseph Peterson wrote in the introduction of his marvelous book *John Dee's Five Books of Mystery*:

> The importance of *Liber Loagaeth* cannot be overemphasized. From it would "be restored the holy bokes, which haue perished euen from the beginning, and from the first that liued." The truths it contains will end religious disputes and restore religious unity. "Which when it hath spread a while, THEN COMMETH THE END."[69] In short, it will usher in the new age. Since the book is so central to these angelic communications, it is amazing that it has remained unpublished.[70]

Amazing indeed, but as I wrote concerning De Heptarchia Mystica, it is only a matter of time before someone cracks the code of this breathtakingly immense body of work. What do I mean by breathtakingly immense?

One surviving manuscript comprises forty-eight leaves, each containing 49 x 49 lettered squares, 115,000 lettered squares in all. Each square was filled, letter-by-letter, according to Kelley's vision. In the end, the magicians were left with forty-nine calls in an angelic language. (Note: These calls were not the same calls in the angelic tongue that would come later and form the centerpiece of the Enochian phase of

Dee and Kelley's partnership.) *Loagaeth* literally means "speech from God," and the magicians were informed that the words of the forty-nine calls were the same as those uttered by God at the dawn of creation—in the same language spoken by Adam when he named all things.

Unfortunately, these calls were never translated (or else the material has been lost), and attempts by modern linguists have failed to find enough landmarks of a properly constructed language to put the calls of *Loagaeth* in the same category as the angelic language that would be received in the third and final phase of the magicians' actions.

Kelley's visionary skills were severely exploited during this period, and his visions were characterized by the presence of a dazzling light that both magicians could see. The light would fly out of the scrying stone and penetrate Kelley's head, putting him in a trance in which he could read and comprehend the text of *Liber Loagaeth*. He was, however, forbidden to translate it and told that God would later provide the translation. At the end of the session, the light would leave Kelley's head and return to the stone. When he returned to normal consciousness, he claimed to have no memory of the experience.

As tempting as it might be, I am, for the time being not incorporating any of the calls from *Loagaeth* in my Enochian-magick preparation ritual. However, something else of great importance came out of this period: the angelic alphabet.

CHAPTER FOURTEEN

The Angelic Alphabet

He wiped his finger on the top of the Table, and there came out above the Table certain Characters enclosed in no line: but standing by them selves, and points between them. He pointed orderly to them with his finger, and looked toward the skryer at every pointing.

—EDWARD KELLEY DESCRIBING HIS VISION OF THE ANGEL'S
REVELATION OF THE ANGELIC ALPHABET, MARCH 26, 1583[71]

I confess, even with clear copies and transcriptions of the source material in front of me, it has been very difficult for me to wrap my mind around the order of the visionary events of Dee and Kelley's years together. Because certain elements of these magical systems were often corrected or amended by the angels in subsequent visions, often occurring months apart, it is extremely difficult (for me at least) to present a clean chronology of events. The circumstances surrounding the reception of the angelic alphabet are no exception.

The alphabet was received during the Loagaeth period, but because the magicians were told to replace the Latin/English letters of the Lamen, Holy Table, and the seven Ensigns of Creation with letters from the angelic script, its influence reached back in time to touch the Heptarchia period as well.

The twenty-one characters of the angelic alphabet appeared fully formed in yellowish letters that rose in Kelley's vision above the table. The images of the individual letters then obligingly hovered over a sheet of paper and stayed visible long enough for him to copy them in ink before fading away.

Words in the angelic language are written from right to left, and that is the order the letters first appeared to Kelley. All twenty-one letters appeared in a single row and were separated by dots. There was also a dot preceding the first letter.

Figure 56: Characters of the angelic alphabet in the order received (read from right to left)

Script	Pa	veh	ged	gal	or	un	graph
Name	Pa	veh	ged	gal	or	un	graph
English	b	c	g	d	f	a	e

Script	tal	gon	na	ur	mals	ger	drux
Name	tal	gon	na	ur	mals	ger	drux
English	m	i	h	l	p	q	n

Script	pal	med	don	ceph	van	fam	gisg
Name	pal	med	don	ceph	van	fam	gisg
English	x	o	r	z	u	s	t

Figure 57: Table of the angelic alphabet (read from left to right)

You will notice that the name for the first letter received, *Pa*, is the only letter whose name is capitalized. *Pa*, *b* in English, has a special significance in the magick of the Heptarchia. For example, the names of all the forty-nine good angels begin with *b*, the letter *b* appears overwhelmingly on the Ensigns of Creation, and each of the four corners of the Holy Table displays an oversized *Pa*.

This abundance of *b*s has caused several knowledgeable modern magical commentators to speculate that *b* must represent the number seven, the number upon which these magical systems seem to be based. While that makes a great deal of sense to me, I have nonetheless found nothing in the original material that would specifically suggest numerical equivalents to any of the single letters of the angelic alphabet.

What is very clear, however, is the fact that the communicating angel wanted Dee and Kelley to immediately memorize the letters of the angelic alphabet and the letters' names. Dee was a busy man and wanted to be excused from this time-consuming duty. The angel Me would have none of it. In this March 26, 1583, exchange, Dee tries to make the angel understand, "Look man, I've got a life!"

Me: I instructed thee before-hand and told thee, that both of you must jointly learn those holy letters (For, so, I may boldly call them) in memory: with their names: to the intent, that the finger may point to the head, and the head to the understanding of his charge.

Dee: You perceive that I have diverse affairs which at this present do withdraw me from peculiar diligence using to these Characters and their names learning by heart: And therefore I trust, I shall not offend, if I bestow all the convenient leisure that I shall get, about the learning thereof.

Me: Peace, Thou talkest, as though, thou understoodest not. We know thee, we see thee in thy heart: Nor one thing shall not let another. For short is the time, that shall bring these things to proof.[72]

BOOK IV

Enochiana

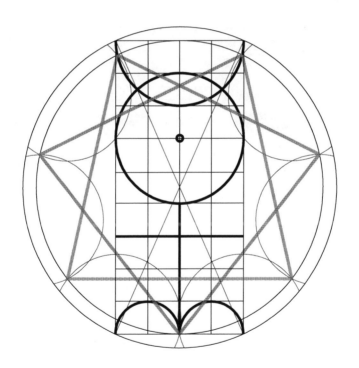

CHAPTER FIFTEEN

Enochian Magick

The Lord appeared unto Enoch, and was merciful unto him, opened his eyes, that he might see and judge the earth, which was unknown to his Parents, by reason of their fall : for the Lord said, Let us shew unto Enoch, the use of the earth : And lo, Enoch was wise, and full of the spirit of wisdom.

—THE ANGEL AVE, MONDAY, JUNE 25, 1584[73]

To my knowledge, Dee and Kelley never used the word *Enochian* to describe the system of magick they received between April 10 and July 13, 1584. Throughout their actions, they simply referred to it as angelic. We cannot, however, be faulted too badly for attaching the biblical patriarch's name to the system. The magicians were told that this was the magick given by God to Enoch (the seventh man from Adam) in the form of a book and that Enoch (before he ascended bodily into the presence of God) passed it on to others. Over the generations, the book fell into wicked hands, and God caused it to be lost. But because of Dee's piety and prayers, God was moved to once again deliver it to mankind.

These final days were an especially difficult period in Dee and Kelley's relationship. They and their families were living in Krakow, Poland. Their actions were regularly interrupted by "evil spirits," who encouraged the magicians to abandon the actions. Kelley was increasingly impatient and uncomfortable with the work, voicing his fear of the possible evil nature of the communications on one hand. Ironically, Kelley was at the time practicing demon magick behind Dee's back. Dee was furious when he learned of this. So were the communicating angels, who warned that such behavior attracted evil spirits into the magician's environment—an annoying and time-consuming distraction. Finally Kelley promised Dee and the angels that he would knock off the black magick.

The angels, too, appeared to be growing impatient with Dee and Kelley, as if they realized the magical chemistry that existed between the two magicians (the personal factors that made them such a perfect operator/receiver team) was rapidly disintegrating. In April, the magicians were told in no uncertain terms that the work had to be completed by August. The magicians met their deadline with time to spare. July 13, 1584, Dee's fifty-seventh birthday, saw the final communication that completed the reception of the angelic calls and provided the names of the thirty Aethyrs. Not only had the Enochian phase of Dee and Kelley's operations ended, but, indeed, the entire angelic adventure had also come to a close. The plug was pulled. The communicating angels fell silent.

The magicians would continue on and off for several years with visionary operations and unsuccessful mago-political adventures in Europe. But, with the exception of only three brief references in their subsequent diaries, they never again mention the angelic magick. One of those latter-day references (the *Tabula Recensa*), however, is very significant to the study of the Enochian magick period. I'll speak more on that very soon.

The reception of the Enochian material was (at least to my impatient attention span) even more confused and topsy-turvy than that which characterized the Heptarchia and *Liber Loagaeth* periods. Sadly, as we discovered in the two earlier cases, the surviving information, while abundant, still does not provide us with adequate information on how it all was supposed to work as a practical system of magick.

And here is where we must again tip our magical hats to S. L. MacGregor Mathers, the adepts of the Golden Dawn, and Aleister Crowley, who at the dawn of the twentieth century developed this material into a remarkably logical system of vision magick—a system possessed of the solid infrastructure lacking in the surviving source material, a system that, for all intents and purposes, offers the diligent practitioner a practical and elegant unified field theory of hermetic and qabalistic magick.

As applied most commonly today, Enochian magick is a two-part magical system: one part focusing on the elemental universe, the other on the aethyric. The former enables the magician to summon or visit in vision the spirits of the myriad levels of the elemental worlds of Fire, Water, Air, Earth, and Spirit; the latter enables the magician to systematically penetrate increasingly higher heavens (or Aethyrs) to access information from those heavenly levels of consciousness.

I will soon show how these two systems are operated. But before I do that, and in keeping with our program of systematic attunement, I need to introduce you to another magick table. It was the first revelation of the Enochian period, but it is also, in my opinion, the final component of the preparation protocol. This tablet was delivered to the magicians by the angel Nalvage in April of 1584. It is an item that was acknowledged by the adepts of the Golden Dawn but never incorporated into any practice. It is something, however, I believe should not escape our attention. No name was given to this object. Some modern scholars designate it simply the Tablet of God. I shall refer to it as the *Round Tablet of Nalvage*.

CHAPTER SIXTEEN

The Round Tablet of Nalvage

The order and knitting together of the parts in their due and perfect proportion, God the Holy Ghost. Lo the beginning and end of all things.

—THE ANGEL NALVAGE, APRIL 10, 1584

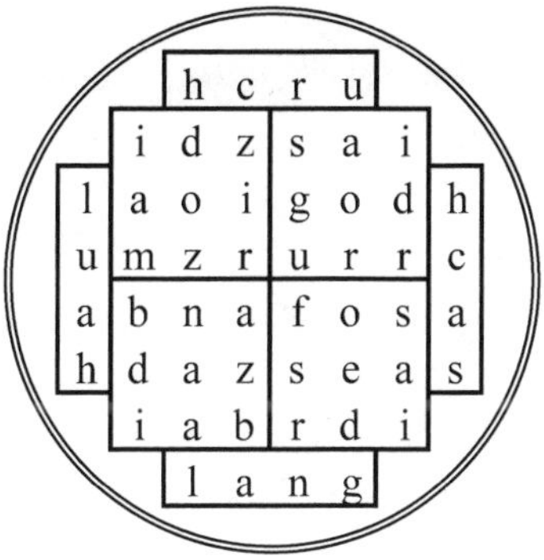

Figure 58: The Round Tablet of Nalvage

"The Method of Science—The Aim of Religion" was the official motto of *The Equinox*, the great magical periodical first published by Aleister Crowley and his colleagues in the early years of the twentieth century.[74] This same phrase could also comfortably serve as the watchwords that describe what the art of magick is to me.

Conversely, superstition (as the word is commonly understood) has, in my opinion, no place in the arsenal of the modern magician. This, I believe, is especially true concerning the practice of Enochian vision magick. In all my years of magical practice and exploration of this system, I have never encountered a single case of so-called psychic attack, demon possession, headache, hives, or hernia—indeed *any* ill effects whatsoever—resulting from the practice of this particular kind of magick.

That being said, strange and unexpected things do occasionally happen to those who practice magick. And while I believe it is bad for one's mental health to ascribe undue importance to these phenomena, it is important that they be dispassionately observed and recorded. So, before I discuss the Round Tablet of Nalvage and its importance to the system of Enochian magick, I feel I must share with you two little stories that might help you understand the level of respect I hold for this particular magical object.

Twenty years ago, I was teaching a class in Enochian vision magick at our home in Costa Mesa. This class was different from the Enochian magick classes I had taught previously, for it was the first time we would study and experiment with using the Round Tablet of Nalvage. In preparation for the first class, I decided to make a copy of the tablet out of wax (as I had done with my Sigillum Dei Aemeth). A friend had given me two massive, black wax candles shaped like giant chessmen (bishops). My plan was to melt these down in a round Christmas cookie tin and carve the squares and the angelic letters of the Tablet of Nalvage on the cooled wax disk.

It was a foolish time to be starting an arts project like this, because our landlord had just informed us he was bulldozing our house in two weeks and building apartments on our lot (thanks a lot!), and we were deep in the midst of packing up our things to move. Still, magick is magick, and life goes on. I put the two black wax bishops in the cookie tin and slid them into the oven. I set the heat on the lowest possible warm level and went out to the garage to help (watch) Constance pack.

As you might imagine, we had some very interesting things in our garage, many of which we hadn't looked at in years. We did more reminiscing than packing. I didn't forget the black wax bishops in the oven, however, and checked on them regularly. It seemed they were taking a long time to melt, so I turned up the heat a little higher.

Back out in the garage we found a stash of psychedelic artwork Constance had painted and drawn in the late sixties, when we were hippies living in the woods of southern Oregon. We hadn't seen them in fifteen years. What a treat! We lingered over them for probably ten minutes before I remembered the black wax bishops for the Round Tablet of Nalvage in the oven.

When I opened the back door, I found the kitchen dark except for a warm orange glow that, like a spectacular sunset, brightened the dark clouds of smoke that filled the house from the ceiling to about four feet from the floor. The oven was completely engulfed in flames. I ran into the living room and found our son, Jean-Paul, lying on the floor watching television completely oblivious to the black smoke pressing its way toward him from above.

Once he and the dog were evacuated, I called for Constance (always a level head in times of emergency), and we proceeded to attack the fire. When I opened the flaming oven, I discovered that one of the bishops had slid to the side of the cookie tin and parts of it had melted down the outside rim. The wax had run to the bottom of the oven and dripped down upon the pilot light, which then become the eternal flame of Costa Mesa. There was nothing we could do to turn off the oven. Constance eventually had to turn off the gas outside, and with the help of baking soda and wet towels, we got the fire out. I rescued the cookie tin and let it cool in the sink. A couple hours later, in the charred ruins of our kitchen, I carved a beautiful black wax Round Tablet of Nalvage.

Now, I'm the first to confess that this story has less to do with magick and superstition and more with my own carelessness and stupidity. (I am now forbidden to use the oven for magical crafts.) The accident did, however, serve to give me a healthy respect for the Round Tablet of Nalvage—a respect that in the last year has increased immeasurably. And that brings me to my second magical tale of Nalvage.

As we'll soon see, there is much we know about the Round Tablet of Nalvage. What we don't know is how it was intended to be used. As I was preparing for the class series that inspired this book, I debated with myself how (or even if) I was going to introduce it into our studies. After all, there is nothing in the source material that hints at what is to be done with it. Late in the afternoon, I prepared our living room temple for the evening's class. The Sigillum and ensigns were set neatly on the Holy Table; the table was covered with its red silk cloth, and the obsidian mirror was set in place.

I went to the closet cupboard in my office and took down my black wax Round Tablet of Nalvage from the topmost shelf. I unzipped its plastic bubble-wrapped envelope and carefully removed it. I had to admit, after all those years, it still looked magnificently magical. I took it into the living room and set it down upon the covered table. I sat down in my comfy chair, and in the warm glow of sunset (which brought to my mind the glow of our blazing kitchen so many years earlier), I meditated about how the Round Tablet of Nalvage fits into the system.

I didn't get much meditating done, because the moment I closed my eyes I fell asleep. I awoke just a few minutes before people would start arriving for class. I still didn't know how or if I was going to the use the tablet for the night's gathering. I hastily decided that if I didn't have sound reasons for using the tablet, I was going to skip it altogether—at least for that night. I took the tablet off the Holy Table, wrapped it back up, and carefully put it back on the top shelf of the closet cupboard.

I went to my desk to turn off the computer and gather things for class, when I was startled by the sound of something smashing against my guitar, which was mounted upright in its stand near the open closet door. With the guitar strings still ringing, I turned to see that the Tablet of Nalvage had flown from its shelf, ricocheted off my guitar, and was resting inches from my feet.

As a reasonably rational man, I am of the opinion that there is nothing supernatural in the world, just natural things that have yet to be explained. I'm sure there is nothing I can say to convince the cynic that the tablet hadn't fallen naturally from the shelf because I hadn't put it there properly. I remain, however, extremely impressed at the distance this object had to travel across physical space in order to strike the guitar and find its way to my feet at the very moment I had decided not to discuss it at that evening's class.

Needless to say, I changed my mind about the importance of the tablet, and in the few moments remaining before class members started to arrive, I composed the two-part chorus that incorporates the dynamics created by the letters of the Round Tablet of Nalvage—a chant that has become the last (and perhaps the most important) component of the Ceremony of Preparation.[75]

Now, let's take a brief look at those dynamics and how a chant based on the Round Tablet of Nalvage can be constructed.

The Tablet of Nalvage is not really round. It is a square divided into four squares (or continents) and surrounded by four outer bars (see figure 59). The continents and bars are subdivided into lettered squares (nine squares per continent and four squares per bar). But before we start filling in the letters, let's see what the angel Nalvage had to say about the continents.

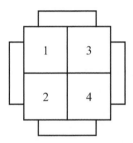

Figure 59: The four continents of the Round Tablet of Nalvage

Nalvage told Dee and Kelley that continents 1 and 2 are "dignified," while 3 "is not yet dignified, but to be dignified," and 4 is "without glory or dignity." Nalvage described them in Latin as follows:

1. *Vita suprema* (highest life), the continent of "joy";
2. *Vita* (life), the continent of "potentiality";
3. *Vita non dignificata, sed dignificanda* (life not dignified, but which shall be dignified), the continent of "creation"; and
4. *Vita est etiam haec, sed quae perperit mors* ("Even this is life, but life which will be paid with death"), the continent of "discord."

Each continent contains nine letters that, when read in various ways, yield words in the angelic language. In order to more easily see these words, I have separated the tablet into its component parts (see figure 60).

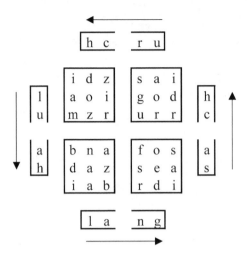

Figure 60: Separated Round Tablet of Nalvage

When read counterclockwise, the outer bars of the tablet spell the names of four classes of angels: *luah* (praising angels), *lang* (ministering angels), *sach* (confirming angels), and *urch* (confounding angels).

These angels circumscribe and contain the angelic forces at work within the continents. Nalvage gave the following Latin meanings to the words inside the continents when the words are read horizontally from left to right (see figure 61).

idz – Gaudium – Joy *aoi* – Praesentia – Presence *mzr* – Laudantes – Praising	*sai* – Actio – Action *god* – Factum – Events *urr* – Confirmantes – Establishing
bna – Potestas – Power *daz* – Motus – Motion *iab* – Ministrantes – Ministering	*fos* – Luctos – Lamentation *sea* – Discordia – Discord *rdi* – Confundantes – Confusing

Figure 61: Words and meanings of the words of the four continents

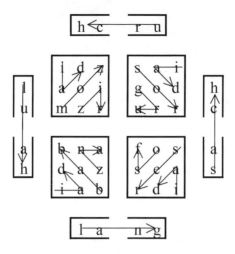

Figure 62: Key to the Round Tablet of Nalvage

Figure 62 shows how the letters of the continents are read to reveal the nature of the divine powers resident in the tablet.

First notice how the three letters of *outer* corners of each of the four continents (upper left corner of upper left continent, lower left corner of lower left continent, and so on) all spell the Enochian word meaning God—*iad*.

Notice next that the three diagonal letters of continents spell the words *moz* (joy), *bab* (power), *sor* (action), and *ser* (lamentation).

Finally, the three letters of the *inner* corners of the continents spell the words *zir* (I am), *zna* (motion), *gru* (deed), and *osf* (discord).

The arrows in figure 62 show the beautiful symmetry the words create within the tablet. If we put the words of each continent together, we arrive at phrases such as:

Continent 1.	*iad moz zir* (I am the Joy of God.)
Continent 2.	*iad bab zna* (God's Power in Motion)
Continent 3.	*iad sor gru* (Result of God's Action)
Continent 4.	*iad ser osf* (God's Discord and Lamentation)

This rich tapestry of joy, movement, creation, and sorrow is contained and encircled by a counterclockwise whirl of the angels: *luah, lang, sach,* and *urch.*

Concerning the tablet as a whole, Nalvage said,"The Substance is attributed to God the Father."[76]

In reference to the letters on the outer bars, Nalvage said, "The first circular mover, the circumference, God the Son, The finger of the Father, and mover of all things."[77]

Referring to the continents and the manner in which their letters are read, he said, "The order and knitting together of the parts in their due and perfect proportion, God the Holy Ghost. Lo the beginning and end of all things."[78]

Like the Holy Table, the Round Tablet of Nalvage, once decoded, displays divine and angelic words and names in perpetual motion in such a way that one can almost sense what is meant by the term *choir of angels*. In group workings, I break the participants up into two voices as we ceremonially chant the words from the tablet.

Voice One: *luah lang sach urch*

Voice Two: *iad moz zir—iad bab zna—iad sor gru—iad ser osf*

The effect is powerful even when I'm alone in the middle of the night and chant one voice at a time.

Once Nalvage described the dynamics of the tablet, he didn't go on to provide instructions on how, or even if, the tablet was to be used. Is it a talisman? Is it to be worn as the Lamen? Is it to be held or placed on the Holy Table? We don't know.

However, we do know that after the two magicians had become attuned to the structure of the Round Tablet of Nalvage, the entire remaining system of Enochian magick was revealed in less than ninety days. This has led more than a few magicians to speculate that the Round Tablet of Nalvage might be the key to a mysterious and unexpressed "first call" of the Enochian system, or perhaps even represent the call itself.

CHAPTER SEVENTEEN

The Forty-eight Calls

Move, therefore, and show yourselves: open the Mysteries of your
Creation: Be friendly unto me: for I am the servant of the same your
God, the true worshipper of the Highest.

—FROM THE FIRST CALL[79]

The centerpiece of the Enochian system is a collection of calls[80] in an angelic tongue that is significantly different from the language delivered in *Liber Loagaeth*. The reception of the calls followed that of the Tablet of Nalvage. They were first dictated to the magicians in the angelic tongue, then afterwards translated into English. Careful examination of the calls and their translations reveal that Enochian is a real language and not simply strings of barbarous names and words. The calls read like evocative hymns or invocations. They are constructed of real, sometimes breathtakingly beautiful sentences that can be translated (not merely transliterated). The language exhibits a remarkable consistency of word meaning from call to call. It has a form of grammar and syntax. This phenomenon, coupled with the multiple double-blind/letter-by-letter method by which it was received, makes this (in my mind at least) one of the most extraordinary aspects of Dee and Kelley's workings.

Technically, there are forty-nine calls. However, as the first call was said to be unexpressed, I will refer to them as if there were forty-eight.

They appear translated in their entirety in appendix II of this book, along with the keys to how they are put to use by modern Enochian magicians (see also chapter twenty-seven).

Beginning on April 10, 1584, the first four calls were painstakingly delivered, letter-by-letter (in backward order, because the angels at first voiced fears that the calls were so powerful it might be too dangerous to deliver them in a straightforward manner). As usual, the letters were drawn from an assortment of lettered grids. The angels also provided translations to the first four calls immediately after their delivery.

Then things changed. It appears that even the angels became impatient with this tedious method. They proceeded to deliver calls five through eighteen in a straightforward manner, but they would wait six weeks before delivering the English translations.

The fact that the translated words from the first four calls (delivered backwards) matched (or were otherwise linguistically compatible with) the translated words of calls five through eighteen (delivered forward and translated six weeks later) all but rules out the possibility that either Dee or Kelley invented the angelic language or the calls.

The nineteenth call (the Call of the Ayres or Aethyrs) and the names of the thirty Aethyrs (or heavens) were received on July 13, 1584, Dee's fifty-seventh birthday, effectively ending Dee and Kelley's angelic magick relationship. However, before that final communication, the angels would deliver an incredible amount of material to the two magicians between April 10 and July 13—material that three hundred years later would inspire the adepts of the Golden Dawn to develop the hybrid system we now call Enochian magick. I call it hybrid because the "Enochian" magick developed by the Golden Dawn and Crowley is based on a number of assumptions that connect the forty-eight calls with other "Enochian" material Dee and Kelley received after the reception of the calls. I refer to what are now commonly called the Elemental Tablets, which I will discuss in detail in chapter twenty-three and beyond. While eminently logical and based on the most anal-retentive hermetic principles, many of the assumptions made by the Golden Dawn and Crowley were nonetheless not clearly made in the original Dee material.

First, however, we need to look at the circumstances that triggered the final and most astounding chapter in the story of the reception of Enochian magick. It all started with Dee wanting to spy on the king of Poland and ended with the reception of what appears to be nothing less than the printed circuit board of the mind of God.

CHAPTER EIGHTEEN

The Ninety-one Parts of the Earth

Dee: Hey Nalvage, I'd sure like to magically eavesdrop on secret meetings between King Stephen of Poland and his ministers. I'd like to know if Count Albert Laski will soon succeed Stephen as king of Poland. Can you help me do this?

Nalvage: No problem, Dr. Dee. But first you have to understand how the universe where this can happen operates. You need to understand how everything in heaven and earth is connected to everything in heaven and earth.[81]

—IMAGINARY CONVERSATION, JOHN DEE AND THE ANGEL NALVAGE

The fantasy dialogue above is more than just another one of my lame attempts to be witty. It describes what, for all intents and purposes, was happening during this phase of the Enochian magick revelations. Dee was indeed trying to squeeze from the angels some information regarding political intrigues in Poland. The angel Nalvage's response was to first try to explain to Dee the mechanics of how specific spirits rule specific parts of the earth. In doing so, Nalvage would ambitiously attempt to demonstrate how everything in heaven and earth is connected to everything in heaven and earth. The results of this revelation Dee would neatly memorialize thirteen months later in *Liber Scientae Auxilii et Vitoriae Terrestris.*[82]

Nalvage started by dividing the universe into thirty segments that would eventually be identified as Aires, or Aethyrs (see column I of figure 63). To the thirty Aires he assigned ninety-one parts of the earth (see column II), which he first referred to by the geographical name recognizable to the sixteenth-century magicians, such as Syria (see second name in column III), then by the name by which it is known in the divine realms, such as Pascomb (see second name in column IV).

He then assigned each of these pairs of names to one of the twelve mythical tribes of Israel, along with their directional coordinates, an angelic king, and a respectable number of good ministers.

All this information and more can be found in figure 63. Columns I through V contain the information Dee and Kelley received at this stage of the reception. The symmetrical characters found in column VI and the names of the good princes of the Air in column VII were delivered to Dee and Kelley at a later date than the information in columns I through V. This fact will have astonishing significance when we examine the circumstances and sequence of events that brought to a close the angelic adventures of the two magicians. The key to the columns of the table is as follows:

Column I   Number of the Aire

Column II   Sequence of the ninety-one parts of the earth

Column III   Names of the ninety-one parts of the earth as
             imposed by man[83]

Column IV   Names of the ninety-one parts of the earth as
             imposed by God (Note: These are also the names
             of ninety-one governors of the Aethyrs; see chapter
             twenty-eight.)

Column V   (from top to bottom) Tribe of Israel, quarter of
             the earth assigned to the dispersed tribes of Israel,
             angelic kind, number of good ministers

Column VI   Divinely ordained symmetrical characters (see
             chapter twenty-one) (Note: The mystery of the
             missing symmetrical characters 28, 29, and 30
             would be revealed to Dee and Kelley later; see
             chapter twenty-four.

Column VII   Names of the good princes of the Air
(Note: These are also the names of the
thirty Aethyrs; see chapter twenty-eight.)

I	II	III	IV	V	VI	VII
1	1	Aegyptus	Occodon	Nephthalim East N-E Zarzilg 7209	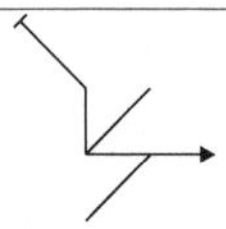	L I L
	2	Syria	Pascomb	Zabulon West S-W Zinggen 2360	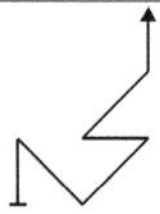	
	3	Mesopotamia	Valgars	Isacaraah West N-W Alpudus 5362	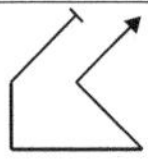	
2	4	Cappadocia	Doagnis	Manasse North Zarnaah 3636	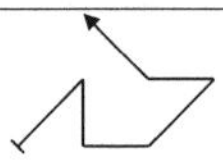	A R N
	5	Tuscia	Pacasna	Reuben South Ziracah 2362		
	6	Parva Asia	Dialiua	Reuben South Ziracah 8962	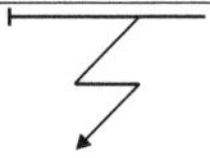	
3	7	Hyrcania	Samapha	Nephthalim East N-E Zarzilg 4400	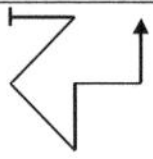	Z O M
	8	Thracia	Virooli	Isacaraah West N-W Alpudus 3660		
	9	Gosmam	Andispi	Gad South S-E Lavavoth 9236	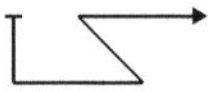	

*Figure 63: The ninety-one parts of the earth, together
with pertinent correspondences*

I	II	III	IV	V	VI	VII
4	10	**Thebaidi**	Thotanp	Gad South S-E Lavavoth 2360		**P** **A** **Z**
	11	**Parsadal**	Axziarg	Gad South S-E Lavavoth 3000		
	12	**India**	Pothnir	Ephraim North N-W Arfaolg 6300		
5	13	**Bactriane**	Lazdixi	Dan East Olpaged 8630		**L** **I** **T**
	14	**Cilicia**	Nocamal	Isacaraah West N-W Alpudus 2306		
	15	**Oxiana**	Tiarpax	Zabulon West S-W Zinggen 5802		
6	16	**Numidia**	Saxtomp	Asseir East S-E Gebabal 3620		**M** **A** **Z**
	17	**Cyprus**	Vauaamp	Ephraim North N-W Arfaolg 9200		
	18	**Parthia**	Zirzird	Asseir East S-E Gebabal 7220		

I	II	III	IV	V	VI	VII
7	19	**Getulia**	Opmacas	Manasse North Zarnaah 6363		D E O
	20	**Arabia**	Genadol	Iehudah West Hononol 7706		
	21	**Phalagon**	Aspiaon	Zabulon West S-W Zinggen 6320		
8	22	**Mantiana**	Zamfres	Asseir East S-E Gebabal 4362		Z I D
	23	**Soxia**	Todnaon	Dan East Olpaged 7236		
	24	**Gallian**	Pristac	Nephthalim East N-E Zarzilg 2302		
9	25	**Illyria**	Oddiorg	Iehudah West Hononol 9996		Z I P
	26	**Sogdiana**	Cralpir	Gad South S-E Lavavoth 3620		
	27	**Lydia**	Doanzin	Nephthalim East N-E Zarzilg 4230		

I	II	III	IV	V	VI	VII
10	28	**Caspis**	LEXARPH	Zabulon West S-W Zinggen 8880		Z A X
	29	**Germania**	COMANAN	Isacaraah West-NW Alpudus 1230		
	30	**Trenam**	TABITOM	Nephthalim East N-E Zarzilg 1617		
11	31	**Bithynia**	Molpand	Gad South S-E Lavavoth 3472		I C H
	32	**Graecia**	Vsnarda	Simeon South S-W Zurchol 7236		
	33	**Licia**	Ponodol	Iehudah West Hononol 5234		
12	34	**Onigap**	Tapamal	Simeon South S-W Zurchol 2658		L O E
	35	**India Major**	Gedoons	Benjamin North N-E Cadaamp 7772		
	36	**Orcheny**	Ambriol	Reuben South Ziracah 3391		

I	II	III	IV	V	VI	VII
13	37	**Achaia**	Gecaond	Gad South S-E Lavavoth 8111		Z
	38	**Armenia**	Laparin	Dan East Olpaged 3360		I
	39	**Cilicia**	Docepax	Isacaraah West N-W Alpudus 4213		M
14	40	**Paphlagonia**	Tedoand Tedoond	Asseir East S-E Gebabal 2673		V
	41	**Phasiana**	Viuipos	Isacaraah West N-W Alpudus 9236		T
	42	**Chaldei**	Ooanamb	Ephraim North N-W Arfaolg 8230		A
15	43	**Itergi**	Tahando	Nephthalim East N-E Zarzilg 1367		O
	44	**Macedonia**	Nociabi	Gad South S-E Lavavoth 1367		X
	45	**Garamantica**	Tastoxo	Ephraim North N-W Arfaolg 1886		O

I	II	III	IV	V	VI	VII
16	46	**Sauromatica**	Cucarpt	Reuben South Ziracah 9920		L
	47	**Aethiopia**	Lauacon	Iehudah West Hononol 9230		E
	48	**Fiacim**	Sochial	Ephraim North N-W Arfaolg 9240		A
17	49	**Colchica**	Sigmorf	Reuben South Ziracah 9623		T
	50	**Coreniaca**	Aydropt	Dan East Olpaged 9132		A
	51	**Nasamonia**	Tocarzi	Nephthalim East N-E Zarzilg 2634		N
18	52	**Carthago**	Nabaomi	Asseir East S-E Gebabal 2346		Z
	53	**Coxlant**	Zafasai	Isacaraah West N-W Alpudus 7689		E
	54	**Idumea**	Yalpamb	Ephraim North N-W Arfaolg 9276		N

I	II	III	IV	V	VI	VII
19	55	**Parstavia**	Torzoxi	Ephraim North N-W Arfaolg 6236		P O P
	56	**Celtica**	Abaiond	Benjamin North N-E Cadaamp 6732		
	57	**Vinsan**	Omagrap	Zabulon West S-W Zinggen 2388		
20	58	**Tolpan**	Zildron	Asseir East S-E Gebabal 3626		C H R
	59	**Carcedonia**	Parziba	Iehudah West Hononol 7629		
	60	**Italia**	Totocan	Isacaraah West N-W Alpudus 3634		
21	61	**Brytania**	Chirspa	Ephraim North N-W Arfaolg 5536		A S P
	62	**Phenices**	Toantom	Benjamin North N-E Cadaamp 5635		
	63	**Comaginen**	Vixpalg	Simeon South S-W Zurchol 5658		

I	II	III	IV	V	VI	VII
	64	**Apulia**	Ozidaia	Ephraim North N-W Arfaolg 2232		L
22	65	**Marmarica**	*PARAOAN *See Chapter 25. Laxdizi	Dan East Olpaged 2326		I
	66	**Concava Syria**	Calzirg	Ephraim North N-W Arfaolg 2367		N
	67	**Gebal**	Ronoamb	Manasse North Zarnaah 7320		T
23	68	**Elam**	Onizimp	Gad South S-E Lavavoth 7262		O
	69	**Idunia**	Zaxanin	Zabulon West S-W Zinggen 7333		R
	70	**Media**	Orcanir	Manasse North Zarnaah 8200		N
24	71	**Ariana**	Chialps	Gad South S-E Lavavoth 8360		I
	72	**Chaldea**	Soageel	Zabulon West S-W Zinggen 8236		A

I	II	III	IV	V	VI	VII
	73	**Sericipopuli**	Mirzind	Manasse North Zarnaah 5632		
25	74	**Persia**	Obuaors	Reuben South Ziracah 6333		U T I
	75	**Gongatha**	Ranglam	Ephraim North N-W Arfaolg 6230		
	76	**Gorsim**	Pophand	Ephraim North N-W Arfaolg 9232		
26	77	**Hispania**	Nigrana	Benjamin North N-E Cadaamp 3620		D E S
	78	**Pamphilia**	Bazchim	Ephraim North N-W Arfaolg 5637		
	79	**Occidi**	Saziami	Reuben South Ziracah 7220		
27	80	**Babylon**	Mathula	Manasse North Zarnaah 7560		Z A A A
	81	**Median**	Orpanib	Asseir East S-E Gebabal 7263		

I	II	III	IV	V	VI	VII
28	82	Idumian	Labnixp	Gad South S-W Lavavoth 2630		B
	83	Felix Arabia	Focisni	Nephthalim East N-E Zarzilg 7236		A
	84	Metagonitidim	Oxlopar	Simeon South S-W Zurchol 8200		G
29	85	Assyria	Vastrim	Iehudah West Hononol 9632		R
	86	Affrica	Odraxti	Manasse North Zarnaah 4236		I
	87	Bactriani	Gomziam	Ephraim North N-W Arfaolg 7635		I
30	88	Afran	Taoagla	Ephraim North N-W Arfaolg 4632		T
	89	Phrygia	Gemnimb	Manasse North Zarnaah 9636		E
	90	Creta	Advorpt	Iehudah West Hononol 7632		X
	91	Mauritania	Dozinal	Simeon South S-W Zurchol 5632		

Using the second of the ninety-one parts of earth, Syria, as our example, we see that its divinely ordained name is Pascomb. The tribe of Zabulon is assigned to Syria/Pascomb, as are the angelic king Zinggen and 2,360 good ministers.

In order for you to appreciate the amazing circumstances surrounding the reception of the Enochian material, it will be important for you to have a general understanding of the chronology of events that took place in the spring and early summer of 1584. This I will try to provide in the following chapter.

CHAPTER NINETEEN

The Golden Talisman and the Watchtowers of the Universe

Now therefore hearken unto me: for I will open unto you the secret knowledge of the Earth, that you may deal with her, by such as govern her, at your pleasure; and call her to a reckoning, as Steward doth the servants of the Lord.

—THE ANGEL AVE, JUNE 20, 1584[84]

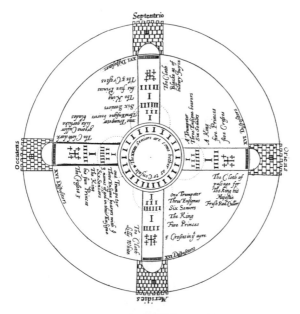

Figure 64a: The Golden Talisman

Very early on the morning of Wednesday, June 20, 1584, Edward Kelley was aroused from a sound sleep by someone (something) patting him on the head. He opened his eyes and beheld an angel, "clothed with feathers, strangely wreathed about him all over, etc." standing at the head of his bed. The angel would later identify itself as Ave, one of the Sons of Sons of Light from the Sigillum Dei Aemeth (see chapter ten). Ave proceeded to project a vision that would dramatize the elements and structure of the entire system of Enochian magick as widely practiced today. The following is from Dee's diary:[85]

> There appeared to him [Kelley] four very fair Castles, standing in the four parts of the world: out of which he heard the sound of a Trumpet. Then it seemed out of every Castle a cloath to be thrown on the ground, of more than the breadth of a Table-cloath . . . [86]

> . . . Out of every Gate then issued one Trumpeter, whose Trumpets were of strange form, wreathed, and growing bigger and bigger toward the end.

> After the Trumpeter followed three Ensign Bearers.

> After them six ancient men, with white beards and staves in their hands.

> Then followed a comely man, with very much Apparel on his back, his Robe having a long train.

> After him came five men, carrying up of his train.

> Then followed one great Crosse, and about that four lesser Crosses.

> These Crosses had on them, each of them ten, like men, their faces distinctly appearing on the four parts of the Crosse, all over.

> After the Crosses followed 16 white Creatures.

After them, an infinite number seemed to issue, and to spread themselves orderly in a compasse, almost before the four foresaid Castles.

The highlights of Kelley's vision would eventually be memorialized upon a round talisman etched in gold, which is today on display at the British Museum. Much as I'd like to believe this object was fashioned by Dee himself, it is almost certainly a forgery patterned upon the flawed image printed in Casaubon's *A True & Faithful Relation*. For reference, however, I will continue to refer to both the vision and the image as the *Golden Talisman*.

The four castles, or Watchtowers, formed a cross, the center of which was a circle supported by twenty-four columns. Figure 64 illustrates the lower quarter of the Golden Talisman.

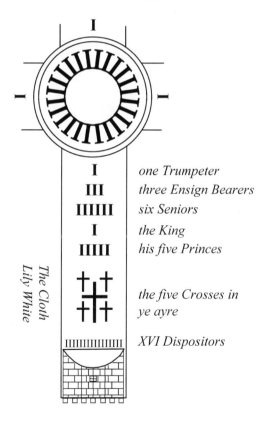

I	*one Trumpeter*
III	*three Ensign Bearers*
IIIIII	*six Seniors*
I	*the King*
IIIII	*his five Princes*
	the five Crosses in
	ye ayre
IIIIIIIIIIIIII	*XVI Dispositors*

The Cloth Lily White

Figure 64: The lowermost of the four castles of the Golden Talisman

Ave would elucidate upon the nature, powers, and hierarchical status of the characters on the Golden Talisman. Eventually he would go into far greater detail by projecting and organizing all of it upon what he called the Great Table or the Great Table of the Watchtowers. The Great Table is the Rosetta stone of Enochian magick. How it was received and how it is connected to the information Dee and Kelley had already received concerning the ninety-one parts of the earth present us with perhaps the most convincing proof that the two magicians were indeed in contact with noncorporeal intelligences of a superior order.

CHAPTER TWENTY

The Unlettered Great Table
and the Four Great Seals

*The seals and authorities of these Houses are confirmed in the begin-
ning of the World. Unto everyone of them be 4 characters, (tokens of
the presence of the son of God: by whom all things were made in
Creation.)*

—THE ANGEL AVE, JUNE 20, 1584[87]

In a working that took place on Wednesday, June 25, 1584, the angel
Ave showed the magicians the image of a table that was divided into
four sections by a central cross. Each of the four sections was identified
as one of the castles of the Golden Talisman vision. Also called
Watchtowers, Watchmen, princes, and mighty angels of the Lord, they
were each represented by a seal. Three of these seals, by their imagery,
bear a direct and unambiguous connection to the Sigillum Dei Aemeth
or the Ensigns of Creation.

The first seal was assigned to the upper left section of the table. It
was the image of a capital letter *T* with four rays beaming vertically
from the top bar. This seal comes from a major landmark of the
Sigillum Dei Aemeth. The 4/T cell is the first (near the top) of the forty
cells that form the perimeter (see figure 23). The 4/T cell is where we
began counting to create the seven Names of God drawn from the
Sigillum.

The second seal was assigned to the upper right section of the table and identified as an alphabet cross. We first saw this cross on the (lower right) corner of the first sevenfold table (see figure 33), which generated the letters of the large outer heptagon of the Sigillum, where the cross appears at the top left (see figure 34).

The third seal was assigned to the lower right section of the Great Table. Its origin was a little harder to track down. Ave said, "It is in that table, which consisteth of 4 and 8." One of the seven Ensigns of Creation that ring the Sigillum on the Holy Table (the one many modern magicians associate with Mercury) is a 4 x 8 table (see figure 54). The square occupying the position of the second column, second row, contains the cross, numbers, and letters exactly as appears on the vision of the third seal.

The forth seal was assigned to the lower left section of the table and was the image of "a little round smoke, as big as a pin's head." It is illustrated in one of the drawings of the Great Table in Sloane 3191 as a tiny circle with twelve rays issuing from it. It is perhaps the stylized representation of the figure that appears on the back of the Sigillum Dei Aemeth: a small circle from which projects the four capital Ts of a cross potent formed from twelve right angles (see figure 51). Perhaps it is connected to the Round Table of Nalvage and the twelve words that occupy its four continents. Frankly I've been unable to find any reference in the original material that would suggest either of these connections.

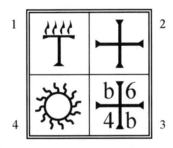

Figure 65: The original positioning of the four Great Seals upon the Great Table

Figure 65 shows the positions of the Great Seals on the Great Table and the order in which they were revealed to Dee and Kelley on June 25, 1584. On April 18, 1587 (nearly three years after the magicians had, for all intents and purposes, discontinued their angelic workings), Kelley would receive a vision that would alter (or reform) several aspects of the Great Table, including the relative positions of the seals and all they represent.

As one might expect, this reformation remains the source of intense frustration to Enochian students and practitioners. To add to all the confusion, Dee at different times assigned different directional attributes to the quarters of the table. Later, the Golden Dawn, in order to develop a workable system from this material, would attribute the quarters of the Great Table to the elements of Air, Water, Earth, and Fire. Eventually, I will do that as well, but for the moment, let's be satisfied with identifying the four quarters of the Great Table by their seals and original numbers as shown in figure 65, while we move on to the wonders of what next took place.

CHAPTER TWENTY-ONE

The Great Table

There was a terrible storm of thunder and rain, toward the end of our yesterdays action: which I said, was somewhat more than natural.

—JOHN DEE, JUNE 26, 1584[88]

I feel I must here briefly outline (if only for my own benefit) the sequential landmarks of the Enochian magick period up to this point:

- The reception of the Round Tablet of Nalvage,
- The beginning of the reception of the forty-eight calls in the angelic language,
- The reception of the order and earthly name of each of the ninety-one parts of the earth, together with:
  - its divinely given name,
  - the tribe of Israel to which it is assigned,[89]
  - the direction assigned to that tribe,
  - the name of its ruling angelic king,
  - the number of good ministers.

(All of the above information is itemized in columns I through IV of the figure 63 in chapter eighteen.)

Then came:

- The vision of the Golden Talisman, with its four sets of castles:

- one trumpeter,
- three ensign bearers,
- six seniors ("six ancient men"),
- the king and his five princes (the "comely man,
  with very much Apparel" and the "five men, carrying up
  of his train"),
- five crosses in the air ("one great Crosse" and "four
  lesser Crosses"),
- sixteen dispositors ("16 white Creatures").
- The vision of the unlettered Great Table and the four Great Seals.

What happened next was so remarkable that I hope I can recount what happened clearly enough for you to appreciate how remarkable it was.

During the working of Monday, June 25, 1584, Kelley was given in vision four blank grids, each of which was twelve squares wide by thirteen squares high. These grids were said to represent the four quarters of the unlettered Great Table of the vision of a few days earlier. As the vision proceeded, "little pricks," or dots, began to appear in the squares. Kelley was then instructed to connect the dots in groups of seven, which created sigils, each forming a curious pattern.

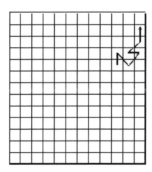

Figure 66: Example of a symmetrical character on a grid

When he was through connecting the dots, all but eight of the 624 squares that make up the four grids were covered by eighty-eight characters, each unique in form, each covering seven squares, but none of which intruded upon another character's squares. These symbols were identified as "the true images of God his Spiritual Creatures."

Now we know what those zigzag lines that fill column *VI* in chapter eighteen's figure 63 are. They are called *symmetrical characters* because each one is formed from the same number of pricks—in this case, seven.

Once the blank grids were filled with the lines of the symmetrical characters, Kelley was instructed to fill in the squares with letters. Starting at the top left of each grid and moving to the right, letters began to appear to Kelley, one by one, as Dee copied them down. Some of the letters were capitalized, but most were not. A few of the capitalized letters appeared to be written backwards.

When all four grids were filled in with letters and characters, it became clear that the characters spelled out names. Not only that, but each of these eighty-eight names also began with a capital letter and contained no other capital letter among the remaining six.

This phenomenon is in itself impressive, but it is nothing compared to what Dee and Kelley would learn next. Within a few hours (and with a few helpful hints from the angels), the two magicians discovered, to their utter amazement, that the symmetrical characters spelled all but three of the divine names of the ninety-one parts of the earth—names they had been given days earlier and in list format. Figure 67 shows an example of how the divine name of the second part of the earth, *Pascomb*, is spelled out by its symmetric character.

All four grids were filled with similar characters all spelling out (with a few minor irregularities) the names of eighty-eight of the ninety-one parts of the earth.

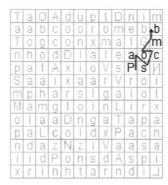

Figure 67: The name Pascomb *drawn from its symmetrical character*

The next day the angels tidied up this array by joining the four 12 x 13 grids with a central cross and turning it into one Great Table. The letters of the three missing divine names of the parts of the earth were found distributed in the central cross (sometimes referred to as the *Black Cross* or the *Great Central Cross*) and a mysterious ninety-second name, *Paraoan*, was created from certain of the backwards letters that occupied the squares left vacant by the symmetrical characters (see chapter twenty-four). Things were wrapped up pretty neatly.

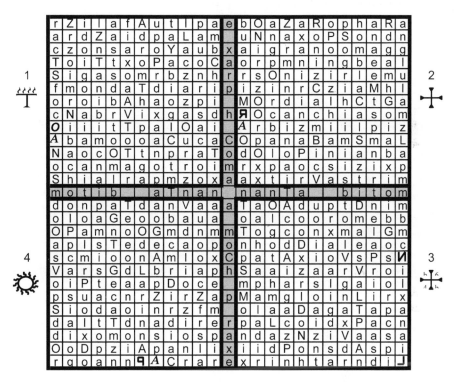

Figure 68: Lettering of the original Great Table

Before we continue, I would like to again stress how impressive was the method of reception. Enochian scholar and magician David R. Jones, wrote:

> The student of Enochian can compare the lists of names with the sigils, which formulate their existence on the Watchtowers, and easily see the correlation. But realize that the names were delivered first and then the Watchtowers horizontally line by line and after having both figures at hand. The Angels demonstrated

that, by discrete (7 letters, the number of letters in each Governor's name) linear connections, all of the letters given in the Watchtowers could be accounted for from the letters that formulate names of the Governors previously given. This would require either a monumental and complex second and third order memorization (2 dimensions to 1 dimension then back to 2 dimensions and with directional correlation from a 3 dimensional origin to a 3 dimensional conclusion) on Kelly's part or an elaborate and extremely obtuse deception on Dee's part. This constitutes one of the chief proofs of the system.[90]

The magicians would eventually be informed that the ninety-one divine names of the parts of the earth are also the names of ninety-one governors who inhabit the thirty Aethyrs, or Aires, or heavens that surround the Watchtowers like a heavenly glass onion. We've yet to discuss the Aethyrs because their names (see figure 63, column VII) were among the last bits of information Dee and Kelley received in their Enochian magick workings. The lowest of these Aethyrs, Tex, is inhabited by four governors. The remaining Aethyrs including the highest, Lil, each have three governors.

I will talk more about the Aethyrs in chapter twenty-five. Here it is important for us to simply understand that linking the ninety-one parts of the earth to the thirty Aethyrs was the Enochian way of identifying and linking all levels of divine consciousness from bottom to top. Thus, the dynamics of the Great Table really are a demonstration of how everything in heaven and earth is indeed connected to everything else in heaven and earth.

CHAPTER TWENTY-TWO

Tabula Recensa

At length, E. K. was willed to go down into his Chamber, and I did remain still at our Dineing Table till his return, which was within an hour or somewhat more. And at his return this he brought in writing . . . .

—JOHN DEE, APRIL 20, 1587[91]

Such was the amazing genesis of the Great Table. How all this is connected to the vision of the Golden Talisman and the practice of modern Enochian magick will be the subjects of the next chapters. Before moving on, however, and in order to more easily illustrate the structure of the system, I need to temporarily tighten up some of the loose ends that the irregularities in the original material often leave dangling in the eyes of the student. The most serious of these concerns the lettering of the Great Table and the various names of angels drawn therefrom. Here's the problem:

After they initially received the Great Table, the magicians were obliged to change or add certain letters in some of the squares. To confuse things further, in documents they received both earlier and later,[92] the names of a handful of the ninety-one governors of the table (whose names are spelled out by the symmetrical characters) and the names of specific angels drawn from the Watchtowers of the Great Table are in subsequent communications spelled a bit differently than they appear in the original table. This difference has proven very frustrating to modern Enochian magicians, who naturally would like to be confident in their ability to accurately identify and spell the name of the angel with whom they wish to communicate.

There are other loose-end inconsistencies that plagued Dee and Kelley, one of which was the uncertainty over which compass directions were to be assigned to the four quarters of the Great Table—a problem that Dee appears never to have resolved to his satisfaction, and one that I have chosen to sidestep completely by not using the directional references to identify the four quarters of the Great Table at all. These inconsistencies, however, pale before what happened in April of 1587, nearly three years after Dee and Kelley had ended their Enochian workings.

For some reason Kelley felt compelled to revisit the mysteries of the Great Table and once and for all settle the questions of unresolved inconsistencies. During a conversation with the archangel Raphael that lasted approximately one hour, he claimed to receive the *Tabula Recensa*, or "Reformed Table." This table, while correcting a few of the letters, was characterized by one very dramatic change: three of the quadrants housing the four Watchtowers were shifted to different positions within the full table. This alteration did not change any symmetrical characters, nor did it tinker all that much with the names of the governors or other angels within the table. What it did do was change the basic construction of the Great Table.

Figure 69 shows the new positioning of the reformed table. (The letters with an asterisk indicate backwards letters.)

For the duration of this book I will, for the sake of consistency, try to use the Tabula Recensa as my main model for both the lettering and arrangement of the Watchtowers of the Great Table. I say "try to use" because for nearly the entire Enochian period the angels referenced the original Great Table (figure 68) when explaining the angelic hierarchies and spelling the names of individual angels. It will be necessary from time to time to refer to the original, unreformed Great Table, especially when we start discussing the Kerubs (see chapters twenty-three and twenty-four), whose names might be dramatically affected by the reformed table's new arrangement.

r	Z	i	ſ	a	f	A	y	t	ſ	p	a	e'	T	a	O	A	d	v	p	t	D	n	i	m
a	r	d	Z	a	i	d	p	a	L	a	m		a	a	b	c	o	o	r	o	m	e'	b	b
c	z	o	n	s	a	r	o	Y	a	v	b	x	T	o	g	c	o	n	x	m	a	ſ	G	m
T	o	i	T	t	z	o	P	a	c	o	C	a	n	b	o	d	D	i	a	ſ	e'	a	o	c
S	i	g	a	s	o	m	r	b	z	n	b	r	p	a	t	A	x	i	o	V	s	P	s	И
ſ	m	o	n	d	a	T	d	i	a	r	i	p	S	a	a	i	x	a	a	r	V	r	o	i
o	r	o	i	b	A	b	a	o	z	p	i		m	p	b	a	r	s	ſ	g	a	i	o	ſ
t	N	a	b	r	V	i	x	g	a	s	d	b	M	a	m	g	ſ	o	i	n	L	i	r	x
O	i	i	i	t	T	p	a	ſ	O	a	i		o	ſ	a	a	D	n	g	a	T	a	p	a
A	b	a	m	o	o	o	a	C	u	c	a	C	p	a	L	c	o	i	d	x	P	a	c	n
N	a	o	c	O	T	t	n	p	r	n	T	o	n	d	a	z	N	z	i	V	a	a	s	a
o	c	a	n	m	a	g	o	t	r	o	i	m	i	i	d	P	o	n	s	d	A	s	p	i
S	b	i	a	ſ	r	a	p	m	z	o	x	a	x	r	i	n	b	t	a	r	n	d	i	Ɉ
m	o	t	i	b		a	T	n	a	n		n	a	n	T	a		b	i	t	o	m		
b	O	a	Z	a	R	o	p	b	a	R	a⁺	a	d	o	n	p	a	T	d	a	n	V	a	a
u	N	n	a	x	o	P	S	o	n	d	n		o	ſ	o	a	G	e'	o	o	b	a	u	a
a	i	g	r	a	n	o	o	m	a	g	g	m	O	P	a	m	n	o	V	G	m	d	n	m
o	r	p	m	n	i	n	g	b	e'	a	ſ	o	a	p	ſ	s	T	e'	d	e'	c	a	o	p
r	s	O	n	i	Z	i	r	ſ	e'	m	v	C	s	c	m	i	o	o	n	A	m	ſ	o	x
i	z	i	n	r	C	z	i	a	M	b	ſ	b	V	a	r	s	G	d	L	b	r	i	a	p
M	O	r	d	i	a	ſ	b	C	t	G	a		o	i	P	t	e'	a	a	p	D	o	c	e'
◌	c	a	n	c	b	i	a	s	o	m	t	p	p	s	u	a	c	N	·r	Z	i	r	Z	a
A	r	b	i	z	m	i	i	ſ	p	i	z		S	i	o	d	a	o	i	n	r	z	f	m
O	p	a	n	a	ſ	a	m	S	m	a	P	r	d	a	ſ	t	T	d	n	a	d	i	r	e'
d	O	ſ	o	P	i	n	i	a	n	b	a	a	d	i	x	o	m	o	n	s	i	o	s	p
r	x	p	a	o	c	s	i	z	i	x	p	x	O	o	D	p	z	i	A	p	o	n	ſ	i
a	x	t	i	r	V	a	s	t	r	i	m	e'	r	g	o	a	n	n	q	A	C	r	a	r

Figure 69: Lettering and arrangement of the reformed
Great Table (Tabula Recensa)

I should remind the reader that in magick it is eminently possible for many contradictory ideas to be simultaneously true. In the pages that follow, the alert reader will notice that the names of certain angels are spelled in a manner inconsistent with the original Great Table, the Tabula Recensa, and/or other obvious references within the text. It is probable that particular inconsistencies are the result of subsequent angelic instructions or other extenuating reasons. For a practical manual such as this it would be distracting to the point of absurdity for me to pause, footnote, cross reference, defend, and explain each and every one of these aberrations, especially considering the fact that in many instances I myself have not been able to track down the source of the differing lettering. For those of you whose research will take you deeper into this subject, I have included in appendix IV versions of the Watchtowers containing all the variations in lettering that I have been able to discover.

Also for convenience sake, I'm going to represent the segue between the Enochian magick of Dee and Kelley and Enochian magick as it is generally practiced today. Up to this point in the chronology of the adventures of Dee and Kelley, each of the four Watchtowers of the Great Table (both the original and reformed) have been identified by the one of the four Great Seals (see figure 65) or by certain landmark letters. At different times in the original material they have been identified by the order they were received or by the directions: east, south, west, or north. Nowhere in the surviving documents have I been able to find the four quadrants of the Great Table overtly identified as the *Elemental Tablets* of Fire, Water, Air, and Earth.

That being said, certain clear references in the continuing communications revealed elemental hierarchies and rulerships both *of* and *within* the individual Watchtowers. Building on this information, the adepts of the Golden Dawn projected an eminently logical elemental structure to the Great Table, its central Black Cross, and its individual subdivisions. These elemental attributions are the heart and soul of the system of Enochian magick taught and practiced by the Golden Dawn, Aleister Crowley, and most modern practitioners.

I personally believe that when these more modern adepts treated the Watchtowers as expressions of the elements they were picking up where Dee and Kelley had stopped and were taking the next logical step in the development of the system. To more easily discuss how all this is going to relate to the practical application of the system, I will now and for the remainder of this book, refer to the four Watchtowers by their modern elemental designations. Please refer to figure 69.

- The *upper left* quadrant of the reformed Great Table I will now refer to as the Watchtower, or Elemental Tablet, of Air.
- The *upper right* quadrant of the reformed Great Table I will now refer to as the Watchtower, or Elemental Tablet, of Water.
- The *lower left* quadrant of the reformed Great Table I will now refer to as the Watchtower, or Elemental Tablet, of Earth.
- The *lower right* quadrant of the reformed Great Table I will now refer to as the Watchtower, or Elemental Tablet, of Fire.

This is how they are identified in most modern Enochian literature. There is a fifth Elemental Tablet—the Tablet of Union—that is attributed to the quintessential element, Spirit. It is much smaller, containing only twenty squares, and its letters are drawn from those on the central Black Cross of the Great Table, which serves to unite the four Watchtowers in precisely the same way Spirit is said to unite and separate the four elements. I will have more to say about this very important tablet in chapter twenty-six.

Figure 70: Elemental Tablets (Watchtowers) are placed in the same positions as found on the pentagram.

CHAPTER TWENTY-THREE

The Great Table Meets
the Golden Talisman

*The Angels of the 4 angles shall make the Earth open unto you,
and shall serve your necessities from the 4 parts of the Earth.*

—THE ANGEL AVE, JULY 2, 1584[93]

Recall, from chapter nineteen, that the vision of the Golden Talisman revealed *four castles* from which flowed four cloths of different colors. Out of each castle, marching in procession came *one trumpeter*, *three ensign bearers*, *six seniors*, and *one king*. The king was followed by five men (who held up his train) and five crosses (one great cross surrounded by four lesser crosses) that floated in the air above them. Each of the four lesser crosses "had on them, each of them ten, like men, their faces distinctly appearing on the four parts of the Crosse, all over."[94]

After the crosses came sixteen *white creatures*, identified as dispositors on the Golden Talisman, and then "an infinite number seemed to issue, almost before the four foresaid Castles."[95]

These images and characters provide, at least partially, the key to the divine hierarchy of the Great Table. This hierarchy represents the spiritual forces that govern not only the phenomenal universe but also heaven. Let's take a moment and project the vision of the Golden Talisman upon the Great Table.

The Four Castles

The castles are obviously the four Watchtowers (Elemental Tablets) themselves, and the rest of the characters in the vision represent the angelic hierarchy resident in each tablet. These angels can be called forth and visited in vision by intoning one or more of the first eighteen calls to activate the Elemental Tablet and the specific area of the tablet where they reside. I will show how that is done in appendix I. First, let's see how the cast of characters from the Golden Talisman fit on the individual Elemental Tablets.

For purposes of illustration, I will use the Elemental Tablet of Fire (the lower right quarter of the reformed Great Table) as our model.

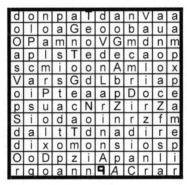

d	o	n	p	a	T	d	a	n	V	a	a
o	l	o	a	G	e	o	o	b	a	u	a
O	P	a	m	n	o	V	G	m	d	n	m
a	p	l	s	T	e	d	e	c	a	o	p
s	c	m	i	o	o	n	A	m	l	o	x
V	a	r	s	G	d	L	b	r	i	a	p
o	i	P	t	e	a	a	p	D	o	c	e
p	s	u	a	c	N	r	Z	i	r	Z	a
S	i	o	d	a	o	i	n	r	z	f	m
d	a	l	t	T	d	n	a	d	i	r	e
d	i	x	o	m	o	n	s	i	o	s	p
O	o	D	p	z	i	A	p	a	n	l	i
r	g	o	a	n	n	ꝗ	A	C	r	a	r

Figure 71: The Elemental Tablet of Fire

The Trumpets (Trumpeter)

The first character to issue from each of the castles was the trumpeter. The trumpeters are the Great Seals of the tablets. In our example (the Elemental Tablet of Fire), the seal is the image of the sun emitting rays.

Figure 72: The Great Seal of the Elemental Tablet of Fire

The Three Ensign Bearers

At the top of the hierarchical ladder of each Elemental Tablet are the three ensign bearers, who represent the *Three Great Secret Names of God*. These names appear in the central horizontal *row* of the Great Central Cross that divides each Elemental Tablet. This cross is made of the two vertical columns that bisect the tablet into left and right; the left column is called the *Line of the Father* and the right column is called the *Line of the Son*, and the single central row that bisects the tablet top and bottom is called the *Line of the Holy Ghost*.

Dee and Kelley were told that the three ensign bearers were respectively of the nature of "3, 4, and 5." This means that the Three Great Secret Names of God are spelled using the first three letters, the next four letters, and the final five letters of the central horizontal row of the central cross. In the case of the Fire tablet, these letter combinations are: *oiP, teaa, pDoce.*

d	o	n	p	a	T	d	a	n	V	a	a
o	l	o	a	G	e	o	o	b	a	u	a
O	P	a	m	n	o	V	G	m	d	n	m
a	p	l	s	T	e	d	e	c	a	o	p
s	c	m	i	o	o	n	A	m	l	o	x
V	a	r	s	G	d	L	b	r	i	a	p
o	**i**	**P-**	**t**	**e**	**a**	**a-**	**p**	**D**	**o**	**c**	**e**
p	s	u	a	c	N	r	Z	i	r	Z	a
S	i	o	d	a	o	i	n	r	z	f	m
d	a	l	t	T	d	n	a	d	i	r	e
d	i	x	o	m	o	n	s	i	o	s	p
O	o	D	p	z	i	A	p	a	n	l	i
r	g	o	a	n	n	9	A	C	r	a	r

*Figure 73: The Three Great Secret Names of God
of the Elemental Tablet of Fire*

If there was any doubt as to the angels' meaning concerning the four sets of the Three Great Secret Names of God, they thoughtfully provided a round diagram with all twelve names neatly represented as ensign flags surrounding a central quartered square. In that diagram, all the letters of the names appeared in uppercase letters: *OIP, TEAA, PDOCE.*

The Three Great Secret Names of all four Elemental Tablets are found in appendix IV.

The Six Seniors

Next came the six seniors. While there is little specific indication in the surviving documents that would suggest the six seniors carry planetary attributions, it is nonetheless a logical assumption; it was made by the adepts of the Golden Dawn and is made by most modern practitioners. For clarity of reference (and for the duration of our discussion), I will adapt the modern planetary designations given to the seniors.

The six seniors of each of the Elemental Tablets are found on the Great Central Cross of each tablet. The seven-letter names of the six seniors radiate from the center two letters of the cross to its extremities.

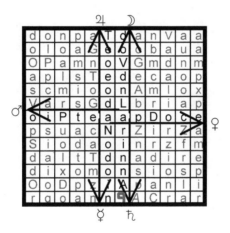

Figure 74: Positions of the six seniors on the Elemental Tablet of Fire

On the Elemental Tablet of Fire, the six seniors are: *aaetPio* (Mars), *adoeoet* (Jupiter), *aLndVod* (Luna), *aapDoce* (Venus), *arinna* (Saturn), and a*Nodoin* (Mercury).

In subsequent references to the seniors (such as in lists and prayers), Dee would standardize the capitalization of the names on all the Elemental Tablets. In our example: Aaetpio, Adoeoet, Alndvod, Aapdoce, Arinna, Anodoin.

The names of the seniors of all four Elemental Tablets are found in appendix IV.

In Kelley's vision of the Golden Talisman, the six seniors from each of the four castles march to the center and meet as pillars that support, as it were, the entire structure. This image is suggestive of the twenty-four elders who surround the throne of God in the Book of the Revelation of John.[96] The twenty-four seniors together are represented on the Golden Talisman as the twenty-four columns that ring the center circle of the talisman (see figure 64).

There is a seventh planetary senior who is attributed to the sun. Just as the sun is the central "king" of our solar system, so too is the sun senior identified as king and found in the center of each Elemental Tablet.

The King

Like the sun, which attracts and holds the planets in orbit, the king of each Elemental Tablet is said to summon and direct the seniors for heavenly duties. When those duties are of a *merciful* nature, the king spells his name a bit differently than when the duties are those of *severity* and judgment.

Like those of the six seniors, the seven letters of the king's name are drawn entirely from the Great Central Cross (the lines of the Father, Son, and Holy Ghost) of the Elemental Tablet. Beginning with the fifth letter from the left in the horizontal line of the Holy Ghost, the name is spelled out in a clockwise whirl that ends in *one* of the two squares that occupies the center of the cross: either at the *sixth letter* from the left for operations of *mercy* (figure 75) or the *seventh letter* from the left for operations of *judgment* (figure 76).

In the case of the Elemental Tablet of Fire, the letters that hold those positions are both *a*s, so both names are *Edlprna*.

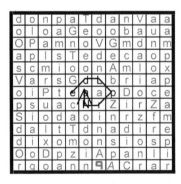 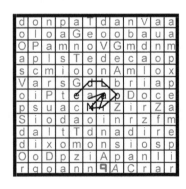

Figures 75 and 76: Clockwise whirl spelling the two names of the king of the Elemental Tablet of Fire, Edlprna *and* Edlprna

Perhaps my use of the Elemental Tablet of Fire is not the best example to illustrate how the name of the king is formed by the clockwise whirls because the resulting names are the same. The other three Elemental Tablets yield distinctly different names.

The names of the Kings of all four Elemental Tablets are found in appendix IV.

The Five Crosses (One Great Cross and Four Lesser Crosses)

Each of the four quarters formed by the Great Central Cross is a rectangle five squares wide by six squares high. These quadrants are often referred to in modern Enochian magick as *lesser angles* or *subangles*. Just as the reformed Great Table positions the Elemental Tablet of Air in its *upper left*, Water in its *upper right*, Earth in its *lower left*, and Fire in its *lower right* quadrants, so too each subangle is assigned one of the four elements and positioned on its Elemental Tablet in the same way.

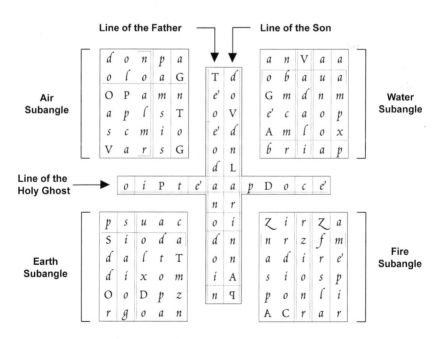

Figure 77: Positions of the subangle elements

Each of the four subangles is dominated by a Calvary cross made up of ten squares (the ten men of the vision of the Golden Talisman), which form the two god names of the subangle. The name drawn from the six letters of the vertical column of the cross (read top to bottom) was said to *summon* the angels of the subangle, and the five-letter god name of the horizontal bar of the cross (read left to right) was said to *command* them. Figure 78 shows the god names *rzionr* and *nrzfm* from the Fire subangle (the lower right quadrant) of the Elemental Tablet of Fire.

Figure 78: God names from the Calvary cross of the Fire subangle of the Elemental Tablet of Fire

The god names of the subangles of all four Elemental Tablets are found in appendix IV.

Sixteen White Creatures (Dispositors)

Next in procession in Kelley's vision (and next in the hierarchy of the Elemental Tablets) are the "16 white Creatures." On the Golden Talisman diagram they are represented as sixteen small columns standing side-by-side at the extremity of each rectangular cloth (see figure 64) where they are labeled "XVI Dispositors."

Among modern magicians there are several schools of thought concerning the identity of the sixteen dispositors. The simplest (and in my opinion the most correct) theory holds they are made up of the four angels who reside beneath the arms of the Calvary cross of each of the four subangles of the Elemental Tablet. Referred to as *good angels* or *servient angels*, they are invoked and commanded by the god names of their Calvary cross and have powers and knowledge that can be of great practical use to the magician (see appendix IV).

The names of the servient or good angels can be spelled with four letters (if you omit the central letter from the vertical bar of the Calvary cross) or with five letters (if you include the letter from the cross). In our example, the names are:

adre or ad[i]re

sisp or si[o]sp

pali or pa[n]li

ACar or AC[r]ar

Figure 79: Servient angels of the Fire subangle of
the Elemental Tablet of Fire

This is a logical and very workable way of looking at the angelic hierarchy of the Elemental Tablet and conforms nicely to the vision of the Golden Talisman and to the way Dee composed his prayers to conjure these good angels.

This theory does, however, leave out in the cold the four letters *above* the arm of each Calvary cross. To address this issue we must bring up the several schools of thought concerning *Kerubs*.

Kerubic Angels

In Christian iconography, every well-appointed crucifix bears a rectangular piece of wood nailed above the head of Christ and displaying the four letters INRI.[97] So too above the arms of the Calvary cross of every subangle we find four letters that spell the name of the Kerub of the subangle, a unique spiritual personage. The Golden Dawn dubbed these angels Kerubs.[98]

Now, if you are paying attention, you might want to point out that there are only four subangles and only four Calvary crosses (one in each Elemental Tablet), and therefore there should only be four Kerub/dispositors, not sixteen, per tablet. Of course, your observation would be accurate—if we restrict ourselves to spelling their names in a straightforward and orderly manner. But according to *this theory*, there are actually four Kerubs hidden in the four letters above the arms of every Calvary cross, and these sixteen Kerubs are actually the sixteen dispositors.

Let's use the Fire (lower right) subangle of the Fire Elemental Tablet and the Kerub ZiZa as our example.

Z	**i**	r	**Z**	**a**
n	r	z	f	m
a	d	i	r	e
s	i	o	s	p
p	a	n	l	i
A	C	r	a	r

Figure 80: Kerub ZiZa of the Fire subangle of the Elemental Tablet of Fire

This subangle's four Kerubs are created from a simple permutation of the four letters above the arms of the Calvary cross; simply slide the four letters to the left, each time placing the displaced first letter to the back of the line:

ZiZa   iZaZ   ZaZi   aZiZ

This dynamic perpetual motion of letters doesn't stop with the Kerub, for each letter of the Kerub's name can also rule a column and row of the sixteen letters of the servient angels residing beneath the arm of the Calvary cross.

In our example, the first *Z* in the Kerub's name rules the column directly beneath it and the arm of the cross: *aspA*.

The *Z* also rules the bottom row of the subangle: *ACar*.

Figure 81 shows how the other letters in the Kerub's name rule the servient angels of the subangle.

Figure 81 (four 5-column grids):

Grid 1:
Z	i	r	Z	a
n	r	z	f	m
a	d	i	r	e
s	i	o	s	p
p	a	n	l	i
A	C	r	a	r

Grid 2:
Z	i	r	Z	a
n	r	z	f	m
a	d	i	r	e
s	i	o	s	p
p	a	n	l	i
A	C	r	a	r

Grid 3:
Z	i	r	Z	a
n	r	z	f	m
a	d	i	r	e
s	i	o	s	p
p	a	n	l	i
A	C	r	a	r

Grid 4:
Z	i	r	Z	a
n	r	z	f	m
a	d	i	r	e
s	i	o	s	p
p	a	n	l	i
A	C	r	a	r

Figure 81: How the letters of the Kerub rule the servient angels of the Fire subangle: The first Z rules column name aspA and row name ACar. The letter I rules column name diaC and row name pali. The second Z rules column name rsla and row name sisp. And finally, the letter a rules column name epir and row name adre.

According to this theory, in order to open a subangle to summon or contact a servient angel, the magician must first invoke the two god names of the Calvary cross of the subangle in question, then invoke the Kerub, then invoke the servient angel of choice. This is a logical and workable system, but one that doesn't appear to have been on Dee and Kelley's menu. In fact, original material suggests that the Kerub is a unique citizen of the subangle, one who is not under the rulership of the Calvary cross, but under a "god" whose name begins with a sacred letter drawn from the Black Cross (the Great Central Cross) of the Great Table.

A Super Kerub?

Neither Dee or Kelley nor the modern magicians of the Golden Dawn ever use the term *Super Kerub*.

There is, however, a variety of kerubic angel who seems to embody that title. Like the variety of kerubs we've just discussed, the names of the Super Kerubs are drawn from the letters above the arms of the Calvary crosses of the subangles of the Great Tablet. But, instead of answering to the two Calvary cross god names of their subangle, the Super Kerubs answer to a higher authority—a supercharged angel who is linked directly to the Black Cross of the unreformed Great Tablet. This angel was the subject of much discussion in the original Dee and

Kelley material, for its existence and posers were central to the understanding of the "wicked" angels.

In order for us to understand the nature of the Super Kerubs and the wicked angels, we will need to take a closer look at the Black Cross.

CHAPTER TWENTY-FOUR

The Black Cross, Super Kerubs, Wicked Angels, Missing Symmetrical Characters, and the Tablet of Union

That shall make the cross that bindeth the 4 Angles of the Table together. The same that stretcheth from the left to right, must also stretch from the right to the left . . .

—THE ANGEL AVE, JUNE 25, 1584[99]

I stated earlier that I have been unable to find in the surviving Dee and Kelley material any overt references to the four Watchtowers as being Elemental Tablets of Fire, Water, Air, and Earth. However, the communicating angels gave every indication that the dynamics and hierarchical structure of the Great Table were, at least in part, elemental in nature. In the communication of Monday, June 25, 1584, the angel Ave speaks of the virtues of the table:[100]

First, generally this Table containeth:

1. All humane knowledge.
2. Out of it springeth Physick.
3. The knowledge of all elemental Creatures, amongst you. How many kindes there are, and for what use they were created. Those that live in the air, by themselves. Those that live in the waters,

by themselves. Those that dwell in the earth, by themselves. The property of the fire—which is the secret life of all things.

4. The knowledge, finding and use of Metal.
   The vertues of them. } They are all of one matter.
   The congelations, and vertues of Stones.

5. The conjoining and knitting together of Natures. The destraction of Nature, and of things may perish.

6. Moving from place to place, [as, into this Country, or that Country at pleasure.]

7. The knowledge of all crafts Mechanical.

8. Transmutatio formalis, sed non effentialis.[101]

If we look at the four quarters of the Great Table as being the Elemental Tablets of Air, Water, Earth, and Fire, the Black Cross that separates and joins the tablets would then obviously represent Spirit—that quintessential force that binds the four elements together in infinite quantities and ratios to create and sustain the universe, while at the same time keeping the elements separated just enough to retain their identities. This push/pull, active/passive nature is a defining characteristic of Spirit. As I mentioned earlier, this characteristic is illustrated (as every good ceremonial magician knows) by the dynamics of the pentagram, which allow for two types of Spirit pentagram, one active and one passive.

The Black Cross contains forty letters that radiate from the central blank square. When we read from the top of the column toward the center, we find the curiously spaced and inconsistently capitalized letters *e xarp* and *h Coma*. When we start at the center square of the Black Cross and read to the right, we find the letters *nanTa* and *bitom*.

We can find identical sets of letters if we read from the bottom of the column toward the center and from the center of the row to the left. In other words, the Black Cross contains mirror images of the letter groups *e xarp*, *h Coma*, *nanTa*, and *bitom*—a phenomenon curiously reflective of the dual nature of Spirit.

During the same June 25 session, Ave would (in remarkably few words) explain the letters on the Black Cross, answer questions concerning the three missing symmetrical characters of the tenth Aire (Lexarph, Comanan, and Tabitom—the twenty-eighth, twenty-ninth, and thirtieth parts of the earth; see chapter eighteen, figure 63), and demonstrate how those three names construct a master table, the *Tablet of Union*, which appears to rule the whole Great Table.

But before discussing all that, we have a small bit of unfinished business to clean up from the last chapter. I am, of course, talking about the Super Kerubs and the wicked angels.

Super Kerubs, or Gods of the Kerubs?

It is my opinion, and I'm sure many will disagree, that there are two hierarchies of angels existing simultaneously in each subangle. The first hierarchy simply begins with the two god names of the Calvary cross, who are invoked before calling upon the four servient angels whose names appear beneath the arm of the cross. In this schema, all the names of the angels in the hierarchy are drawn neatly and exclusively from within the subangle itself. The Kerub plays no role at all.

The second hierarchy, I believe, does not use the two god names of the Calvary cross at all, nor does it necessarily concern itself with the servient angels. Instead, it places a new character, a Super Kerub, or kerubic god, above a group of angels whose names are drawn exclusively from the four letters above the arms of the cross.

Figure 82 is a version of the original, unreformed Great Table that I've highlighted to, hopefully, make this all clear. I realize it may sound crazy for us to bounce back to using the unreformed table when locating these angels, but it is the unreformed table the angels used in 1584 when this information was received. For the moment, please ignore the circled backwards letters on the diagram.

The letters of the Black Cross are the key to creating the kerubic gods. Note how four of the letters in the column are isolated from others that appear neatly in groups of four. Reading from the top toward the center, the *e* of *e xarp* and the *h* of *h Coma* are isolated. Reading from the bottom toward the center, the *p* of *exar p* and the *a* of *hCom a* are also isolated. Note that these four isolated letters appear in the same rows as the Kerubs who live above the arms of the Calvary crosses of all sixteen subangles.

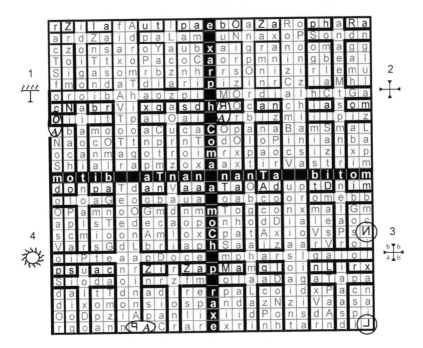

Figure 82: Key to the Black Cross and Kerubs

To determine the name of a subangle's kerubic god, simply insert the isolated letter (that appears on the same row as the Kerub's name) at the beginning of the Kerub's four-letter name. For example, the Kerub of the Fire subangle of the Fire tablet, *ZiZa*, would be transformed into the Super Kerub, *pZiZa* (see figure 80). Instead of ruling the servient angels, this Super Kerub *pZiZa* directly rules four angels whose names are created by the permutation of the Kerub's own name: ZiZa, iZaZ, ZaZi, and aZiZ. A table containing all the kerubic gods and their Kerubs can be found in appendix IV.

The important thing to remember is that in this system there are two hierarchies of angels in each of the sixteen subangles: one hierarchy that simply uses the god name of the Calvary cross to summon or contact the serviant angels living under the arms of the cross, and one hierarchy that selects a letter from the Black Cross (outside the Elemental Tablet) and adds it to the Kerub's name to create a kerubic god who rules four Kerubs whose names are created by the permutation of the regular Kerub's own name.

When to use one hierarchy and not the other in a magical operation remains a subject of debate among modern magicians. One thing is certain, the more the magician understands about the nature and dynamics of the Great Table, the more he or she will be able to devise a logical and workable mode. So let's discover more wonders of the Black Cross. Let's start with something we haven't encountered before in Enochian magick—wicked angels.

Wicked Angels

The letters of the Black Cross are also the key to creating the names of the four wicked, or evil or malevolent, angels of each subangle. Up to now we've been dealing with angels whose names are representative of complete and balanced segments of the Great Table and its Elemental Tablets. But during the June 25 session, as the angel Ave was expounding on the virtues of the Black Cross, he also introduced Dee and Kelley to a set of angels that are not complete and balanced—angels he referred to as being "wicked." These malevolent angels manifest aversely the powers of their good-angel subangle neighbors. For example, if the good angels are useful for healing, the wicked angels bring sickness and affliction (see appendix IV).

But some of the wicked angel duties seem rather tempting and are said to be useful in obtaining money and for gambling. Kelley initially got pretty excited about such prospects and was very disappointed when Ave in no uncertain terms told him hands off the evil angels. Why Ave would give details of these critters and turn around and tell the magicians not to use them remains a mystery. Or does it?

The name of an evil angel is a portrait of incompleteness and imbalance supercharged with an injection of the immense power of the Black Cross—a dangerous recipe if there ever was one. Creating it is very simple. Here's how to do it.

Remember how we created the name of a kerubic god by prefacing the name of a regular Kerub with the letter from the Black Cross occupying the same row? Well, that's almost exactly what we do to create the name of a wicked angel. However, instead of prefacing the four letters of a Kerub's name, we preface only the *first two letters* of the servient angel's name with its neighboring letter from the Black Cross. This three-letter supercharged perversion of the first half of a servient angel's name is a wicked angel.

Figure 83 is the Air (upper left) subangle of the Elemental Tablet of Earth (upper right Elemental Tablet in the *unreformed* Great Table) with the adjoining Black Cross letters. The four evil angels of this subangle are *xai*, *aor*, *rrs*, and *piz*.

e	b	O	a	ʒ	a
	u	N	n	a	x
x	a	i	g	r	a
a	o	r	p	m	n
r	r	s	O	n	i
p	i	z	i	n	r

Figure 83: Names of wicked angels of the Air subangle of the Elemental Tablet of Earth (unreformed Great Table)

And how does one, if one were inclined, call forth these evil angels? Who are their hierarchical rulers? As one might expect, the adverse god names that call forth the evil angels are the names on the Calvary cross *spelled backwards*. In the case of our example they are *iOpgna* and *xanNu*.

You can easily work out the names of the other evil angels and their rulers by referring to figure 82 or consulting the table in appendix IV.

Paraoan

Ave was particularly concerned that Dee and Kelley locate the name *Paraoan* on the Great Table. The significance of this great angel has not (at least to my satisfaction) been adequately explored or explained. The name *Paraoan* first appeared among the ninety-one parts of the earth as one of the three divine names (number 65) in the twenty-second Aire. *Paraoan* is the divine name of the part of the earth designated as Marmarica. According to Enochian scholar Robin Cousins, in Dee and Kelley's day, *Marmarica* was a North African coastal region straddling the Egyptian and Libyan coasts, bounded on the east by the River Nile (see appendix III).

Oddly enough, a perfectly good sixty-fifth symmetrical character already existed. It is found in the lower right section of the Elemental Tablet of Water, and spells the name *Laxdizi*.

Nevertheless, Paraoan seems to also hold the title of the sixty-fifth part of the earth known as Marmarica. The obvious and inescapable similarity between the names *Marmarica* and *America* inserts (into my mind at least) an added dimension of mystery to this curious anomaly. Add to this the enigmatic and direful comments Ave made concerning the final *n* in *Paraoan*:

> As far as that N. stretcheth in the Character, so far shall that Countrey be consumed with fire, and swallowed into Hell, as Sodom was for wickednesse. The end of all things is even at hand: and the earth must be purified, and delivered to another.[102]

A bit later, Dee presses Ave on this:

> Dee: I beseech you say somewhat of the N in Paraoan, of which you said, so far as that stretched, should sink to hell.

> Ave: Every letter in Paraoan, is a living fire: but all of one quality and of one Creation. But unto N is delivered a viol of Destruction, according to that part that he is of Paraoan the Governour.[103]

The letters of the name *Paraoan* are created from seven of the eight backward letters that appear scattered among the four Elemental Tablets of the Great Table. See the circled letters in figure 82. The eighth backwards letter, the backward *L* found in the lowermost square on the right of figure 82, has another very important job to do.

The Three Missing Symmetrical Characters of the Tenth Aire

Recall from the table in chapter eighteen (figure 63) that there were no symmetrical characters for the three parts of the earth assigned to the tenth Aire (those whose divine names were *Lexarph*, *Comanan*, and

Tabitom). Neither can these three names be found within the available letters in any of the four Elemental Tablets. They are, however, to be found on the Black Cross, and the angel Ave, in his highly productive lecture of June 25, 1584, shows how it is done.

Ave instructed Dee and Kelley to pluck the backward capital *L* from the lower right corner of the lower right Watchtower (I've circled it in figure 82) and preface the lowercase letters *e*, *x*, *a*, *r*, *p*, and *h* from the column of the Black Cross to form dual versions of the divine name *Lexarph*.

Then starting with the capital letter *C* in the column, moving down from the top *C* (or up from the bottom *C*), then continuing to read either right or left into the horizontal row, dual versions of the divine name *Comanan* are formed.

Then, starting with the capital letter *T* in the left and right arms of the Black Cross and reading toward the extremities, we discover dual versions of the divine name *Tabitom*.

Lexarph, *Comanan*, and *Tabitom* are respectively the divine names of the twenty-eighth, twenty-ninth, and thirtieth parts of the earth in the tenth Aire, whose symmetrical characters were missing from the original material concerning the ninety-one parts of the earth. Their characters are simply the straight lines and rotating *L*s that spell out their names on the Black Cross.

Obviously, angelic beings whose names are drawn from the Black Cross are of a nature that sets them apart from their neighbors in the Elemental Tablets. Their presence in the tenth Aire also distinguishes that portion of the ninety-one parts of the earth for special attention— something that will be important to us later.

The Four Names of the Tablet of Union

Lexarph, *Comanan*, and *Tabitom* also contain within themselves the four names that appear in pairs on the Black Cross, names that are very familiar to practicing Enochian magicians: *EXARP*, *HCOMA*, *NANTA*, and *BITOM*. These are the four divine names of the elements that (in the practice of modern Enochian magick at least) rule the four Elemental Tablets.

These four names are arranged into a table five squares wide by four squares high. This *Tablet of Union*, in its profound simplicity, extracts the essence and hierarchical dynamics of the entire Great Table. The Tablet of Union is quite literally the Great Table distilled.

E	X	A	R	P
H	C	O	M	A
N	A	N	T	A
B	I	T	O	M

Figure 84: The Tablet of Union

We'll soon learn much more about the Tablet of Union. But first, we are almost ready to bring the story of Dee and Kelley's Enochian period to an end. It was not long after Ave's revelations concerning the Black Cross, Kerubs, wicked angels, missing symmetrical characters, and the Tablet of Union that the two magicians' great angelic adventure, for all intents and purposes, came to a close. There remained only a couple of loose ends to tie up. But my heavens, what loose ends those were!

CHAPTER TWENTY-FIVE

"There Is All."

*Nalvage is called away and cannot be in Action with you until
Wednesday. Then shall you have the Calls that you look for.
And so enter into the knowledge and perfect understanding of
the 49 Gates and Tables if you will.*

—THE ARCHANGEL GABRIEL, MONDAY, JULY 9, 1584[104]

In early July of 1584, the two magicians were busy trying to tie up loose
ends before a mysterious August deadline. On July 7, the angel Ave
waxed eloquent about how Enoch made tablets such as those Dee and
Kelley now possessed, and had labored fifty days in prayer and confes-
sion before receiving a supreme revelation. It appears from the communication[105] that the two magicians were to do likewise.

In a breathtakingly short amount of time, Dee and Kelley received
the translations of the remaining angelic calls (five through eighteen),
which they had six weeks earlier received in the angelic tongue,
together with tantalizing hints that the eighteen calls might be connected to the Tablet of Union and the four Elemental Tablets.

On Thursday, July 12, the angel Ilemese[106] began to deliver a nineteenth call, together with its translation. This call was said to be actually
thirty calls, bringing the total number of calls to forty-eight. Add the
unexpressed "first" call (see chapter sixteen), and we have a grand total

of forty-nine (7 x 7) calls. The next day, Friday the thirteenth, 1584, John Dee's fifty-seventh birthday, Ilemese delivered the remaining portion of the nineteenth call and revealed that it was the key to accessing the thirty Aires (the heavens connected to the ninety-one parts of the earth). Lastly, he revealed the names of the thirty Aires, which until then had only been identified by numbers (see chapter nineteen, figure 63, columns I and VI).

The nineteenth call was a master call to be used to access each of the thirty Aires or Aethyrs. The only thing that differentiated the thirty calls from one another was insertion of the name of the particular Aire in the first line. Ilemese delivered the names of the Aires as a simple list and then engaged in a brief exchange with Dee.

The first Aire is called ———————— Lil.

The second ———————— Arn.

The third ———————— Zom.

4. ———————— Paz.

5. ———————— Lit.

6. ———————— Maz.

7. ———————— Deo.

8. ———————— Zid.

9. ———————— Zip.

10. ———————— Zax.

11. ———————— Ich.

12. ———————— Loe.

13. ———————— Zim.

14. ———————— Uta.

15. ———————— Oxo.

16. ———————— Lea.

17. ———————— Tan.

18. ———————— Zen.

19. ———————— Pop.

20. ———————— Chr.

21. ———————— Asp.

22. ———————— Lin.

23. ————————————	Tor.
24. ————————————	Nia.
25. ————————————	Uti.
26. ————————————	Des.
27. ————————————	Zaa.
28. ————————————	Bag.
29. ————————————	Rii.
30. ————————————	Tex.

Ile: There is all—Now change the name, and the Call is all one.

Δ: Blessed be he who onely is always one.

I take these names to be as primus, secudus, tertius, and to 30.

A voice . . . Not so, they be the substantial names of the Aires.

Δ: It was said they had no proper names; but were to be called, O thou of the first Aire, O thou of the second, etc. I pray you reconcile the repugnancy of theses two places, as they should seem.[107]

Dee's testiness evoked a response from none other than the archangel Gabriel, who was sitting nearby in Kelley's vision during Ilemese's discourse. The great angel stood and informed the magicians they now possessed the knowledge they needed. He encouraged them to study and prepare for the August operation and then, after one more little jab at Dee's cheekiness, delivered a most poignant valediction.

E. K. The Curtain is opened.

E. E. [sic] Now Gabriel standeth up.

Gabr . . . Thus has God kept promise with you, and hath delivered you the keyes of his storehouses: wherein you shall find, (if you enter wisely, humbly, and patiently) Treasures more worth than the frames of the heavens.

But it is not August come: Notwithstanding the Lord hath kept his promise with you be the time. Therefore, Now examine you Books, Confer one place with another, and learn to be perfect for the practice and entrance.

See that your garments be clean. Herein be not rash: Nor over hasty; For those that are hasty and rash, and are loathsomely appareled, may knock long before they enter.

There is no other reading of the Book, but the appearing of the Ministers and Creatures of God: which shewing what they are themselves, shew how they are conjoyed in power, and represented formally by those letters.

E. K. Now he taketh the Table, and seemeth to wrap it up together.

Δ: Seeing I have moved the doubt of their names I pray you to dissolve it.

Gab . . . You play with me childishly.

Δ: I have done.

Gab . . . Thinkest thou that we speak any thing that is not true?

Thou shalt never know the mysteries of all things that have been spoken.

If you love together, and dwell together, and in one God; Then the self-same God will be merciful unto you: Which bless you, comfort you, and strengthen you unto the end. More I would say, but words profit not. God be amongst you.

E.K. Now they both be gone in a great flame of fire upwards . . . [108]

Thus, in a dramatic burst of flame, the angels of Enochian magick fell silent, and the most amazing magical operation ever recorded came to an end. Unfortunately, we don't know if the two magicians actually performed the fifty-day operation scheduled for August. Surviving diary entries for the month treat on other matters. What we are left with, however, is an elegant and remarkably coherent system of vision magick.

For those of us who have made Enochian magick a part of our spiritual quest, Gabriel's parting words ring profoundly true. God did keep promise with Dee and Kelley and delivered unto them (and us) the keys to the storehouses wherein we shall find, if we enter wisely, humbly, and patiently, treasures worth more than the frames of the heavens.

BOOK V

Putting It Together

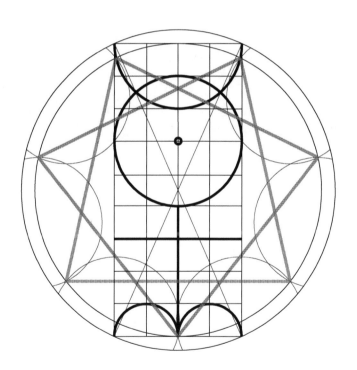

CHAPTER TWENTY-SIX

Rulership of the Tablet of Union

The Tablet of Union is a Great Table *you can put in your briefcase; but EHNB is a* Tablet of Union *you can put in your pocket.*

—LON MILO DUQUETTE

I have purposefully placed this brief overview of practical Enochian vision magick after the chronology of Dee and Kelley's great Enochian adventure. I do so because Enochian vision magick as it is generally practiced today is a system that depends heavily on innovations that were developed long after the great magicians passed into history. Not that I think that modern Enochian magick is an affront to the memories of these two giants of magick. But I do think it is important for us to know the difference between the foundational material and the structures that have later been built upon it.

I think it is also important to remember that there is nothing particularly sacrosanct about the methods and techniques developed by the Golden Dawn, Crowley, or any other latter-day magicians. As an informed and competent magician, you are just as free as these individuals were and are to develop your own Enochian magick art form based and structured on your personal interpretation and understanding of Dee and Kelley's experiences and material. After all, in order for you to justly claim the title of magician you must *be* a magician, not merely a one-man or one-woman Society for Creative Anachronism dedicated to simply recreating the lives and works of real magicians of the past.

Enochian vision magick as practiced today can be divided into two broad categories: elemental and aethyric. Both require the ability to scry and to keep a faithful written record of one's workings. Scrying the Aethyrs has, in my later years, become the focus of most of my Enochian operations, because that process deals most directly with the current state of my personal initiatory career—by that I mean my personal transformational process, my spiritual journey, the lifting of my consciousness.

However, it has not always been so. Indeed, I would never encourage any magician, especially in the early stages of his or her Enochian career, to neglect either branch of Enochian exploration. I spent many years honing my visionary skills by exploring the elemental worlds that not only make up my physical, mental, and emotional environment but also actually represent everything that my limited senses tell me is *me*.

It is the elemental branch of Enochian vision magick that I will first discuss. To help me do this, I'm going to talk briefly about the structure of another great magical tool, the tarot.

Rulership of the Tablet of Union

The classic tarot image of the Magician shows the magician standing behind a table, upon which are four magical tools; a wand, a cup, a sword, and a disk. These are the four elemental weapons of the magician. They represent respectively the four suits of the tarot and the elements Fire, Water, Air, and Earth.

The master card of each suit is the ace. The ace is the "Spirit" of the suit—the "Spirit" of the element. The other cards in the suit are given life by the spirit of the ace. They are essentially subdivisions, components, and aspects of the ace—they all "live" inside the ace.

If we put an ace under a magick microscope, we would first see that it is composed of four major components.[109] These are the four court cards (commonly titled king, queen, prince, and princess) that represent respectively the elements Fire, Water, Air, and Earth. For example, if we put the Ace of Wands (Fire) under our magick microscope, we would see that it was composed of the King of Wands (the fiery aspect of Fire), the Queen of Wands (the watery aspect of Fire), the Prince of Wands (the airy aspect of Fire), and the Princess of Wands (the earthy aspect of Fire).

In the Enochian model, we can actually see Spirit's influence inter-penetrating the heart and every quadrant of the Elemental Tablet in the form of the Great Central Cross and the Calvary crosses of the suban-gles. The Black Cross of the Great Table reveals Spirit's influence on an even larger scale. It literally holds together and separates the four Elemental Tablets. The Black Cross is like the ace of aces. All this is expressed most simply and elegantly in the Tablet of Union.

I draw your attention to figure 85 and the four rows of names in the Tablet of Union.

Subangles

	✵	◬	▽	▽	△
◬	E	X	A	R	P
▽	H	C	O	M	A
▽	N	A	N	T	A
△	B	I	T	O	M

Elemental Tablets

Figure 85: The elemental key to the Tablet of Union

Recall that *Exarp, Hcoma, Nanta,* and *Bitom* are the four names found in pairs on the Black Cross of the Great Table. In modern Enochian magick, these Black Cross letters represent the element Spirit. The four names on the Tablet of Union are not merely the master keys to the elemental universe—they are the elemental universe.

Starting with the top row, we see that EXARP is the elemental world of Air; HCOMA the world of Water; NANTA, Earth; and BITOM, Fire.[110] (Note the little symbols of the elements to the left of each row of names.)

Now let's look at the five columns of the Tablet of Union. The left-most column is made from the four first letters of the names, giving us the name *EHNB*. At the top of this column is a little circle with spokes inside. This is the symbol of Spirit. It tells us that *EHNB* is the column of Spirit and the essence of the entire tablet.

Obviously, the angelic entity described by the letters *EHNB* is profoundly powerful. It is a name that represents and contains within itself the entire Great Table and all the angelic forces within it. *E* represents the entire the Elemental Tablet of Air, *H* the Elemental Tablet of Water, *N* the Elemental Tablet of Earth, and *B* the Elemental Tablet of Fire.

In a real sense, the remaining sixteen letters all live inside *EHNB* in just the same way the sixteen court cards of the tarot live inside their aces. Put *E* under a microscope and see the letters *XARP*. Put *H* under a microscope and see *COMA*. Put *N* under a microscope and see *ANTA*. Put *B* under a microscope and see *ITOM*.

As we move right, the next column is *XCAI*, whose letters represent the four Air subangles of the four Elemental Tablets and all the resident angels inside the Air subangles. (XCAI would be the four princes of the tarot.)

AONT does the same for the Water subangles (queens of the tarot), *RMTO* for the Earth subangles (princesses of the tarot), and *PAAM* for the Fire subangles (kings of the tarot).

Now are you starting to see the power resident in the Tablet of Union? If we were to call EXARP, HCOMA, NANTA, and BITOM archangels of the elements, then we would have to say that EHNB is the archangel of archangels of the elements. The Tablet of Union is a *Great Table* you can put in your briefcase, but EHNB is a *Tablet of Union* you can put in your pocket.

The Tablet of Union and the four Elemental Tablets are activated and penetrated in vision by intoning one or two of the first eighteen calls in the angelic tongue. I give details showing how this is done in appendix II, but here is a brief overview:

The first two calls are dedicated to the Tablet of Union exclusively and are never used to call or visit the angels of the Elemental Tablets.

The next four calls (three through six) deal with the angels of the individual letters of EXARP, HCOMA, NANTA, and BITOM, and/or are used to activate and penetrate the *native subangles* of the Elemental

Tablets. (A native subangle is the subangle of an Elemental Tablet that represents the same element as the Elemental Tablet—e.g., the Air Subangle of the Air Tablet, the Water Subangle of the Water Tablet.)

The next twelve calls (seven through eighteen) are used to activate and penetrate the remaining three subangles of the Elemental Tablets. How these calls are allotted to the various subangles is an exercise in routine hermetic logic.

As I mentioned earlier, it is not necessary for you to have elaborate or expensive models of the Elemental Tablets and the Tablet of Union in order to perform Enochian magick. But it is important that you have a good understanding of them and have the equipment "installed" in your mind. When I work with the angels of the Elemental Tablets or the Tablet of Union, I simply have my four colored Elemental Tablets (positioned as they appear in the reformed Great Table) on a table before me and place my small Tablet of Union on the top of them in the center.

Now on to the business of actually doing Enochian vision magick.

CHAPTER TWENTY-SEVEN

Elemental Workings, Temple Openings, and Addressing the Hierarchies

Sylphs and Gnomes and Undines too,

Salamanders beckon you . . .

—"THEME FROM MOUNT OREAD"[III]

Why on earth would anyone wish to call upon an angel of the elements? What can a salamander (Fire elemental) do for me? When does an undine (Water elemental) come in handy? Does a sylph (Air elemental) really look like Tinkerbell? Are gnomes (Earth elementals) really grumpy? Is exploration of the elements a necessary prerequisite to higher magical workings?

As I wrote in the prologue, the question of, "why magick?" is one that is not easily answered. The supreme goal of the magician is spiritual enlightenment and liberation of the soul. Do I expect to accomplish that end through the aid of elemental spirits?

Not directly. But the elementals are a part of my world, a part of my being. They move within me and around me. They dwell among themselves in their infinite number, ratios, and proportions. "Know

Thyself" was chiseled above the doors of the ancient temples of initiation. How can I know myself when the mysteries of the elements of my own heart and soul remain undiscovered?

Enochian elemental magick is not a matter of calling up a spirit to command it to do a job for you, to cause the girl next door to fall in love with you, to bewitch your neighbor's cow, or to kill an enemy at a distance. Instead, when you visit an Enochian elemental angel in vision, you are exploring a specific aspect of creation, a highly specialized area of which the angel is the visual and metaphoric embodiment. You see things the way they *are* in that narrow quadrant of the universe. Once armed with the insights these spiritual specialists can provide, you are better prepared to know how to go about causing the girl next door to fall in love with you or bewitching your neighbor's cow. (I understand that killing at a distance is less satisfying than one might imagine.)

Does this really help the magician? First and most obviously, it broadens his or her understanding of how the spirit world is the subjective and underlying reality of the objective world. Just as the educated and seasoned traveler is better equipped than the novice to understand rewards and pitfalls of world travel, a magician experienced with elemental work is endowed with a greater understanding of existence. That in and of itself is a spiritual reward.

But more than that, each willed encounter with the angels of the elements activates, readjusts, and rebalances the magician's own internal elemental components. Like the computer user who periodically defragments the hard drive of his or her computer in order to make things to run more efficiently, the magician is changed and (hopefully) improved with every thoughtful and seriously examined elemental encounter.

At our Monday night magick class, we've developed a series of simple questions we first ask every angel we call from an Elemental Tablet. Just as we would not expect any two computer hard drives to be fragmented in exactly the same way, no two magicians should expect the exact same answers to these questions. Here are a few of them. The first questions are the simplest yet most important:

- What is your name? (Confirm you have who you've called.)
- What is your nature?

The next questions deal with how the angel is perceived by the human senses:

- What is your color?
- What is your sound (musical note, if possible)?
- How do you feel to the human touch?
- What do you taste like?
- How do you smell?

The next questions deal with how the angel makes itself known to us through our thoughts and emotions:

- How do I express you through emotions?
- In what form of images and ideas are you most revealed to me?
- When are you most manifest in my daily life?

Other questions could concern things more specific to one's own personal magical issues, but I think you get the picture.

Now that we know a little more about why to practice Enochian elemental magick, let's look at how to do it. It is likely that my opinion on this subject will be slightly at odds with a number of practicing Enochian magicians. It is even more certain to receive condemnation by legions of others who don't actually perform Enochian magick but instead enjoy speculating how Enochian magicians should operate.

Dee and Kelley contacted the angels by praying. Boy, did they pray! There is nothing in the surviving records that suggests that they performed banishing rituals, drew pentagrams or hexagrams in the air, made knocks or magical gestures, or called upon the strings of classic qabalistic Hebrew divine names from the sephiroth of the Tree of Life. The operating procedures of the Golden Dawn and Crowley, however, do all those things and more.

Here is an example of a Golden Dawn–style temple opening appropriate for working with the Elemental Table of Earth. It is a ceremony that incorporates ritual components from the GD's neophyte degree, the grade that represents Malkuth, the tenth and lowest sephirah on the Tree of Life. As you can see, the ritual invokes the qabalistic hierarchy of divine names, archangels, and angels traditionally attributed to Malkuth and the element Earth.

The Opening of the Temple in the Grade of 1° = 10 ☐

Give the Sign of the God SET fighting.

Purify with Fire and Water, and announce

"The Temple is cleansed."

Knock.

"Let us adore the Lord and King of Earth! Adonai ha Aretz, Adonai Melehk, unto Thee be the Kingdom, the Sceptre, and the Splendour: Malkuth, Geburah, Gedulah, The Rose of Sharon and the Lily of the Valley, Amen!"

Sprinkle Salt before Earth tablet.

"Let the Earth adore Adonai!"

Make the Invoking Hexagram of Saturn.

Make the Invoking Pentagram of Spirit Passive and pronounce . . .

"AHIH AGLA NANTA"

Make the Invoking Pentagram of Earth, and pronounce . . .

"ADNI MLK." And Elohim said: "Let us make Man in Our own image; and let them have dominion over the Fish of the Sea and over the Fowl of the Air; and over every creeping thing that creepeth upon the Earth. And the Elohim created ATh-h-ADAM: in the image of the Elohim created They them; male and female created They them. In the Name of ADNI MLK, and of the Bride and Queen of the Kingdom; Spirits of Earth, adore your Creator!"

Make the Sign of Taurus.

"In the Name of Auriel, great archangel of Earth, Spirits of Earth, adore your Creator!"

Make the Cross.

"In the Names and Letters of the Great Northern Quadrangle, Spirits of Earth, adore your Creator!"

Sprinkle water before Earth Tablet.

"In the three great secret Names of God, MOR, DIAL, HCTGA, that are borne upon the Banners of the North, Spirits of Earth, adore your Creator!"

Cense the Tablet.

"In the name of ICZHIHA, great king of the North, Spirits of Earth, adore your Creator! In the Name of Adonai Ha-Aretz, I declare that the Spirits of Earth have been duly invoked."

Knock. 4444—333—22—1

For many modern Enochian magicians, rituals such as this qabalistically formatted degree opening ceremony are perfect vehicles for establishing the proper elemental environment in which to operate. For years they were an indispensable part of my operating procedure as well. I discontinued, however, about ten years ago.

As we myopically focus on the fascinating intricacies of different magical systems, we often forget the big picture and the fact that we have only one universe to play with. There is no such thing as a separate qabalistic magick universe, or a separate Solomonic magick universe, or a separate Enochian magick universe. These various systems simply oblige us to view the same universe from different angles. Granted, when we look from differing points of view, we see certain similarities. After all, it's the same universe. There are certain to be recognizable landmarks. But we can't expect the structure of one system's point of view to neatly match or define the other.

It is my opinion that the spiritual forces inherent in Enochian magick are expressed units of living consciousness that reflect a uniquely structured and organized point of view of the universe—one that the communicating angels obliged Dee and Kelley to build from scratch. It is a perfect, self-referential system of looking at things that cannot be expected to be consistently compatible with other self-referential systems.

With all due respect to the knowledgeable and eloquent magicians who created the above temple opening, I believe that (unless your sensitivities as a magical artist demands it) most of it is completely unnecessary in order for you to properly activate an Elemental Tablet and effectively address the hierarchy of angels who rule the angel you may wish to contact. The use of the various pentagrams and the hexagram, the assumption of a Samo-Thracian elemental god-form, the invocation of the various names of the Hebrew deity and traditional angels, and the recitation of Bible verses are all tried-and-true magical methods to access the elemental world of Earth, but they are tools used in *another* kind of magical system—a system that views the magical universe from a slightly different angle, music played using a different scale of notes.

Please don't misunderstand me. Qabalistic temple openings such as the one above work effectively enough for Enochian elemental operations. But what makes them work, in my opinion, is not the pentagrams, Hebrew god names, or Bible verses. They work because, nestled within the ramblings and tossing about of salt and water, the magician is required to recognize and address by name the spiritual forces of the elements as they are uniquely organized and expressed in the Enochian magick system. In our example above, those names are Nanta (the great angel of Earth from the Tablet of Union), Mor, Dial, Hctga (the Three Great Secret Names of God from the Elemental Tablet of Earth), and Iczhiha (the king of the Elemental Tablet of Earth). The hierarchy of high elemental forces that the *other* magical system calls Adonai ha Aretz, Adonai Melehk, Malkuth, the Rose of Sharon, and the Lily of the Valley—everything the *other* system calls forth by means of pentagrams, gestures, and Bible verses—are all wrapped up and neatly addressed in the Enochian system in the names Nanta, Mor, Dial, Hctga, and Iczhiha.

If you conclude that my thoughts on this subject have some merit, I encourage you to customize for yourself a simply formatted little speech that addresses by name and in proper order the various angelic personages of the hierarchies of each Elemental Tablet. I will outline my address to the hierarchies at the end of this chapter. But first, let's discuss what the proper procedure for an elemental working might be.

DuQuette's Protocol for Enochian Elemental Vision Magick

The lower the angel you wish to contact is in the hierarchy of the Elemental Tablet, the more superior angels there are above it who must be named and addressed. Therefore, for our example I will use Adre, a lowly servient angel found under the arms of the Calvary cross of the Fire Subangle of the Elemental Tablet of Fire. (See chapter twenty-three, figures 71 through 79.)

I. Preliminaries

Before embarking on any formal magical operation it is helpful, indeed necessary, to feel good about oneself. Therefore, I always recommend that the magician first bathe, dress in clean clothing, and operate in a clean and uncluttered space. It is also wise to formally purify and banish the area before operating. These preliminary ceremonies can be as simple or as elaborate as you feel necessary. I always begin with a simple Lesser Banishing Ritual of the Pentagram that I've customized to reflect my own taste and spiritual proclivity. A classic version if the pentagram ritual can be found at the beginning of appendix I.

I next perform the Ceremony of Preparation that is outlined in chapter one and appendix I of this book. I consider this ritual an Enochian magick temple opening par excellence. I believe it serves to purify, banish, and consecrate both the temple and the magician in a manner that is in harmony with the universe as perceived by the Enochian angels. It also establishes and sanctifies the magical environment for the black mirror or scrying stone.

II. The Call(s)

A complete list of the angels of all four Elemental Tablets, together with their traditional duties, can be found in appendix IV.

In order to contact any angel from an Elemental Tablet, one need first activate the tablet by intoning the proper call or calls in the Enochian tongue. The calls and the key to their use can be found in appendix II.

Only one call is necessary if your target angel resides in the Great Central Cross (one of the Three Great Secret Names of God, a senior, or a king). Also, only one call is necessary if your target angel resides in the *native* subangle of the Elemental Tablet (e.g., the Fire Subangle of the Fire Tablet, the Water Subangle of the Water Tablet, etc.). But if your target angel resides in a non-native subangle (e.g., the Earth Subangle of the Water Tablet, the Air Subangle of the Fire Tablet, etc.), you must also recite an additional call assigned specifically to the subangle.

Our target angel, Adre, resides in the native subangle (Fire Subangle of the Fire Tablet), so we need only recite the sixth call (see appendix II).

Reciting the sixth call switches on the power of the Elemental Tablet of Fire, as it were, and puts it in standby mode to await more specific actions from the magician.

III. Addressing the Hierarchy

Whether you feel it or not,[112] your recitation of the sixth call has put you in an altered state of consciousness. Magically speaking, you are now present within the environment of the Element Tablet of Fire. You have awakened the spiritual forces of the tablet, and they are waiting to see if you are worthy of their attention. If you can convince the spirits of the tablet that you know where you are and how you got there, they will acknowledge you as a natural citizen of their well-ordered magical universe. Once you've established rapport with its superiors, the target angel will have no choice but to be compliant and ready to open its mysteries to you.

You prove your worthiness by remembering your manners and addressing by name the angels who reign over your target angel. In the case of a servient angel like Adre, the hierarchy is essentially the whole cast of characters. Starting from the top we have:

1. The Supreme Name of Fire from the Tablet of Union: *Bitom*.
2. The Three Great Secret Names of God of the Elemental Tablet of Fire: *Oip*, *Teaa*, *Pdoce*.
3. The name of the king of the Elemental Tablet of Fire: *Edlprna*.
4. The names of the six planetary seniors of the Elemental Tablet of Fire: *Aaetpio*, *Adoeoet*, *Alndvod*, *Aapdoce*, *Arinna*, and *Anodoin*.
5. The first god name of the Fire subangle: *Rzionr*.
6. The second god name of the Fire subangle: *Nrzfm*.
7. And finally, the name of our target servient angel: *Adre*.

If the target angel is higher on the hierarchical ladder, there are fewer names to include in your little speech. For example, to call a senior, you only need to use the names in steps 1, 2, and 3 before calling on the name of the target senior. If your target angel is the king of the Elemental Tablet, you only have to use the names in steps 1 and 2.[113]

And what about the kerubic angels who, as we learned earlier, have a separate hierarchy that skips the god names of the subangle?

In the case of the Fire subangle of the Elemental Tablet of Fire, simply replace the name in step 5 with the name of the god Kerub (*Pziza*) and replace the name in step 6 with the name of the Kerub (*ZiZa*, *iZaZ*, *ZaZi*, or *aZiZ*).

IV. Calling Your Target Angel

Repeat out loud the name of the target angel, Adre, several times. State why you have called it; ask your questions and/or make your requests, then sit quietly and scry. If necessary, repeat the call to induce a deeper state of mind. If you wish, have a tape recorder running and describe your vision as it unfolds. Don't tire yourself. Conclude your visionary business at the first signs of fatigue. Thank the angel and formally close the session with a banishing ritual of your choice.

V. Write It All Down

Immediately transcribe everything into your magical journal. I mean *everything*: the date and time, weather conditions, astrological aspects (if you know them and care about such things). Even if you think there is nothing to report, write that down, along with your thoughts of why things might not have worked.

Sample of a Hierarchical Invocation

The invocation below is what I currently use to acknowledge and invoke the hierarchy of the Elemental Tablet. I will provide the English translation of it first so you will know what it is saying. You may easily customize your own by referring to an Enochian dictionary.[114]

With the Elemental Tablet before me, I utter each angel's name and I wave my wand over the squares that spell it.

I invoke and move thee, O thou, Spirit (name of target angel).

And being exalted above you in the power of the Most High, I say unto you come forth and obey!

In the name of (Supreme Name from the Tablet of Union; e.g., Exarp, Hcoma, Nanta, or Bitom);

and in the name of (the Three Great Secret Names of God of the Elemental Tablet),

and in the name of (the name of the king of the Elemental Tablet),

and in the name of (the names of the six seniors of the Elemental Tablet),

and in the name of . . . ,

and in the name of. . . ,

and in the name of . . . (as many names in hierarchy as necessary),

I invoke and move thee, O thou Spirit (name of target angel).

Here is the same invocation in the Enochian angelic language:

Ol vinu od zacam, Ils gah (name of target angel).

Od lansh vors gi Iad, gohus pugo ils niiso od darbs!

Dooiap (Supreme Name from the Tablet of Union),

od dooiap (the Three Great Secret Names of God),

od dooiap (the name of the king),

od dooiap (the names of the six seniors),

od dooiap . . . ,

od dooiap . . . ,

od dooiap . . . (as many names in hierarchy as necessary),

Ol vinu od zacam, Ils gah (name of target angel).

CHAPTER TWENTY-EIGHT

Aethyric Workings

Everything in heaven and earth is connected to everything in heaven and earth.

Everything in heaven and earth is the reflection of everything in heaven and earth.

Everything in heaven and earth contains the pattern of everything in heaven and earth.

Look hard enough at anything and you will eventually see everything.

—RABBI LAMED BEN CLIFFORD[115]

In order to more easily understand what follows, I ask that you turn back to chapter eighteen and refer to the columns in figure 63.

Right up until the last day of the Enochian period, Dee and Kelley believed that the thirty Aires (column I) were simply the numbered segments of creation that organized in groups of three[116] the ninety-one parts of the earth. Furthermore, they believed that the ninety-one divinely appointed names of the parts of the earth (column IV) were merely the angelic language names for the geographic areas of the earth named in column III. But in his final communication of July 13, 1584, the angel Ilemese revealed that the thirty Aires had names and a certain connection with the nineteenth call. As we saw in chapter twenty-five, this concept appeared to confuse and irritate Dee, who seemed comfortable with merely identifying the Aires by their sequence number.

Even though there is very little in the surviving material to suggest the thirty Aires are anything other than containers for the parts of the Earth, many modern magicians believe they carry a more profound significance. Indeed, it appears to me that this is an excellent example of modern magicians picking up the football where Dee and Kelley dropped it and running with it for a very big touchdown. The basic idea is this.

In keeping with the most fundamental hermetic and qabalistic axiom, "As above, so below," the *micro*cosmic world (the physical universe and humanity) is the reflection of a heavenly *macro*cosmic world of divine consciousness. So too, the thirty Aires containing the ninety-one parts of the earth are the microcosmic reflection of thirty Aethyrs, or heavens, that surround and enclose the four Watchtowers of the Great Table in thirty heavenly spheres, like layers of a glass onion.

Like the ten sephiroth and the twenty-two paths on the Tree of Life, the thirty Aethyrs can be viewed as emanations of divine consciousness. The thirtieth or lowest Aethyr would represent a level of divine consciousness that is so low that it has almost descended into matter. The first or highest Aethyr would represent the pure and undifferentiated mind of Deity.

Using this model, the ninety-one parts of the earth (column IV of figure 63) have their counterparts in the Aethyrs, and the divine names of the parts of the earth (e.g., Pascomb for Syria) also serve as the names of angelic governors, who, in groups of three, inhabit the thirty Aethyrs. The only exception to this is the thirtieth Aethyr, Tex, which has four governors.

There is a great temptation among modern practitioners to project this thirty-Aethyr model upon classic schema of the qabalistic Tree of Life with its ten sephiroth and twenty-two paths that also represent levels of consciousness. Some magicians go so far as to suggest the thirty Aethyrs can simply be divided by three into ten units and superimposed upon the ten sephiroth of the Tree. I wish I could believe things were as simple as that, but, as I wrote in the previous chapter, the classic qabalistic and Enochian models oblige us to view the same universe from different angles.

Aleister Crowley gave perhaps the most comprehensible way of viewing the relationship of the thirty Aethyrs and the Tree of Life:

> It is to be remarked that the last three æthyrs have ten angels attributed to them, and they therefore represent the ten Sephiroth. Yet these ten form but one, a Malkuth-pendant to the next three, and so on, each set being, as it were, absorbed in the higher. The last set consists, therefore, of the first three æthyrs with the remaining twenty-seven as their Malkuth.[117]

The angels Crowley is referring to are the governors of the Aethyrs. Because Tex contains four governors instead of three, Crowley considered the last three Aethyrs (Tex, Rii, and Bag) as a set containing ten governors who could be projected on a Tree of Life (see figure 86).

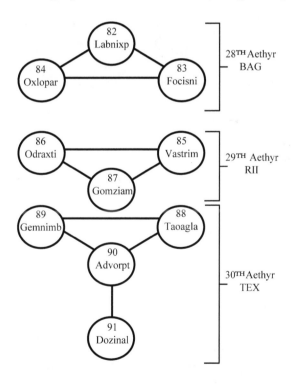

Figure 86: The first (lowest) set of governors (of the thirtieth, twenty-ninth, and twenty-eighth Aethyrs) projected on a single Tree of Life

He then posited that this entire Tree of Life becomes the Malkuth (the tenth and lowest sephirah) of a higher Tree of Life made up of the nine governors of the next three Aethyrs (Zaa, Des, and Vti), which, in turn, become the Malkuth of the next three Aethyrs, and so on all the way to the top.

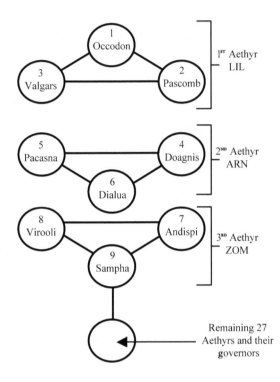

Figure 87: The last (highest) set of governors (of the first, second, and third Aethyrs) with the remaining twenty-seven Aethyrs and their governors encapsulated in a master Malkuth

You may or may not resonate with Crowley's view on this subject. Still, it is not unreasonable to compare the thirty Aethyrs to the sephiroth of the Tree of Life, especially when we understand both of them to be levels of personal initiation. This is precisely how Aleister Crowley viewed them. His systematic scrying of the Aethyrs as he walked across the North African Sahara in 1909 are chronicled in his visionary masterwork,

The Vision & the Voice, a text I believe should be studied by anyone interested in Enochian aethyric vision work.

While I certainly am not yet ready to compare my aethyric adventures with those of Crowley's, I have on multiple occasions engaged in a systematic exploration of the Aethyrs. I have, on a number of occasions, scryed each Aethyr, starting with number thirty, Tex, and worked my way to number one, Lil. Even my Monday night magick class is obliged to now and again undergo thirty weeks of scrying the Aethyrs.

Am I suggesting that we all actually achieve the sublime levels of consciousness represented by the higher Aethyrs? Of course I am not. But most of us receive provocative and highly personal visions, especially in the lower Aethyrs. That is because the lower Aethyrs represent levels of consciousness that we visit all the time in the natural course of daily life—in dreams, reveries, ecstasies, even deliriums. Even as I write these words, I am probably dipping into the lower Aethyrs as my memory and imagination conjure images that help me crystallize ideas I can put into words on the page. (I probably spent my entire senior year of high school staring into space and cruising in the lower Aethyrs!)

As the magician moves upwards through the Aethyrs, he or she progressively breaks into higher and higher levels of consciousness. If we are prepared for this new territory, our visions are characterized by a certain spontaneity and lucidity. However, when we begin to get out of our depth—when we haven't yet achieved the level of consciousness necessary to take the next step—our visions become murky and forced, as if we were watching it through a glass darkly. When this happens, the vision is usually characterized by a clear message announcing in no uncertain terms that we have not completely penetrated the Aethyr.

But that is not a bad thing. In fact, it is exactly what we want to happen, because we then know where we are on the initiatory ladder. Moreover, we have a chance of knowing what it is we need to do (or, more accurately, we will know who we need to become) to take the next step in our initiatory career. Allow me to illustrate with a hypothetical example.

Let's say you've resolved to systematically scry all thirty Aethyrs, one per night, from thirty to one, over a one-month period. Each night after your scrying session, you dutifully record in your journal the details of your vision. Everything is going along nicely until you attempt to penetrate in vision the fifteenth Aethyr, Oxo. You recite the nineteenth call in the proper manner and call for the three governors of Oxo (Tahando, Nociabi, and Tastoxo; see figure 63 column IV).

As the vision begins, three angels appear in the mirror, crystal, or your mind's eye, and march in a circle around you so that you cannot move in any direction. They will not respond to your questions or vouchsafe a proper vision. When something like this happens, you know that your present level of consciousness (your personal initiatory grade) is not refined enough to penetrate, let alone appreciate, the next Aethyr. It's as though you are a radio receiver not yet equipped to pull in higher broadcast frequencies. In order for you to do so, you will need to upgrade your equipment by raising your level of consciousness.

You will need to undergo an initiatory experience that will turn you into a more refined visionary traveler. And, as in all initiations, there is an obstacle that needs to be overcome. This obstacle can be anything from a psychological issue to a personal demon or character flaw. In order to conquer it, you might need just a tiny illumination concerning life, or a magical shift of focus, or to successfully achieve a more profound meditative state or trance.

You won't need to look far to discover what this obstacle is. It should be right there in your magical diary, in the record of the last Aethyr you could successfully penetrate. Somewhere in that vision there is a message telling you what it is you must do in order to take the next step in your spiritual journey through the heavens. It is sublimely simple and personal. It makes Enochian aethyric magick, in my opinion, a far more effective and user-friendly method of magical self-transformation than guided meditations or qabalistic pathworkings.

The method I use is straightforward. After performing a banishing and the Ceremony of Preparation, I simply recite the nineteenth call using the name of the particular Aethyr I wish to visit. Then I repeat the names of the three governors of the Aethyr until the vision begins.

The vision is usually characterized by the appearance of one or more of the governors, who stand ready to answer my inquiries and demonstrate the nature of the Aethyr. As in elemental workings, I try not to tire myself, and afterward make a detailed record of my experiences in my diary.

A complete list of the governors is found in chapter eighteen, in column IV of the table designated figure 63, and in appendix II, figure 90.

Epilogue

In the Middle of the Night

Isn't it enough to see that a garden is beautiful without having to believe that there are fairies at the bottom of it too?

—DOUGLAS ADAMS

It's 3:15 a.m. For the last few days, I have arranged to sleep through the afternoon heat of an unseasonably hot late summer so that I may write undisturbed in the cool peace and quiet of the wee hours. This book of magick has taken me much longer to complete than I anticipated. Did I say "complete"? It's a well-worn cliché that a writer never finishes a work, but merely abandons it. I've finally come to the place where I'm ready to abandon this book. For as slim as it is, it might be hard for you to believe that it has dominated my life for nearly three years. My publisher expected it in their hands over a year ago, and for their patience I am profoundly grateful.

This is far from the end of the material, however. I've worked hard and long on the appendices, which for the practicing Enochian magician will likely become the most worn and dog-eared section of the book.

I must confess that my attitudes concerning Enochian magick have changed many times in the thirty years it has been part of my life. My respect for the magical art form, however, has never diminished and has continued to grow unabated. I feel like the musician who is moved to tears by listening to a great symphony, but who can play only a few tunes himself and those only moderately well.

Perhaps you will never choose to make Enochian magick a part of your spiritual repertoire. Perhaps you will. In either case, as I abandon this book, it is my sincerest hope that I have been able to help you in some small measure attune your magical ear to the music of the spheres.

Adieu.

Appendix I

The Ceremony of Preparation

The magician purifies and banishes the temple as he or she has skill to do so. Below is a standard version of the Lesser Banishing Ritual, a ceremony used by many modern magicians.

Touching the forehead, say, *Ateh* ("Unto Thee").

Touching the breast, say, *Malkuth* ("the Kingdom").

Touching the right shoulder, say, *ve-Geburah* ("and the Power").

Touching the left shoulder, say, *ve-Gedulah* ("and the Glory").

Clasping the hand upon the breast, say, *le-OLAHM, AMEN* ("to the Ages, Amen").

Turning to the east, make the banishing pentagram (that of Earth) with the wand. Say, *IHVH* ("Ye-ho-wau").

Figure 88: Banishing pentagram (Earth)

Turning to the south, again draw the pentagram but say, *ADNI* ("Adonai").

Turning to the west, again draw the pentagram but say *AHIH* ("Eheieh").

Turning to the north, again draw the pentagram, but say *AGLA* ("Agla").

Extend the arms in the form of a cross say:

> *Before me Raphael,*
> *Behind me Gabriel,*
> *On my right hand, Michael,*
> *On my left hand, Auriel,*
> *For about me flames the pentagram*
> *And in the column stands the six-rayed star.*

Touching the forehead, say, Ateh ("Unto Thee").

Touching the breast, say, Malkuth ("the Kingdom").

Touching the right shoulder, say, ve-Geburah ("and the Power").

Touching the left shoulder, say, ve-Gedulah ("and the Glory").

Clasping the hand upon the breast, say, *le-OLAHM, AMEN* ("to the Ages, Amen").

The Ceremony of Preparation

The Temple

The Holy Table is set in the middle of the room upon a carpet of red silk. Four small versions of the Sigillum Dei Aemeth rest under the table legs. In the center of the Holy Table rests the Sigillum Dei Aemeth surrounded by the seven Ensigns of Creation. All are covered and draped by a red silk cloth with gold tassels at the corners. The black mirror or scrying crystal is placed upon the covered Sigillum. The Ring and Lamen are at hand upon the covered table.

A chair is positioned before the table so that the face of the scryer may be reflected in the mirror. The chair must also rest upon the red silk carpet. When operating at night or in a dimly lit room, one or two candles can also be place upon the covered Holy Table.

The Ceremony

After banishing, the magician sits down and prays:

> Teach me (O creator of all things) to have correct knowledge and understanding, for your wisdom is all that I desire. Speak your word in my ear (O creator of all things) and set your wisdom in my heart. Amen.

The magician picks up the Ring and prays:

> Behold the Ring. Lo, this it is. This is it, wherewith all miracles, and divine works and wonders were wrought by Solomon: this is it, which the Archangel Michael has revealed to me. This is it, which Philosophy dreameth of. This is it, which the Angels scarce know. This is it, and blessed be his name: yea, his Name be blessed forever. Without this I shall do nothing. Blessed be his name, that encompasses all things: Wonders are in him, and his name is WONDERFUL: PELE. His Name works wonders from generation to generation. Amen.

The magician picks up the Lamen and prays:

> Behold the Lamen. As the Holy Table conciliates Heaven and Earth, let this Lamen which I place over my heart conciliate me to the Holy Table. Amen.

The magician recites seven complete rounds of the chant of the Holy Table's Perimeter Letters. If possible, the magician traces with the wand the covered letters he or she is chanting:

Pa Med Fam Med Drux Fam Fam Ur Ged Graph Drux Med Graph Graph Med Med Or Med Gal Ged Ged Drux.

Pa Drux Un Tal Fam Don Ur Graph Don Or Gisg Gon Med Un Ged Med Graph Van Ur Don Don Un.

Pa Drux Ur Ur Don Ur Drux Un Med Graph Graph Med Med Graph Ceph Ged Ged Ur Mals Mals Fam Un.

Pa Gon Med Un Graph Fam Mals Tal Ur Pa Pa Drux Un Un Van Un Med Un Gon Drux Drux Ur.

The magician chants seven rounds of the twelve letters of the Holy Table's central square:

Med Gon Gisg, Don Ur Van, Ur Don Ur, Med Med Graph. Med Don Ur Med, Gon Ur Don Med, Gisg Van Ur Graph.

The magician chants one round of the names of the forty-nine angels upon the Sigillum Dei Aemeth:

Galas Gethog Thaoth Horlωn Innon Aaoth Galethog

Zaphkiel Zedekiel Cumael Raphael Haniel Michael Gabriel

E(l) Me Ese Iana Akele Azdobon Stimcul

I Ih Ilr Dmal Heeoa Beigia Stimcul

S Ab Ath Izad Ekiei Madimi Esemeli

E An Ave Liba Rocle Hagonel Ilemes

Sabathiel Zadkiel Madimiel Semeliel Nogahel Corabiel Lavanael

Finally, the magician quietly whispers the Holy Names of the Round Table of Nalvage. First the angel names of the corners:

luah lang sach urch

Then the god names of the four continents:

Iad moz zir—iad bab zna—iad sor gru—iad ser osf.

The magician then proceeds to the business at hand—calling an angel of an Elemental Tablet or scrying an Aethyr.

When the magician's work is done, he or she dismisses the spirit with thanks and prays:

Thy Name be mighty, O God, which canst open the veil whereby Thy All-Powerful Will may be opened unto men. Power, Glory, and Honor be unto Thee, For Thou art the same God of all things, and art life eternal. Amen.

Appendix II

The Enochian Calls (Keys)

The genuineness of these Keys, altogether apart from any critical observation, is guaranteed by the fact that anyone with the smallest capacity for Magick finds that they work.

—ALEISTER CROWLEY[118]

Invocations?

Enochian magick as developed by the Golden Dawn and widely practiced today uses the first eighteen calls to activate the Elemental Tablets and contact the resident angels. However, in the hectic last days of the Enochian period, Dee was instructed in several places to write his own invocations. It remains unclear to me whether or not the angels were suggesting that additional "homemade" invocations were to be created as appendages to the calls. What *is* clear to me, after more than a quarter century of practical application, is the fact that the calls by themselves (with only the briefest of additional verbiage to awaken target angels and their hierarchy) serve admirably as the only invocations a magician needs.

Naturally, if it appeals to your magical sense of art to compose additional invocations to utter before and/or after the call, I encourage you to do so.

Pronunciation

You will probably be very surprised at how little time I spend on this subject. In fact, I am very tempted to simply paraphrase Rabbi Ben Clifford's heretical comment about the Hebrew language and tell you bluntly, "There is no such thing as correct Enochian pronunciation!" On a few occasions, the communicating angels gave Dee and Kelley suggestions as to how certain words are pronounced. But, by and large, we modern magicians are left to our own devices as to how to push these awkwardly constructed words out of our mouths.

Dee notated the words of the calls in columns. The left column contained the Enochian word in all uppercase letters—*PIRIPSOL*, for example. The right column contained the word in upper- and lowercase letters, which split the word into syllables and characterized certain letters as if to suggest pronunciation: *Pe ríp sol*. Sometimes the translation of the word appeared in a center column: "of the heavens."

The Golden Dawn and Crowley use a pronunciation method that they felt rolled more fluidly off the tongue. This method obliged the magician to insert a natural Hebrew vowel sound after every Enochian consonant. For example, the word *butmon* (meaning "mouth") would be pronounced, "but-a-mon-u." This is wonderful for words such as this one, giving it an almost Italian lilt. But things get a little crazy when in comes to the letter *z*, which the English currently pronounce as "zed" and in Dee and Kelley's day was pronounced "zod."

The angels did on occasion instruct Dee when and when not to use "zod," but its universal application to a language that uses the letter *z* very often becomes, in my opinion, laughably cumbersome. Using the Golden Dawn pronunciation method, the simple, one-syllable Enochain word *zims* ("clothing") becomes the unwieldy, four-syllable "zod-I-me-zod." You tell me which rolls off the tongue better.

The most obvious alternative to the GD pronunciation is simply sounding out the words as they are written (which appears to be what the angels generally wanted Dee and Kelley to do). For the last fifteen years, this is what I have done, and it is what I recommend to students who are learning Enochian magick. Before that, however, I used the GD/Crowley pronunciation method and was perfectly happy with it. In fact, I still use the Italian sounding method when I recite the first and second calls because I have them memorized and they hold a special place in my heart.

Both methods work just fine. In fact, any sincere effort on the part of the magician to sound out the words as they appear in the call works. Some of the best group scrying sessions I have experienced have followed the most horribly butchered recitations of the calls. It's as though the Enochian angels (like the French) appreciate any attempt on your part to speak their language. I often use the example of a mouse. If a mouse hopped up on your shoe and squeaked, you'd just shoo it away. But if it hopped up on your shoe and started to talk to you in your native tongue, you'd be impressed. You wouldn't even care if it spoke with a thick accent!

I have tried to present the calls below as close as possible to the original spelling, breaks, letter characterization, and punctuation. The English translation that follows each call is generally punctuated in the same way as the Enochian.

The Calls, the Tablet of Union, and the Elemental Tablets

According to the Golden Dawn, Crowley, and many modern Enochian magick practitioners, the first eighteen calls activate the Tablet of Union, the Elemental Tablets, and the hierarchy of angels resident in the tablets in a very specific (and demonstrably logical) manner. Although the Dee and Kelley source material does not support this arrangement, it has become the foundation of a remarkably workable system. This table is the key to their use.

The First Call

Ol sonf vorsg, gohó Iad balt lansh calz vonpho, sobra z-ol ror i ta nazpsad Graa ta Malprg Ds hol-q Qa-a nothóa zimz, Od commah ta nobloh zien: Soba thil gnonp prge aldi Ds urbs óbôleh grsam: Casarm ohoréla cabá pir Ds zonrensg cab erm

Iadnah. Pilah farzm od znrza adna od gono Iädpil Ds hom od tóh, Soba Iaod Ipam Ul Ipâmis, Ds lóhôlo vep zomd Poamal od bogpa aäi ta piap piamos od vaoan: ZACARe c-a od ZAM-RAM: odo cicle Qaa: zorge, lap zirdo noco MAD: Hoath Iaida.

CALL	ELEMENTAL TABLET	CALL USED FOR . . .
1	TABLET OF UNION	The first call is to be used first in all invocations of angels of the Tablet of Union. According to the Golden Dawn, it is never used for actions dealing with angels of the Elemental Tablets.
2	TABLET OF UNION	The second call is to be used second (after call 1) to invoke Angel EHNB of Tablet of Union. According to the Golden Dawn, it is never used with Elemental Tablets.
3	AIR	The third call can be used in one of three ways: 1. Used third (after calls 1 and 2) to invoke angels of EXARP of the Tablet of Union. 2. Used first for operations involving the Elemental Tablet of Air. 3. Used by itself for invocations of the Seniors from the Elemental Tablet of Air or for angels from the Air Subangle of the Elemental Tablet of Air.
4	WATER	The fourth call can be used in one of three ways: 1. Used third (after calls 1 and 2) to invoke angels of HCOMA of Tablet of Union. 2. Used first for operations involving the Elemental Tablet of Water. 3. Used by itself for invocations of the Seniors from the Elemental Tablet of Water or for angels from the Water subangle of the Elemental Tablet of Water.
5	EARTH	The fifth call can be used in one of three ways: 1. Used third (after calls 1 and 2) to invoke angels of NANTA of Tablet of Union. 2. Used first for operations involving the Elemental Tablet of Earth. 3. Used by itself for invocations of the Seniors from the Elemental Tablet of Earth or for angels from the Earth subangle of the Elemental Tablet of Earth.

Figure 89: Key to the calls

CALL	ELEMENTAL TABLET	CALL USED FOR . . .
6	FIRE	The sixth call can be used in one of three ways: 1. Used third (after calls 1 and 2) to invoke angels of BITOM of Tablet of Union. 2. Used first for operations involving the Elemental Tablet of Fire. 3. Used by itself for invocations of the Seniors from the Elemental Tablet of Fire or for angels from the Fire subangle of the Elemental Tablet of Fire.
7	AIR	The seventh call is used after call 3 to call forth or visit the angels of the Water subangle of the Elemental Tablet of Air.
8	AIR	The eight call is used after call 3 to call forth or visit the angels of the Earth subangle of the Elemental Tablet of Air.
9	AIR	The ninth call is used after call 3 to call forth or visit the angels of the Fire subangle of the Elemental Tablet of Air.
10	WATER	The tenth call is used after call 4 to call forth or visit the angels of the Air subangle of the Elemental Tablet of Water.
11	WATER	The eleventh call is used after call 4 to call forth or visit the angels of the Earth subangle of the Elemental Tablet of Water.
12	WATER	The twelfth call is used after call 4 to call forth or visit the angels of the Fire subangle of the Elemental Tablet of Water.
13	EARTH	The thirteenth call is used after call 5 to call forth or visit the angels of the Air subangle of the Elemental Tablet of Earth.
14	EARTH	The fourteenth call is used after call 5 to call forth or visit the angels of the Water subangle of the Elemental Tablet of Earth.

CALL	ELEMENTAL TABLET	CALL USED FOR . . .
15	EARTH	The fifteenth call is used after call 5 to call forth or visit the angels of the Fire subangle of the Elemental Tablet of Earth.
16	FIRE	The sixteenth call is used after call 6 to call forth or visit the angels of the Air subangle of hte Elemental Tablet of Fire.
17	FIRE	The seventeenth call is used after call 6 to call forth or visit the angels of the Water subangle of the Elemental Tablet of Fire.
18	FIRE	The eighteenth call is used after call 6 to call forth or visit the angels of the Earth subangle of the Elemental Tablet of Fire.

I reign over you, sayeth the God of Justice, in power exalted above the firmaments of wrath: in whose hands the Sun is as a sword and the Moon as a through-thrusting fire which measureth your garments in the midst of my vestures, and trussed you together as the palms of my hands: Whose seats I garnished with the fire of gathering and (which) beautified your garments with admiration: to whom I made a law to govern the holy ones and delivered you a rod with the ark of knowledge. Moreover you lifted up your voices and swear obedience and faith to him that liveth and triumpheth whose beginning is not, nor end can not be, which shineth as a flame in the midst of your palace and reignneth amongst you as the balance of righteousness and truth. Move, therefore, and show yourselves: open the Mysteries of your Creation: Be friendly unto me: for I am the servant of the same your God, the true worshipper of the Highest.

The Second Call

Adgt v-pa-âh zongom fa-á-ip sald viv L sobam Iál-prg I-zâ-zaz pi-ádph, Cas-arma abramg ta talho paráclêda Q-ta lors-l-q turbs öoge Baltoh. Giui chis Lusd orri. Od micalp chís bia ózôngon. Lap noán trof cors ta ge, o-q manin Ia-í-don. Torzu góhel. ZACAR ca c-nó-qod: ZAMRAN micalzo: Od ozazm vrelp Lap zir Ioiad.

Can the wings of the winds understand your voices of wonder, O you the second of the first, whom the burning flames have framed within the depth of my Jaws, whom I have prepared as Cups for a wedding, or as the flowers in their beauty for the Chamber of righteousness. Stronger are your feet than the barren stone. And mightier are your voices than the manifold winds. For you are become a building such as is not, but in the mind of the All powerful. Arise, sayeth the First. Move therefore unto his Servants: Show yourselves in power: And make me a strong Seer: for I am of him that liveth forever.

The Third Call

Micma gohó Piad zir cómselh azien biab Os Lón-doh. Norz chis óthil Gigîpah, und-l chis tá pû-im: Q mos-pleh teloch Qui-i-n

toltorg chis I-chis-ge, m ozíen dst brgda od torzul í-lí E ól
balzarg od áála Thiln os ne-tâ-ab dluga vomsarg Lonsa cap-mi-áli
vors cla homil cocasb, fafen izízop od miinôag de gne-táab
vaun na-ná-ê-el: panpir Malpirgi caósg Pild noan unalah balt
od vooán. do-ó-i-ap MAD Gohólor gohús amiran. Micma
Iehúsoz ca-cá-com od do-o-â-in noar mi-cá-olz a-aí-om.
Casármg gohia: ZACAR, unîglag od Im-uâ-mar pugo plapli
anánael Qáan.

Behold, sayeth your god, I am a Circle on whose hands stand 12
Kingdoms. Six are the seats of Living Breath, the rest are as sharp sickles:
or the horns of death wherein the Creatures of ye earth are to are not,
except mine own hand which sleep and shall rise. In the first I made you
Stewards and placed you in seats 12 of government, giving unto every
one of you power successively over 456, the true ages of time, to the
intent that from your highest vessels and the corners of your govern-
ments you might work my power: powering down the fires of life and
increase continually on the earth. Thus you are become the skirts of
Justice and Truth. In the Name of the same your God, lift up, I say, your
selves. Behold his mercies flourish and Name is become mighty
amongst us. In whom we say: Move, Descend and apply your selves
unto us, as unto the partakers of the Secret Wisdom of your Creation.

The Fourth Call

Othíl lasdi babâge od dorpha Gohól G-chisge avávâgo Cormp
pd dsonf viv-di-v Casármi Oali Mapm Sobam ag cormpó
c-rp-l Casarmg croódzi chis od vgeg dst capimáli chis
Capimaon lonshin chis ta Lo Cla: Torgú Nor quasáhi, od F
caósaga: Bagle Zirenáiad, Dsi od Apâla. Do-ó-â-ip Q-á-al
ZACAR, od ZAMRAN Obelisong rest-el aaf Nor-mô-lap.

I have set my feet in the south and have looked about me, saying,
are not the Thunders of increase numbered 33 which reign in the second Angle under whom I have placed 9639 Whom none hath yet numbered but one, in whom the second beginning of things are and wax
strong, which also successively are the number of time: and their powers
are as the first 456: Arise, you Sons of pleasure, and visit the earth: for
I am the Lord your God, which is, and liveth. In the name of the

Creator, Move and show yourselves as pleasant deliverers that you may praise him amongst the sons of men.

The Fifth Call

> Sapáh zímii du-i-v od noas ta-qa-a-nis adroch dorphal Ca ósg od faonts péripsol tablior Casarm amipzi nazarth af od dlugar zizop z-lida caósgi toltórgi od z-chis esîasch L taviu od iaád thild ds peral hubar Peóal soba cormfa chis ta la vls od Q-có-casb. Ca niis od Darbs Q-á-as, Feth-ar-zi od blióra. ia-ial ed-nas cicles: Bágle? Geiad i L.

The mighty sounds have entered into the third Angle and are become as olives in the olive mount, looking with gladness upon the earth and dwelling in the brightness of the heavens as continual comforters, unto whom I fastened pillars of gladness 19 and gave them vessels to water the earth with her creatures and they are the brothers of the first and second and the beginning of their own seats which are garnished with continually burning lamps 69636 whose numbers are as the first, the ends and the contents of time. Therefore come you and obey your creation, visit us in peace and comfort. Conclude us as receivers of your mysteries: for why? Our Lord and Master is all One.

The Sixth Call

> Gah s díu chis em micálzo pilzin sobam El harg mir babálon od obloc samvelg dlugar malprg arcaósgi od Acám canal sobólzar f-bliard caosgi od chis anétab od miam ta viv od d. Darsar sol-peth bien: Brita od zácam g-micálzo, sob-há-hath trían Lu-iá he odecrin MAD Q-a-a on.

The spirits of the 4th Angle are Nine, Mighty in the firmament of waters: whom the first hath planted a torment to the wicked and a garland to the righteous giving unto them fiery darts to vanne the earth and 7699 continual Workmen whose courses visit with comfort the earth and are in government and continuance as the second and the third. Wherefore hearken unto my voice: I have talked of you and I move you in power and presence, whose Works shall be a song of honor and the praise of your God in your Creation.

The Seventh Call

Raas isâlman paradiz oécrîmi aao ial-pîrgah qui-in enay but-mon od inóas ni paradîal casarmg vgéar chirlan od zonac Luciftian cors to vaul zirn tol-hâ-mi Soba Londóh od miam chis tad o dés vmadêa od piblîar Othílrit od miám. Cnoquol Rit, ZACAR, ZAMRAN, oëcrimi Q-a-dah: od omicaolz aaîom Bagle papnor idlúgam lonshi od vmplif vgêgi Biglîad.

The East is a house of virgins singing praises amongst the flames of first glory wherein the Lord hath opened his mouth and they are become 28 living dwellings in whom the strength of man rejoiceth, and they are appareled with ornaments of brightness such as work wonders on all creatures. Whose Kingdoms and continuance are as the third and fourth strong towers and places of comfort, the seats of mercy and continuance. O you Servants of Mercy, Move, Appear, sing praises unto the Creator and be mighty amongst us. For to this remembrance is given power and our strength waxeth strong in our Comforter.

The Eighth Call

Bazmêlo i ta pirípson oln Nazâvábh ox casarmg vrán chis vgeg dsa-bramg baltôha gohó î-ad soba miam trian ta lól-cis Abaíuônin od aziágîer rior. Irgil chís da ds pá-â-ox busd Caósgo ds chis odípûran téloâh cacrg O isâlman loncho od Vouéna carbaf. Niíso, Bagle aváuâgo gohón: Niíso, bagle mómâo siáîon od mábza Iad-oiás-mômar poilp. Niis ZAM-RAN ciaofi caósgo od bliors od corsi ta a-brâmig.

The Midday the first is as the third heaven made of Hyacinth Pillars 26 in whom the Elders are become strong which I have prepared for my own righteousness sayeth the Lord whose long continuance shall be as bucklers to the stooping Dragons and like unto the harvest of a Widow. How many are there which remain in the glory of the earth, which are, and shall not see death until this house fall and the Dragon sink? Come away, for the Thunders have spoken: Come away, for the Crowns of the Temple and the coat of him that is, was, and shall be crowned are divided, Come, Appear to the terror of the earth and to our comfort and of such as are prepared.

The Ninth Call

Mi-ca-ôli bransg prgel napta ialpor (ds brin efáfâfe P vonpho oláni od obza: sobca vpâah chis tatan od tranan balye) alar lusda sobôln od chís hôlq Cnoquódi cial. vnál aldon mom caósgo ta las óllor gnay limlal: Amma chiis sobca madrid zchis, oöanôan chiis auíny drilpi caósgin od od butmôni parm zumvi Cníla: Daziz ethámz a-chíldao od mirc ózól chis pidiai collal vlcínin a-sóbam vcim. Bagle? Iadbáltoh chirlan par Niiso od ip ofafâfe Bagle acósasb icórsca vnig blior.

A mighty guard of fire with two-edged swords flaming (which have vials 8 of wrath for two times and a half: whose wings are of wormwood and of the marrow of salt) have settled their feet in the West and are measured with their Ministers 9996. These gather up the moss of the earth as the rich man doth his treasure: Cursed are they whose iniquities they are, in their eyes are millstones greater than the earth, and from their mouths run seas of blood: their heads are covered with diamond, and upon their hands are marble sleeves. Happy is he on whom they frown not. For why? The God of righteousness rejoiceth in them! Come away, and not your Vials, for the time is such as requireth comfort.

The Tenth Call

Coráxo chis cormp od blans Lucal azíâzor pæb, Soba Lilônon chis virq op eôphan od Raclir maâsi bagle caosgi, ds ialpon dosig od basgim: od oxex dazís siâtris od salbrox cynixir fabôan Vnâl-chis coust ds dâox cocasg ol oánîo yor eors vóhim ol gizyax od math cocasg plosi molui ds pagêip Larag om droln matorb cocasb emna. L patralx yolci math nomig monons olôra gnay angêlard Ohio Ohio Ohio Ohio Ohio Ohio noib Ohio Caósgon Bagle madrid I, ziróp, chiso drilpa. Niiso crip ip nidâli.

The Thunders of Judgment and Wrath are numbered and are harbored in the North in the likeness of an oak, whose branches are Nests 22 of lamentation and weeping laid up for the earth, which burn night and day: and vomit out the heads of scorpions and live sulfur mingled with poison. These be The Thunders that 5678 times in the 24th part of a moment roar with a hundred mighty earthquakes and a thousand times as many surges. which rest not neither know any echoing time here. One rock bringeth forth 1000, even as the heart of man doth his thoughts. Woe, Woe, Woe, Woe, Woe, Woe, yea Woe be to the earth! For her iniquities is, was and shall be great. Come away: but not your noises.

The Eleventh Call

Oxiayal holdo od zirom O coráxo ds zildar raâsy, od vabzir comlîax od báhal, Niiso. salman telóch Ca-sár-man hol-q od ti ta z-chis soba cormf i ga. Niisa. Bagle abramg noncp. ZACARe ca od ZAMRAN. odo cicle qaá. Zorge lap zirdo noco Mad, Hoath Iaida.

The Mighty Seat groaned and they were 5 thunders which flew into the East, and the Eagle spake and cried with a loud voice, Come away. And they gathered themselves together in the house of death of whom it is measured and it is as they are, whose number is 31. Come away. For I have prepared for you. Move therefore, and show your selves. Open the Mysteries of your Creation. be friendly unto me: for I am the servant of the same your God, the true worshipper of the Highest.

The Twelfth Call

Nonci dsonf Babage od chis ob, hubíâo tibibp, allar atraâh od ef. drix fafen Mian ar E nay ovof soba dooâin aai i VONPH. ZACAR, gohus, od ZAMRAM, odo cicle Qaa. Zorge, Lap zirdo noco MAD, Hoath Iaida.

O you that reign in the South and are 28, the lanterns of sorrow, bind up your girdles and visit us. Bring down your train 3663 that the Lord may be magnified whose name amongst you is Wrath. Move, I say, and show yourselves, open the Mysteries of your Creation. Be friendly unto me, for I am the servant of the same your God, the true worshipper of the Highest.

The Thirteenth Call

Napêai Babâgen dsbrin vx ooáôna lring vonph doâlim, eôlis ollog orsba ds chis affa. Micma isro MAD od Lon-shi-tox ds ivmd aai GROSB. ZACAR od ZAMRAN. odo cicle Qäa, Zorge, Lap zirdo Noco MAD, Hoath Iaïda.

O you swords of the South which have 42 eyes to stir up the wrath of sin, making men drunken which are empty. Behold the promise of God and his power which is called amongst you a Bitter Sting. Move and show your selves. Open the Mysteries of your Creation: be friendly unto me: for I am the servant of ye same your God, the true worshipper of the Highest.

The Fourteenth Call

Norómi bagíe pasbs oîad ds trint mirc ol thil dods tolham caósgo Homin, ds brin oroch Quar, Micma bial oîad aîsro tox dsivm aai Baltim. ZACAR od ZAMRAN. odo cicle Qäa. Zorge, Lap zirdo Noco MAD, hoath Iaïda.

O you sons of fury, the daughters of the Just, which sit upon 24 seats vexing all creatures of the earth with age, which have under you 1636, behold the Voice of God promise of him which is called amongst you Fury or Extreme Justice. Move and show your selves. Open the Mysteries of your Creation. Be friendly unto me. For I am the servant of the same your God, the true worshipper of the Highest.

The Fifteenth Call

Ils tabâan Liálprt casarman vpaáhi chis darg dsoâdo caôsgi orscor ds ômax monasci Bæôuib od emetgis iaíâdix. ZACAR od ZAMRAN, odo cicle Qäa, zorge, Lap zirdo noco MAD, hoath Iaïda.

O Thou the governor of the first flame under whose wings are 6739 which weave the earth with dryness which knowest of the great name Righteousness and the Seal of Honor. Move and show your selves, open the Mysteries of your Creation, be friendly unto me, for I am the servant of the same your God, the true worshipper of the Highest.

The Sixteenth Call

Ils viuíâlprt salman blat ds acroódzi busd od bliôrax balit, dsinsi caosg lusdan Emod dsom od tliob drilpa geh yls Madzilodarp. ZACAR od ZAMRAN, odo cicle Qöa, zorge, Lap zirdo noco MAD, hoath Iaída.

O Thou second flame the house of Justice which hast thy beginning in glory and shalt comfort the just, which walkest on the earth with feet 8763 that understand and separate creatures, great art Thou in the God of Stretch Forth and Conquer. Move and show your selves, open the Mysteries of your Creation, be friendly unto me, for I am the servant of the same your God, the true worshipper of the Highest.

The Seventeenth Call

Ils dialprt soba vpâah chis nanba zixlay dodsih, od brint Faxs hubaro tustax ylsi, sobaíad I vónpôvnph, Aldon daxil od toá-tar. ZACAR od ZAMRAN, odo cicle Qäa, zorge, Lap zirdo Noco MAD hoath Iaïda.

O Thou third flame whose wings are thorns to stir up vexation, and hast 7336 lamps living going before thee, whose God is Wrath in Anger, gird up thy loins and harken. Move and show yourselves, open the Mysteries of your Creation, be friendly unto me, for I am the servant of the same your God, the true worshipper of the Highest.

The Eighteenth Call

Ils Micaólz Olprit ialprg Bliors ds odo Busdir oîad ouôars caósgo, Casarmg Laíad erán brints casâsam, ds ivmd á-q-lo adóhi MOZ od maóffas, Bolp comobliort pambt. ZACAR od ZAMRAN, odo cicle Qäa, zorge, Lap zirdo Noco MAD, hoath Iaïda.

O Thou mighty Light and burning flame of comfort which openest the glory of God to the center of the earth, in whom the Secrets of Truth 6332 have their abiding, which is called in thy kingdom JOY and not to be measured, be Thou a window of comfort unto me. Move and show your selves, open the Mysteries of your Creation, be friendly unto me: for I am the servant of the same your God, the true worshipper of the Highest.

The Call of the Thirty Aethyrs

The nineteenth call is used to open each of the thirty Aethyrs. Only the name of the Aethyr itself (the third word in the first sentence) is changed.

Each Aethyr (with the exception of the thirtieth) is inhabited by three governors, who could be considered personifications of the nature of the Aethyr. I believe that after you recite the call and before you settle down to scry, it is important to pronounce, vibrate, or otherwise incorporate the names of the governors in a brief invocation.

The names of the Aethyrs and their governors are listed in figure 90. If you wish to incorporate the sigils of the governors (the symmetrical characters) for visualizations or to create talismans, the sigils can be found in chapter eighteen, in column VI of figure 63.

The Nineteenth Call

Madriax dspraf [name of Aethyr, e.g., *TEX, RII,* or *BAG*] chis Micaólz saánir Caósgo, od físis balzizras Iaída, nonca gohúlim, Micma adoían MAD, Iáod bliorb, sabaooáôna chis Lucíftîas perípsol, ds abraássa noncf netááib Caósgi od tilb adphaht dámploz, toóat noncf gmicálzôma Lrásd tófglo marb yárry IDOIGO od torzulp iáodaf gohól, Caósga tabaord saánir od christéós yrpóil tióbl, Busdir tilb noaln paid orsba od dodrmni zylna. Elzáptilb parmgi perípsax, od ta qurlst booapiS. Lnibm ovcho symp, od Christéos Agtoltorn mirc Q tióbl Lel. Ton paombd dilzmo aspian, Od christêos ag L tortorn parach asymp, Cordziz dodpal od fifalz Lsmnad, od fargt bams omaóas, Conísbra od auâuox tonug, Orscatbl noâsmi tabges Levithmong, unchi omptilb ors. Bagle? Mooóah ol córdziz. L capîmao ixomaxip od cacócasb gsâa. Baglen pii tianta abábâlond, od faórgt telocvovim. Mádrîiax torzu oádriax orócha abóâpri. Tabáôri priáz artabas. Adrpan corsta dobix. Yolcam priazi arcoazior. Od quasb qting. Ripir paaoxt sagácor. vml od prd-zar cácrg Aoivéâe cormpt. TORZV, ZACAR, od

ZAMRAN aspt sibsi butmôna ds surzas tia baltan. ODO cicle Qáa, od ozama plapli Iadnâmad.

O you heavens which dwell in the First Ayre are mighty in the parts of the Earth, and execute the Judgment of the Highest, to you it is said, Behold the face of your God, the beginning of comfort, whose eyes are the brightness of the heavens, which provided you for the government of the Earth and her unspeakable variety, furnishing you with a power of understanding to dispose all things according to the providence of Him that sitteth on the Holy Throne, and rose up in the beginning say-ing: the Earth let her be governed by her parts and let there be division in her, that the glory of her may be always drunken and vexed in it self. Her course, let it run with the heavens, and as a handmaid let her serve them. One season let it confound an other, and let there be no creature upon or within her the same, All her members let them differ in their qualities, and let there be no one creature equal with an other: the rea-sonable Creatures of the Earth let them vex and weed out one an other, and the dwelling places let them forget their names: the work of man, and his pomp, let them be defaced: his buildings let them become caves for the beasts of the field. Confound her understanding with darkness. For why? It repenteth me I made Man. One while let her be known and an other while a stranger: because she is the bed of a Harlot, and the dwelling place of Him that is Fallen. O you heavens arise: the lower heavens underneath you, let them serve you! Govern those that govern: cast down such as fall! Bring forth with those that increase, and destroy the rotten! No place let it remain in one number: add and diminish until the stars be numbered! Arise, Move, and Appear before the Covenant of his mouth, which he hath sworn unto us in his Justice. Open the Mysteries of your Creation: and make us partakers of Undefiled Knowledge.

1	1	Occodon	**11**	31	Molpand	**21**	61	Chirspa
LIL	2	Pascomb	**ICH**	32	Vsnarda	**ASP**	62	Toantom
	3	Valgars		33	Ponodol		63	Vixpalg
2	4	Doagnis	**12**	34	Tapamal	**22**	64	Ozidaia
ARN	5	Pacasna	**LOE**	35	Gedoons	**LIN**	65	PARAOAN
	6	Dialiua		36	Ambriol		66	Calzirg
3	7	Samapha	**13**	37	Gecaond	**23**	67	Ronoamb
ZOM	8	Virooli	**ZIM**	38	Laparin	**TOR**	68	Onizimp
	9	Andispi		39	Docepax		69	Zaxanin
4	10	Thotanp	**14**	40	Tedoand Tedoond	**24**	70	Orcanir
PAZ	11	Axziarg	**VTA**	41	Viuipos	**NIA**	71	Chialps
	12	Pothnir		42	Ooanamb		72	Soageel
5	13	Lazdixi	**15**	43	Tahando	**25**	73	Mirzind
LIT	14	Nocamal	**OXO**	44	Nociabi	**UTI**	74	Obuaors
	15	Tiarpax		45	Tastoxo		75	Ranglam
6	16	Saxtomp	**16**	46	Cucarpt	**26**	76	Pophand
MAZ	17	Vauaamp	**LEA**	47	Lauacon	**DES**	77	Nigrana
	18	Zirzird		48	Sochial		78	Bazchim
7	19	Opmacas	**17**	49	Sigmorf	**27**	79	Saziami
DEO	20	Genadol	**TAN**	50	Aydropt	**ZAA**	80	Mathula
	21	Aspiaon		51	Tocarzi		81	Orpanib
8	22	Zamfres	**18**	52	Nabaomi	**28**	82	Labnixp
ZID	23	Todnaon	**ZEN**	53	Zafasai	**BAG**	83	Focisni
	24	Pristac		54	Yalpamb		84	Oxlopar
9	25	Oddiorg	**19**	55	Torzoxi	**29**	85	Vastrim
ZIP	26	Cralpir	**POP**	56	Abaiond	**RII**	86	Odraxti
	27	Doanzin		57	Omagrap		87	Gomziam
10	28	LEXARPH	**20**	58	Zildron	**30**	88	Taoagla
ZAX	29	COMANAN	**CHR**	59	Parziba	**TEX**	89	Gemnimb
	30	TABITOM		60	Totocan		90	Advorpt
							91	Dozinal

Figure 90: Aethyr/governor table

Appendix III

The Geographical Location of the Ninety-one Parts of the Earth Named by Man, as Detailed in John Dee's *Liber Scientiae Auxilii Et Victoriae Terrestris*[119]

by Robin E. Cousins

Liber Scientiae Auxilii et Victoriae Terrestris, which forms part of Sloane Manuscript 3191, provides the details necessary to operate a system of magic, by which the magician can discover

> 'how to compare . . . [the] divisions of provinces according to the Divisions of the Stars, with the Ministry of the Ruling Intelligences, and Blessings of the Tribes of Israel, the Lots of the Apostles, and Typical Seals of the Sacred Scripture, [so that he] shall be able to obtain great and prophetical oracles, concerning every region, of things to come.'[120]

On Wednesday 23 May 1584, while in Krakow, John Dee and Edward Kelley received from the Spirit Nalvage the names of ninety-one regions and provinces of the physical world, as defined by man. At this time America was no longer considered to be a group of islands; but Australia had yet to be discovered and the search for the North-West Passage had just commenced. The names of the ninety-one parts relate to the Ptolemaic ancient world of about AD 150 with some additions. The Spirit Nalvage explains:

> 'Notwithstanding the Angel of the Lord appeared unto Ptolemie, and opened unto him the parts of the Earth: but

some he was commanded to secret: and those are Northward under your Pole. But unto yon, the very true names of the World in her Creation are delivered.'[121]

The list is not altogether satisfactory. Dee, who was well-versed in geography, had not heard of some of the places and even Nalvage said, 'Here are 15, which were never known in these times . . . The rest are'. Many of the strange locations are indeed in the Polar Regions, which were uncharted at the time. In fact, a considerable Arctic land mass was believed to exist and was featured on sixteenth century maps. Nevertheless, locations for this region are desirable and there are many areas in the extreme north, whether land or sea, which can be covered by the descriptions. The belief of a south polar continent (Tolpam, Part 58) was not inaccurate, a location which can usefully extend to Australasia which was undiscovered at the time.

Two points emerge at the end of the communication relating to known lands not included in the list. Firstly, when Dee asks of 'Polonia, Moschovia, Dania, Hibernia (Ireland), Islandia, and so of many others', Nalvage replies: 'Polonia and Moscovia, are of Sarmatia (Russia); Denmark, Ireland, Frizeland, Iseland, are of Britain: And so it is of the rest.'[122] Does this imply that Brytania (Part 61) can be used to gain access to lands not included within the ninety-one parts? Secondly, when Dee presses Nalvage as to which part governs 'Atlantis and the annexed places, under the King of Spain called the West Indies', Nalvage replies: 'When these 30 appear, they can each tell you what they own. Prepare for tomorrows Action'. The communication is, therefore, incomplete. Unfortunately, 'tomorrows Action' never occurred, because Kelley believed Nalvage to have taken the descriptions from books, including Agrippa's *Occult Philosophy*, and refused to communicate further. 'E. K. remained of his wilful intent', noted a frustrated Dee. However, Onigap (Part 34) may refer to these lands and there is the possibly implied use of Brytania, as described above. Note that Dee held that the term 'West Indies' was very misleading and preferred to use 'Atlantis' instead of 'America', as a name for the new lands. Nevertheless, the additional thirty parts wait to be realised, which would bring the total of the parts of the Earth to 121. It is interesting to speculate, whether they would affect the design of the Great Table.

Dee bought Gerhard Mercator's *Universal Chart of the World* and the geographical work of Pomponius Mela to help him with his locations. He does not record his success. Ultimately, the advice of Nalvage in relation to Chaldei (Part 42) and Chaldea (Part 72) is the only way to establish the locations of the obscure and ambiguously described parts of the world: 'You shall finde the difference of it, in practice'.

The Ninety-One Parts of the World

Many of the locations are well-known. However, for the obscurer areas Dee's Spiritual Diaries (*Cotton Appendix XLVI, Parts 1 & 2*, published as *A True and Faithful Relation of What passed for many Yeers Between Dr. John Dee and Some Spirits*, edited by Meric Casaubon, 1659) are often the only guide. In these instances, supportive quotations are given. Other parts, especially those located by Kelley or Nalvage in the Far Orient or in the Arctic regions, are difficult to place on the world map today, as in Dee's time these regions were largely unexplored and uncharted.

1 **AEGYPTUS**: Egypt.

2 **SYRIA**: Southern Syria.

3 **MESOPOTAMIA**: Land between the Tigris and Euphrates rivers in Northern Iraq and North-East Syria.

4 **CAPPADOCIA**: Extensive province of Central Turkey, stretching from the Black Sea in the north to Cilicia (Part 14) in the south. The original territory, Cappadocia Proper, occupied the southern areas.

5 **TUSCIA**: Tuscany or Etruria, a province in Central Italy including Florence.

6 **PARVA ASIA**: Asia Minor, Anatolia or Asiatic Turkey.

7 **HYRCANIA**: Area south-east of the Caspian Sea in Iran.

8 **THRACIA**: Thrace includes Eastern Greece, Turkey in Europe, and Southern Bulgaria.

9 **GOSMAM**: According to Kelley, 'Here appear great Hills, and veins of the Gold Mines appear: the men seem to have baskets of leather. This is one of the places under the Pole Artick.'

10 **THEBAIDI:** Thebes (Egypt) and surrounding area.

11 **PARSADAL:** Kelly, 'Here the sun shineth fair.' Most probably Pasargardae or Parsagarda ('the habitation of the Persians'), the ancient capital of Parsa/Persis/Persia Proper or the modern Iranian province of Fars (Part 74). Parsagarda is located about 60 miles northeast of Shiraz.

12 **INDIA:** Includes Indian provinces along the Indus River, roughly present-day Pakistan and India West of the Ganges (India Intra Ganges).

13 **BACTRIANE:** Bactriana covers Northern Afghanistan and the south-east of the Turkmenistan, the River Amu Darya (Oxus) forming the northern boundary. For lands to the north of the river, see Sogdiana (Part 26).

14 **CILICIA:** Coastal country bordering the Mediterranean in South-East Turkey.

15 **OXIANA:** Alexandreia Oxiana, a town and its surrounding area on the Oxus River (Amu Darya) on the borders of Northern Afghanistan and Uzbekistan.

16 **NUMIDIA:** Eastern Algerian coastal district between Africa (Part 86) and Mauretania (Part 91).

17 **CYPRUS:** Cyprus.

18 **PARTHIA:** North-East Iran, to the south of Hyrcania (Part 7). The region has a common border with Turkmenistan.

19 **GETULIA:** The Western Sahara, south of Morocco, including Southern Algeria, Mali and the modern state of Mauritania.

20 **ARABIA:** Saudi Arabia.

21 **PHALAGON:** Dee: 'I have never heard of it.'

Kelley: 'It is toward the North, where the veines of Gold . . . appear . . . The men have things on their shoulders of beasts skins.'

Dee: 'Groynland as I think' (i.e. Greenland).

22 **MANTIANA:** This is Matiana or the Mattieni by Lacus Matianus, now Lake Urmia in North-Western Iran. The population is mainly Kurdish. Lake Van, approximately 200 miles west in Eastern Turkey, was once called Lake Mantiana.

23 **SOXIA**: Sacae/Sachia/Sakas approximates with Xinjiang Uygar or Sinkiang Uighur region, North-West China. It is also known as Chinese Turkistan.

Kelley: 'People here appear of reddish colour.'

24 **GALLIA**: A 'greater' France with the Rhine forming the northern and eastern boundaries, thereby including Belgium, Luxembourg, and the Southern Netherlands.

25 **ILLYRIA**: At its greatest extent, Illyria included Central and Eastern Austria, Western Hungary or Transdanubia, the former Yugoslavia excluding Macedonia, Northern Bulgaria and Romania.

26 **SOGDIANA**: District between the rivers Amu Darya (Oxus) and Syr Darya (Jaxartes) including Uzbekistan, with the cities of Bokhara and Samarkand, and Western Tajikistan. Afghanistan is to the south, for which see Bactriana (Part 13).

27 **LYDIA**: Coastal region in Western Turkey.

28 **CASPIS**: Area to the south-west of the Caspian Sea in Iran.

29 **GERMANIA**: Includes modern Germany, Poland, the Czech Republic, Slovakia, and extends to the Italian border in the south, incorporating Switzerland and the Tyrol in Western Austria. In the north, Germania can include Denmark, Norway and Sweden, although Dee was told that Brytania (Part 61) could be used for Denmark, which at that time governed Norway as well.

30 **TRENAM**: Kelley: 'Here appear Monkies, great flocks. The people have leather Coats, and no beards, thick leather, and Garthers . . . '

Nalvage: 'These people are not known to you?'

Dee: 'Are they not in Africa?'

Nalvage: 'They be.'

Probably Teniam, a region on Jodocus Hondius's *World Map* (1608) straddling the Ivory Coast/Upper Volta/Ghana borderlands.

31 **BITHYNIA**: Black Sea coastal region in the north of Turkey, west of Paphlagonia (Part 40), including Istanbul (Asian side).

32 **GRAECIA**: Nalvage: 'A great Citie, and the Sea hard by it.'

Dee: 'Is not that great Citie Constantinople?'

Nalvage: 'It is . . .'

Graecia is thus Istanbul, not Greece; for which use Achaia (Part 37).

33 **LICIA**: Lycia is a country on the south coast of Turkey or Anatolia.

34 **ONIGAP**: Kelley: 'Here appear handsome men, in gathered tucked garments, and their shoes come up to the middle of their legs, of diverse coloured leather.'

Nalvage: 'These be beyond Hispaniola.'

Kelley: 'It is a low Countrey. Here appear great piles of Stones like St Andrews Crosses . . . There are on this side of it (a great way) a great number of dead Carkases . . .'

Nalvage: 'It is beyond Giapan.' (That is, beyond Japan across the Pacific to the Americas. Note that Onigap is an anagram of Giapon.)

Dee: 'Then it is that land, which I use to call Atlantis.'

Nalvage: 'They stretch more near the west.'

This can only be Mexico, particularly the Yucatan. Beyond Hispaniola (Haiti and Domenica) and west of 'Atlantis' or America is Central Mexico and the Yucatan, which is a low-lying peninsula. The people wore bright colours; the temples could resemble St Andrew's crosses; and, many people were slaughtered by the Spanish Conquistadores.

35 **INDIA MAJOR**: India Extra Gangem or India east of the Ganges, which includes all of South-East Asia.

36 **ORCHENY**: Nalvage: 'A great many little Isles.'

> Dee: 'Do you mean the Isles of Orkney?'
>
> Nalvage: 'No.'
>
> Dee: 'They seem to be the Isles of Malacha.'

Dee is mistakenly thinking of the islands around Malaya (Malacha or Malacca) or even the Moluccas. The Orcheni were a people south of Chaldea (Part 72), living on or by islands in the marshlands of the lower Tigris and Euphrates.

37 **ACHAIA**: Southern Greece, including Athens and the Peloponnisos.

38 **ARMENIA**: Extensive region which, most comprehensively, stretches

from the Euphrates in eastern Turkey to the Caspian Sea, thereby including Armenia and Azerbaijan.

39 CILICIA (NEMROD): Nalvage: 'You never knew this Cilicia. This is Cilicia where the Children of Nemrod dwell. It is up in the Mountains beyond Cathay.' Probably Calatia, a region in this location featured on Emery Molyneux's terrestrial globe of 1592. It equates with the extreme north-eastern province of Russia by the Bering Straits, the Magandan Oblast. Cilicia in Turkey is Part 14.

40 PAPHLAGONIA: Black Sea coastal country in the north of Turkey.

41 PHASIANA: Mainly Kurdish region in Eastern Turkey, north of Lake Van, not to be confused with Phazania/Fezzan in Libya, for which see Garamantica (Part 45).

42 CHALDEI: The people of Chaldea (Part 72).

43 ITERGI: Nalvage: '. . . the people are yellow, tawney . . . They are to the south of the last Cilicians.' This is possibly Mongolia, Manchuria (North-East China), and Korea. The name appears in this region on a terrestrial globe, dated 1492, of German geographer Martin Behaim (c.1459–1507).

44 MACEDONIA: Northern Greece and the Former Yugoslav Republic of Macedonia.

45 GARAMANTICA: Garamantes, a large area in Inner Africa, covering the Eastern Sahara, including the south of Libya (Fezzan), extreme South-Eastern Algeria, Niger and Chad.

46 SAUROMATICA: Sarmatia or European Russia.

47 AETHIOPIA: Includes Ethiopia south of Egypt and also the entire unknown African continent south of the Equator, which was known as Ethiopia Interior in Dee's time. Unexplored parts of Africa north of the Equator were known as Libya Interior.

48 FIACIM: Kelley: 'Now he sheweth by the North Pole and the great Mountain.'

This is the North Pole. A great mountain was believed to exist at the Pole.

49 COLCHICA: Colchis roughly equates with the modern Republic of Georgia, located to the east of the Black Sea.

50 **CIRENIACA**: Cyrenaica, a Mediterranean coastal region of Eastern Libya.

51 **NASAMONIA**: Ill-defined north-eastern Libyan coastal district by the Gulf of Sirte in the west of Cireniaca (Part 50).

52 **CARTHAGO**: Carthage, Tunisia.

53 **COXLANT**: Nalvage: 'It appeareth very Eastward.'

Kelley: 'It is on high ground. There come four Rivers out of it, one East, another West, another North, and another South . . . Is this the Paradise that Adam was banished out of?'

Nalvage: 'The very same.'

A discussion follows which does not help to locate Coxlant. The search for the Earthly Paradise, like the Eldorado, was the dream of early explorers. The four rivers are the Pison (The Persian Gulf?), Gihon (The Nile?), Hiddekel (Tigris), and Euphrates. The favourite location of Paradise was considered to be a little north of the confluence of the Tigris and Euphrates. However, other locations favoured sites further north in Mesopotamia and Armenia. Tibet could be another location. It is very easterly; on high ground; and the four rivers are the Mekong (east), the Indus (west), the Yangtze (north), and the Brahmaputra (south). Ultimately, however, the location of Coxlant or the Earthly Paradise must rest with the spirituality of the individual.

54 **IDUMEA**: Also called Edom, this is Southern Israel and Jordan.

55 **PARSTAVIA**: Actually Bastarnia, approximately Bessarabia or Moldavia to the east of Romania.

56 **CELTICA**: Nalvage: 'It is that which you call Flandria, the Low Country.'

This is North-West France and Belgium, not Central Gaul which is usually known as Celtica.

57 **VINSAN**: Kelley: 'Here appear men with tallons like Lions. They be very devils. There are five isles of them.'

Suggest the ancient kingdom of Wu-Sun, south of Lake Balkhash in Kazakhstan. The 'isles' could be communities near the lake.

58 **TOLPAM**: Kelley: 'Under the South Pole.' This is Antarctica and Australasia.

59 CARCEDONIA: Carchedonia or modern Tunisia.

60 ITALIA: Italy, including the Istrian Peninsula in Croatia.

61 BRYTANIA: The British Isles, Scandinavia, and possibly places not included in the 91 parts.

62 PHENICES: Phoenicia, approximately the Lebanon and Northern Israel.

63 COMAGINEN: Commagene, a land-locked district in Southern Turkey, bounded on the east by the Euphrates and on the south by Syria. Cilicia (Part 14) is to the west.

64 APULIA: Province in south-east Italy between the Apennines and the Adriatic, bounded on the south by Calabria or the 'heel' of Italy.

65 MARMARICA: North African coastal region straddling the Egyptian and Libyan border. The Nile forms the eastern boundary.

66 CONCAVA SYRIA: Hollow Syria, usually known as Coele Syria, now forms Northern Syria.

67 GEBAL: Later Byblos, now Jubayl, about twenty miles north of Beirut, Lebanon.

68 ELAM: Also known as Susiana, it is approximately the same as the modern Iranian province of Khuzestan at the north of the Persian Gulf, bordering Iraq and including Abadan.

69 IDUNIA: Nalvage: 'It is beyond Greenland.'

70 MEDIA: North-Western Iran, south of Caspis (Part 28) and Hyrcania (Part 7). Includes Teheran.

71 ARIANA: Eastern Iran, Pakistan west of the Indus, Southern Afghanistan.

72 CHALDEA: A tract of country in South Iraq running along the Euphrates from the Persian Gulf to Babylon (about 50 miles south of Bagdad). The Shamiya Desert forms the western boundary.

73 SERICIPOPULI: A people in Eastern Asia. Serica or Seres equates with China and the Far East.

74 PERSIA: Persis or Parsa, this is approximately the modern Iranian province of Fars. Located in South-West Iran and bounded on the west by the Persian Gulf, the province was the kernel of ancient Persia and includes the ancient cities of Parsagarda (Part 11) and Persepolis.

75 GONGATHA: Kelley: 'Towards the South Pole.'

This is Gongala, an area to the south of Libya Interior by the Equator. In the sixteenth century Kelley's description is apt, but today the region equates with South Sudan.

76 GORSIM: Kelley: 'Beares and Lions here.'

Most probably Chorazin/Korazim/Gorazim, an ancient site to the north of Lake Tiberias (Sea of Galilee), Israel, with the ruins of a black basalt synagogue. The place was condemned by Jesus and legend claims the Antichrist will be born there. Note also Chorasmia/Khorezm/Khiva, south-east of the Caspian Sea in Turkmenistan.

77 HISPANIA: Spain and Portugal.

78 PAMPHILIA: Southern Turkish coastal land, between Lycia (Part 33) and Cilicia (Part 14), forming a narrow strip of land around the Bay of Antalya.

79 OACIDI: This is Oasitae ('. . . of the Oasis'), the oasis area west of the Nile, which includes the great oasis of the Oracle of Amon.

80 BABYLON or **BABYLONIA:** Region in Southern Iraq, extending north from the Persian Gulf between the Lower Tigris and the northeastern Arabian desert. Babylon, the capital, is about fifty miles south of Bagdad.

81 MEDIAN: Kelley: 'It is much Northward.'

Note, however, Midian—the land of the Midianites by Sinai; or, even the people of Media (Part 70).

82 IDUMIAN: Kelley: 'They are two Isles environed with an arm of the Scythian Sea, which goeth in at Maspi.'

Most probably the region to the north-east of the Aral Sea in the Kazakhstan. Suggest 'Maspi' is a corruption of the Aspisii Montes/Mons Aspisii, which shortened to M. Aspisii, distorts to Maspi. The mountains were supposedly located in this region, but in the sixteenth century much of this land and especially the far north of Siberia or Scythia was Terrae Incognita. Mercator's map of North-East Asia, which is dated 1569, shows a hypothetical arm of the Scythian Sea (Laptev and East Siberian seas) almost reaching to the north-east of the Aral Sea with the M. Aspisii nearby. The Aspisii Scythea were the people dwelling to the west of the mountains and to the north of the River Jaxartes (Syr Darya). Note also, however, the Arimaspi detailed in Part 88 below. The Maspii, a noble Persian tribe, are too far south to be considered.

83 **FELIX ARABIA**: Arabian Red Sea coastlands, particularly the southwestern areas, including the Yemen.

84 **METAGONITIDIM**: The Metagonitae were a people living in Tangiers and the surrounding area. The district forms the west of Mauretania (Part 91) or modern Northern Morocco.

85 **ASSYRIA**: Eastern Iraq between the Tigris and the Iranian border.

86 **AFRICA**: Mediterranean coastal region of Libya, including Tripoli and the modern province of Tripolitania, but excluding the eastern part, for which see Cireniaca (Part 50) and Nasamonia (Part 51). The region also includes the eastern Algerian coastlands and the Algerian/Tunisian border. This is not the continent of Africa.

87 **BACTRIANI**: The people of Bactriana (Part 13).

88 **AFNAN** or **AFRAN**: Kelley: 'Here appear people with one eye in their head, seeming to be in their breast, towards the Equinoctial.'

Dee: 'I remember of people called Arimaspi.'

Dee is confused here, as the Arimaspi ('the one-eyed') were a people on the left bank of the Middle Volga, north of the Caspian Sea. The Afran are the people Ptolemy called the Aphricerones, located just north of Equatorial Africa in North Zaire. The ancient scholars considered that all the southern parts of Africa were uninhabitable (as with many unexplored lands) and populated with strange beasts. Herodotus included in his conjectures on unknown Africa descriptions of peoples with 'one eye in the breast instead of the usual head', which must be the people referred to.

89 **PHRYGIA**: Large province in Central Turkey. Greater Phrygia was bounded on the east by Cappadocia (Part 4).

90 **CRETA**: Crete.

91 **MAURITANIA** or **MAURETANIA:** Morocco and the north Algerian coastlands, not to be confused with the modern state of Mauritania, which is located further south and for which see Getulia (Part 19).

References

Geography of Claudius Ptolemy, New York, 1932.

Kiepert, H. *Formae Orbis Antiqua*, Berlin, 1894.

Louis, V. de St Martin. *Atlas dresse pour l'histoire de la geographie et des decouvertes geographiques*, Paris, 1874.

Oestergaards Handatlas durch alle Welt, Peter J. Oestergaard Verlag, Berlin, 193–.

Skelton, R. A. *Decorative and Printed Maps of the Fifteenth to Eighteenth Centuries*, London, 1965.

Smith, W. *Dictionary of Greek and Roman Geography*, London, 1878.

Taylor, E. G. R. *Tudor Geography: 1485–1583*, London, 1930.

Appendix IV

Angels of the Elemental Tablets

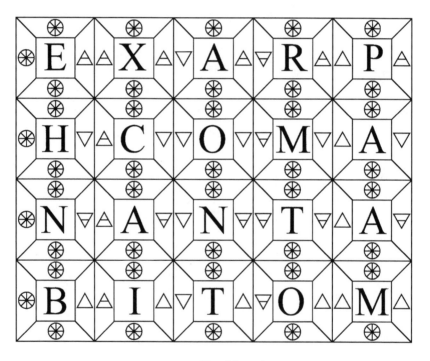

Figure 91: Full Tablet of Union

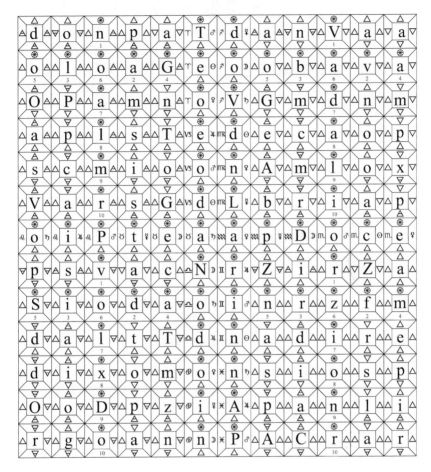

Figure 92: Full Elemental Tablet of Fire

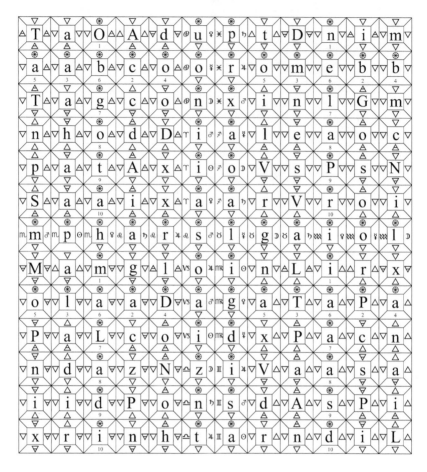

Figure 93: Full Elemental Tablet of Water

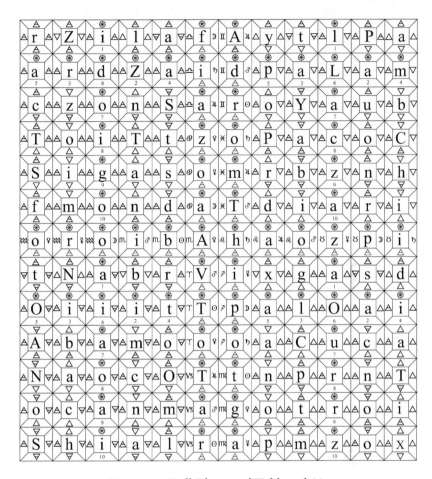

Figure 94: Full Elemental Tablet of Air

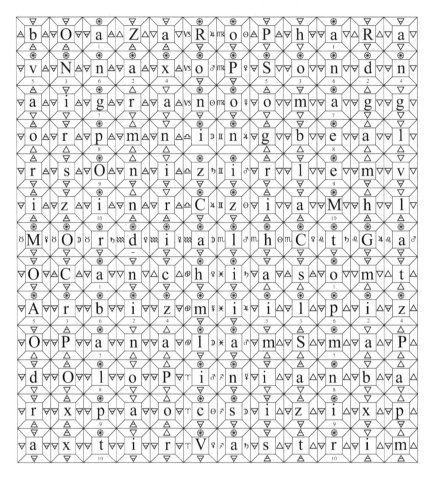

Figure 95: Full Elemental Tablet of Earth

The Three Great Secret Names of God

At the very top of the hierarchy of the Elemental Tablet are the Three Great Secret Names of God. In the practice of modern Enochian magick, prior to contacting any angel from the Elemental Tablet, the Three Great Secret Names of God should be first be invoked. The Golden Dawn and Crowley incorporated the names in a preliminary temple opening. Whether you use these temple openings in your own work, or if you design your own opening ritual, you must never neglect to recognize by name the Three Great Secret Names of God who rule the Elemental Tablet you are working with.

Elemental Tablet	Three Great Secret Names of God		
Air	ORO	IBAH	AOZPI
Water	MPH	ARSL	GAIOL
Earth	MOR	DIAL	HCTGA
Fire	OIP	TEAA	PDOCE

Figure 96: The Three Great Secret Names of God of the Elemental Tablets

The Seniors and the Kings

Next in hierarchical order are the six seniors and the king of the Elemental Tablet. After invoking the Three Great Secret Names of God, these seven angels must also be recognized by name and made part of the magician's opening ritual.

If you are invoking an individual senior, you may omit the names of the other seniors (but not the king) in your ritual opening.

Elemental Tablet	Planets Assigned to the Seniors					
	Mars	Jupiter	Luna	Venus	Saturn	Mercury
Air	Abioro	Aaozaif	Htmorda	Ahaozpi	Hipotga	Autotar
Water	Lsrahpm	Saiinou	Laoaxrp	Slgaiol	Ligdisa	Soniznt
Earth	Laidrom	Aczinor	Lzinopo	Alhctga	Liiansa	Ahmlicu
Fire	Aaetpio	Adoeoet	Alndvod	Aapdoce	Aarinnap	Aarinnap

Figure 97: The seniors of the Elemental Tablets

Elemental Tablet	Name of King for Operations of Mercy	Name of King for Operations of Severity
Air	Bataiva	Bataivh
Water	Raagios	Raagiol
Earth	Iczhhca	Iczhhcl
Fire	Edlprna	Edlprna

Figure 98: The kings of the Elemental Tablets

Air

Air Subangles	Elemental Tablet of ….				Duty
	Air	Water	Earth	Fire	
Servient Angels	C z|o|ns To|i|tt So|g|as Fm|o|nd	To|g|co Nh|o|dd Pa|t|ax Sa|a|iz	Ai|g|ra Or|p|mn Rs|o|ni Iz|i|nr	Op|a|mn Ap|l|st Sc|m|io Va|r|sg	Sixteen good angels most skilled and powerful in medicine and the curing of diseases.
Invoke with god Name -	Idoigo	Olgota	Angoi	Noalmr	
Command with god Name -	Ardza	Oalco	Unnax	Oloag	
Kerubic god Name	Erzla	Ataad	Eboza	Adopa	
Kerubs	Rzla Zlar Larz Arcl	Taad Aadt Adta Dtaa	Boza Ozab Zabo Aboz	Dopa Opad Pado Adop	Sixteen good angels who are most powerful and skilled in the mixing together of natural substances.

Water

Water Subangles	Elemental Tablet of ….				Duty
	Air	Water	Earth	Fire	
Servient Angels	Oy|a|ub Pa|c|oc Rb|z|nh Di|a|ri	Ma|l|gm Le|a|oc Vs|p|sn Rv|r|oi	Om|a|gg Gb|e|al Rl|e|mu Ia|m|hl	Gm|d|m Ec|a|op Am|l|ox Br|i|ap	Sixteen good who are powerful & learned in the finding. collection use and virtues of metals. and in the coagulations and powers of jewels.
Invoke with god Name -	Palam	Nelapr	Anaeem	Vadali	
Command with god Name -	Llacza	Omebb	Sondn	Obaua	
Kerubic god Name	Eutpa	Atdm	Ephra	Aanaa	
Kerubs	Utpa Tpau Paut Autp	Tdim Dimt Imtd Mtdi	Phra Hrap Raph Aphr	Anaa Naaa Aaan Aana	Sixteen good angels who are powerful in transporting from place to place.

Earth

Earth Subangles	Elemental Tablet of ….				Duty
	Air	Water	Earth	Fire	
Servient Angels	Ab|a|mo Na|o|ca Oc|a|nm Sh|i|al	Pa|l|co Nd|a|zn Ii|d|po Xr|i|nh	Op|a|na Do|l|op Rx|p|ao Ax|t|ir	Da|l|tt Di|x|om Oo|d|pz Rg|o|an	Sixteen good who are powerful and learned in Transformation.
Invoke with god Name -	Aioaoi	Maladi	Cbalpt	Ulxdo	
Command with god Name -	Oiiit	Olaad	Arbiz	Sioda	
Kerubic god Name	Hcnbr	Pmagl	Hroan	Ppsac	
Kerubs	Cnbr Nbrc Brcn Rcnb	Magl Aglm Glma Lmgl	Roan Oanr Anro Nroa	Psac Sacp Acps Cpsa	Sixteen good angels who are skilled and powerful in the Mechanical Arts.

Fire

Fire Subangles	Elemental Tablet of ….				Duty
	Air	Water	Earth	Fire	
Servient Angels	Ac|u|ca Np|r|at Ot|r|oi Pm|z|ox	Xp|a|cn Va|a|sa Da|s|pi Rn|d|il	Ms|m|al Ia|n|ba Iz|i|xp St|r|im	Ad|i|re Si|o|sp Pa|n|li Zc|r|ar	Sixteen good angels who liveth in and knoweth the quality and use of all four elements.
Invoke with god Name -	Aourrz	Iaaasd	Spmnir	Rizionr	
Command with god Name -	Aloai	Atapa	Ilpiz	Nrzfm	
Kerubic god Name	Hxgsd	Pnlrx	Hiaom	Pziza	
Kerubs	Xgzd Gzdx Zdxg Dxgz	Nlrx Lrxn Rxnl Xnlr	Iaom Aomi Omia Miao	Ziza Izaz Zazi Aziz	Sixteen good angels who are skilled and powerful in the discovering the secrets of all men.

Figure 99: Good angels, god names, and Kerubs of the subangles, with their duties

	Elemental Tablet of...			
	Air	***Water***	***Earth***	***Fire***
Subangles of Air	Xcz Ato Rso Pfm	Mto Onh Cpa Hsa	Xai Aor Rrs Piz	Mop Oap Csc Hva
Invoke with reverse god name	**Ogiodi**	**Atoglo**	**Iogna**	**Rmlaon**
Command with reverse god name	**Azdra**	**Pclao**	**Xannau**	**Gaolo**
Subangles of Water	Xoy Apa Rrb Pdi	Mma Ole Cvs Hrv	Xom Agb Rrl Pia	Mgm Oec Cam Hbr
Invoke with reverse god name	**Malap**	**Rpalen**	**Meeana**	**Iladav**
Command with reverse god Name	**Azcall**	**Bbemo**	**Ndnos**	**Auabo**
Subangles of Earth	Cab Ona Moc Ash	Rpa And Xii Exr	Cop Odo Mrx Aax	Ada Adi Xoo Erg
Invoke with reverse god name	**Ioaoia**	**Idalam**	**Tplabc**	**Odxlu**
Command with reverse god name	**Tiiio**	**Daalo**	**Zibra**	**Adois**
Subangles of Fire	Cac Onp Mot Apm	Rxp Ava Xda Ern	Cms Oia Miz Ast	Rad Asi Xpa Ezc
Invoke with reverse god name	**Zrruoa**	**Dsaaai**	**Rinmps**	**Rnoizir**
Command with reverse god name	**Iaola**	**Apata**	**Zipli**	**Mfzrn**

Figure 100: Wicked angels of the subangles and the adverse gods that invoke and command them

d	o	n	p	a	T	d	a	n	V	a	a
o	l	o	a	G	e	o	o	b	a	u v	a i
O	P	a	m	n	o	V O	G	m n	d	n	m
a	p b	l	s	T	e	d c	e	c	a	o	p
s	c	m	i	o	o a	n	A	m	l	o	x
V	a	r	s	G	d	L	b v	r	i	a	p
o	i	P	t	e	a	a	p	D	o	c	e
p	s	u v	a	c	n	r	Z	i	r	Z	a
S	i	o	d	a	o	i	n	r	z	f	m
d	a	l b	t	T	d	n	a	d	i	r	e
d	i	x	o	m	o	n	s	i	o	s	p
O	o	D	p	z	i	A	p	o	n	l	i
r	g	o	a	n	n	q* o	A*	C	r	a	r

Figure 101: Multiple-lettered Elemental Tablet of Fire

T	a	O	A	d	u(v)	p	t	D	n	i	m
a(o)	a	b(ſ)	c	o	o	r	o	m	e'	b	b
T	o(a)	g	c	o	n	x(z)	m(i)	a(nu)	ſ	G	m
n	h	o	d	D	i	a	ſ(ia)	e'(aſ)	a	o	c
P(f)	a	t(c)	A	x	i	o(uv)	V	s	P	s	M*(ſyh)
S	a	a	i	x(z)	a	a	r	V	r	o	i
m	p	h	a	r	s	ſ	g	a	i	o(c)	ſ(h)
M	a	m	g	ſ	o	i	n	L	i	r	x
o	ſ	a	a	D	n(a)	g	a	T	a	p	a
p	a	L	c	o	i	d	x	P	a	c	n
n	d	a	z	N	z(x)	i	V	a	a	s	a
i(r)	i	d	P	o	n	s	d	A	s	p	i
x	r	i(r)	n	h	t	a	r	n(a)	d	i	J*

Figure 102: Multiple-lettered Elemental Tablet of Water

r	Z	i	ſ	a	f	A	y(u)	t	ſ(i)	p	a
a	r	d	Z	a	i	d	p	a	L	a	m
c	z	o	n	s	a	r	o	Y	a	u	b
T	o	i	T	t	z(x)	o	P	a	c	o	C
S	i	g	a	s	o	m(n)	r	b	z	n	h
ſ	m	o	n	d	a	T	d	i	a	r	i(ſ)
o	r	o	i	b	A	h	a	o	z	p	i
t(c)	N	a	b	r(a)	V	i	x	g	a	s(z)	d
O*	i	i	i	t	T	p	a	ſ	O	a	i
A*	b	a	m	o	o	o	a	C	u(v)	c	a
N	a	o	c	O	T	t	n	p	r	n(ua)	T
o	c	a	n	m	a	g	o	t	r	o	i
S	h	i	a	ſ	r	a	p	m	z	o	x

Figure 103: Multiple-lettered Elemental Tablet of Air

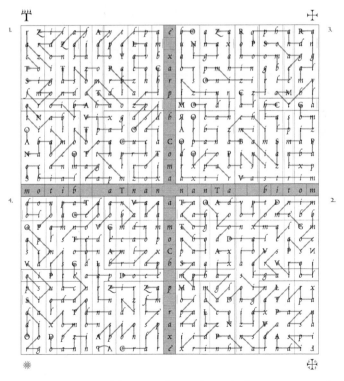

b	O	a	Z	a	R	o	p	h	a	R	a
u v	N	n	a	x	o	P	S	o	n	d	n
a	i	g	r	a	n	o	o a	m	a	g	g
o	r	p	m	n	i	n	g	b	e'	a	ʃ
r	s	O	n	i	z	i	r	ʃ	e'	m	v
i	z	i	n	r	C	z	i	a	M	h	ʃ
M	O	r	d	i	a	ʃ	h	C	t	G	a
O* Я*	c O	a c	n a n m	c	h c	i h	a ibt	s a	o s	m o	t m
A*	r	b	i	z	m	i	i ʃ	ʃ	p	i	z
O	p	a	n	a	ʃ B	a	m	S	m	a	P LT
d	O	ʃ	o	P F	i	n	i	a	n	b	a
r	x	p	a	o	c	s	i	z	i	x	p
a	x	t	i	r	V	a	s	t	r	i	m

Figure 104: Multiple-lettered Elemental Tablet of Earth

Figure 105. The Great Table (Unreformed) with the Symmetrical Characters

Appendix V

Three Examples of Enochian Magick Visions

Nanta, elo Hoath zorge ef.

"Spirit of Earth, first worshiper friendly visit."
—LAIDROM, MARS SENIOR OF EARTH

Example 1[123]

First Session (September 25, 1980) Laidrom, Mars senior of the Elemental Tablet of Earth. Scryer: David P. Wilson.

For our first evocation session I decided we would work as Dee and Kelley did. One person would act as seer, and one as operator. The seer would recite the appropriate call, receive the vision, and communicate it during or after the session. The operator would banish, open and close the temple, and question the seer. I would be the operator, but I did not know who in our little class would be the first to sit in the visionary driver's seat. On class night there was only one rather reluctant volunteer.

David P. Wilson was not new to the world of magick. In the years leading up to his affiliation with our lodge he sat in with a host of magical groups and workshops in the Los Angeles area upon whom he later heaped scorn and ridicule because of their inability to show him "real magick." He was the boldest member of the class, also the most impatient and sarcastic. I could see the Enochian class going down in flames on opening night because David the curmudgeon once again "saw nothing!" He had done none of the preliminary Enochian work with the rest of the class. He hadn't painted a set of tablets or studied any of the calls. Still, he was our only volunteer.

I can't recall why but I decided we would to try to contact LAIDROM, the Mars Senior of the Elemental Tablet of Earth. In the spirit of *better safe than sorry*, we placed the Earth tablet in the South (Capricorn/Cardinal Earth) and enclosed the entire class in a circle cast with a clothesline cord. I banished with the rituals of the lesser and greater pentagrams and hexagrams, then opened the temple and invoked the hierarchical names as indicated in *Liber Chanokh*. David was seated on the floor at the southern edge of the circle, just inches away from the Earth tablet. Leaning against the wall behind the tablet was a huge cardboard version of the [Elemental] Tablet of Earth that I placed there for the other members of the class to focus upon. I turned on the tape recorder and gave David a copy of the Call to read. I sat down behind him while he read it aloud.

He did rather well considering he had never read it before. When he was finished, he closed his eyes and took a deep breath. Nothing happened. I asked him to read the Call again. He did so and after only a few seconds he said, "I have a landscape. I see a landscape."

I was relieved beyond words. "What does it look like?"

David proceeded to describe in surprising detail a desert vista of flat, trackless white crystalline powder stretching to the horizon. Great gray columns of volcanic rock towering over the plain broke the monotony of the scene. Between the columns the ground was pockmarked with countless gaping pits.

That was it. Nothing else was occurring. I asked him to read the Call a third time. This time there was movement. From out of a pit in the center of his field of vision arose a black cone. He said it sparkled from the inside and upon its surface with thousands of little sparks that jumped from one star to another.

I asked, "Is this LAIDROM?"

David grabbed his pencil and notepad and quickly scribbled something. I looked at what he had drawn. It looked like four very poorly drawn Enochian letters. At the time it meant nothing to me. I asked for a clearer answer. "Is this LAIDROM?"

"It's him! It's him! I see him."

He described a humanoid figure draped in the same material from which the cone was constructed. He had an egg-shaped head but no face. His hands were like mittens—there were no fingers. He reached his arm toward the ground and "drew" a diagram in the sand in front of him. David quickly copied the figure on the notepad. It was a square divided diagonally by two lines with a small circle in the lower left-hand corner. We took this to be LAIDROM's signature.

We were all very excited. It was as if the entire class saw David's vision in our mind's eye. Then it occurred to me. Now that we've got this guy, what the hell are we to do with him? Before I could think of what to do next, David said, "Lon, I feel like . . . I feel . . . I could make strange sounds."

This was a twist. "Let yourself." I told him. "Go with it." I tried to sound calm.

"*Naw-n tahelo hoh athayzo raygayeff. . .* this is bullshit!"

"No! Relax, let it happen!"

"I mean it, I feel like an idiot. I'm too . . . *zil-zi-anzilzi-lo-da-arp nan-ta* . . . (inaudible) . . . *ef* . . . *efee thar-zi.* I am sorry. That's all. Nothing like this has ever happened before. I just felt like doing it." David's apology was comical. We all broke into nervous giggles.

It had been quite an evening. As we had planned nothing particular to do with LAIDROM, I thought it wise to quit while we were ahead. I asked David to thank our spirit guest for his visit and proceeded to banish and close the temple.

One of the class members had brought along his Enochian Dictionary[124] and suggested we try to use it to see if David's strange babbling actually meant something. I rewound the tape and played it back from the beginning. Everything was crystal clear right up to the time of LAIDROM's appearance, when the tape developed an irritating distortion. We joked that it was the fault of malicious spirits and expected it to soon clear up. It did not. In fact, by the time the tape reached David's babbling we could hardly pick his voice out from behind the bank of white noise. As soon as the good stuff was over, the distortion suddenly stopped.

Noise notwithstanding, after replaying the section of tape a dozen times or more, we picked up enough of what was being said to write down three audible strings of syllables:

naw-n tahelo hoh athayzo raygayeff.

zil-zi-anzilzi-lo-da-arp nan-ta . . . (inaudible) and

ef . . . efee thar-zi.

Starting at the beginning, we painstakingly played with the phonetics of each word (and the word/words following) and attempted to match them with words in the Enochian Dictionary. Obviously we weren't being very scientific, nor, I confess, very objective. This was all very exciting and romantic, and I am sure that night we would have squeezed *some* profundity out of any string of sounds. Be that as it may, it took less than an hour to break the sounds up as follows:

Nanta, elo Hoath zorge ef.—Which translated neatly to: "Spirit of Earth, first worshiper friendly visit."

Zil zien—"stretch forth hands"

Zilodarp Nanta—"stretch forth and conquer Spirit of Earth"

Ef etharzi—"visit in peace."

Needless to say we were all very impressed. At the end of the evening it was agreed that from now on class would meet two times a week to pursue Enochian magick. Sadly, David's ability to break spontaneously into the Enochian language would diminish rapidly as his familiarity with the language of the Calls increased. After the fourth or fifth session, he lost the ability completely. His visions, on the other hand, became clearer, more informative, and more provocative.

Example 2

Monday Night Magick Class (July 17, 2006) Twenty-ninth Aethyr Rii. Scryer: Jill Belanger

Enochian scrying sessions sometimes trigger emotional, physical, even sexual reactions. This is a clip from the transcription of a recording of a Monday night magick class scrying of the twenty-ninth Aethyr, Rii, and its governors: Vastrim, Odraxti, and Gomziam. The main scryer in this session was Jill Belanger, one of the class's most talented seers. It demonstrates that Enochian visions need not take the form of biblical-esque landscapes and heavy magical pronouncements. I thank

Jill for being a very good sport and allowing us to eavesdrop on part of this provocative session.

This session started with the full opening ritual as outlined in chapter one.

As soon as I closed my eyes I was pulled into a vortex, an upside down six, and I was pulled in with an . . . um . . . another gentleman, a lover, a man, and we were instantly in sexual ecstasy going in water in the form of six, and just flying around, the flame was in the middle, and the water was swirling around, and I was lost in that ecstasy for a while. And then I thought, No, I've got to figure out what this message is about. So I tried to push him away. (Laughter from class.) And I said (very drunkenly), "Gumziam [sic], where are you? And I kept flying around in the water vortex. I then saw two triangles together but three dimensional, in sort of like (garbled) with three or four sides instead of eight sides, and then the two triangles . . . one split off from the other one. One on top, one on bottom, and the widest parts were together, and I was standing in the middle . . . and it was like the floor and ceiling were separating and apart.

And I looked down, and the floor was split into four parts, not like the Watchtowers, more like pyramids, and one was Fire, Water, Earth, and Air. Then it was stuck back together again, and I was swirling with the vortex again. I said, "Fire creates, but water solidifies," and the two pyramids went back together, and I was with this lover again, floating around, and I was like, "OK! Let's . . . well . . . OK!" (Laughter from class.) I'm still kind of hot! (More laughter.)

Example 3

Public Workshop (July 22, 2006) Thirtieth Aethyr, Tex. Scryer: name withheld

The following is a letter I received a few days after I returned home from a workshop series on Enochian vision magick. The vision the young woman describes occurred during a scrying session that concluded a half-day public workshop. She, like most of the attendees at this event, had never performed Enochian magick before.

After I had outlined a brief history of Dee and Kelley's adventures and the fundamentals of Enochian magick, the entire class took part in

the ritual and chanting of the Ring/Lamen/Holy Table/Sigillum/Table of Nalvage opening ceremony. Over their two-part chorus of the Table of Nalvage words, I recited the nineteenth call to penetrate the thirtieth Aethyr, Tex. Here is her experience.

Hi, Lon!

Thanks again for making the trek here . . . last weekend. I learned a lot more than I had expected to, which is why I'm writing you this. I didn't get a chance to talk to you about the things I saw/did when you led the class foray into the Enochian aethyrs, and initially I was hesitant to because of the rather personal nature of some of it. But after talking to [my brother] about it, I realized I should tell you; in fact, he insisted I do so. So here goes.

We had just finished chanting the Holy Table, and you indicated we should close our eyes while you continued chanting and just follow the images that came to us. Initially I got not images per se, but random geometric shapes in dark shades of purple and green, mostly pyramids, and pyramids of one color in front of squares of a slightly darker shade. I realized that I was falling forward, swiftly, down a triangular corridor filled with a dark purplish haze, with occasional lighter purple flashes—like falling through layers and layers and layers, whoosh, whoosh, whoosh, with something spinning all around me at the same time. Then I realized I wasn't going down anymore, but rising, still through this triangular purple infused corridor, whoosh, whoosh, whoosh, still the spinning, and I began to feel my heart pounding like it would burst inside me, I felt dizzy and slightly nauseous, and just when I thought I couldn't stand it for another moment longer, I stopped speeding forward, and the purple mist cleared, and I was standing on a grassy plain, almost a hilltop, that rose slightly upward in front of me. I realized that the thing that had been spinning seemed to be the petals of an enormous flower, a lotus, perhaps, and that the hillside on which I stood was contained within its perimeter, like a low wall going around it. It occurs to me now that I was facing north.

Beyond the border of the wall were two more hills in the distance, one to the left and one to the right, covered in vibrant dark green vegetation, and I knew vaguely that there were Things in those hills, in those trees, but I didn't have time to think about them. There were four pillars that stretched up around me, at the outside edge of the wall, and as I watched, a pyramid rose up out of the hillside in front of me, or perhaps I simply moved swiftly up the hillside towards it. It wasn't large, maybe only one or one and a half stories high; it was four sided and made of a smooth golden brick or stone. A blinding light issued from the center of it, and, as I watched, the form of a person appeared in the center of this light and was walking towards me.

My impression was that he came from inside the pyramid, and he seemed to be coming from some distance, though the pyramid was just in front of me. He was tall and blond and blue eyed and wore a garment of brilliant white and a golden circlet about his temples. And he was smiling, he was so glad to see me. As he came close to me, he opened up the robe to reveal a column of blinding white light running down the centerline of his body. As my eyes adjusted to the light, I realized that the light was coming from his chakras, which were blazing yellow-white light and shaped sort of like flowers. I realized that my chakras were also blazing, and the light from his heart chakra leapt forward in a thin white-yellow tongue of flaming light and entered my heart chakra. Then his throat chakra flamed and leapt into mine, and then all of them at once seemed to, and that blazing sharing of chakra light continued for a few blissful, amazing moments.

He held his hands out in front of him, palms facing toward me, and I placed my palms against them, and the chakras in our hands blazed with light and fire for a moment. Then he took my hands and pulled them straight into his chest so that I held his heart chakra in my hands, and then he indicated that I should put his heart chakra inside my chest. I was amazed that he would suggest that, and slightly hesitant, but he was insistent, and together we thrust it into my chest. I was stunned at the force of the heat of the union of our two heart chakras. Then he gestured to his throat chakra, and again, I took his chakra in my hands, and lifted it out of him and into myself, with another flash of heat. Then I lifted out his third-eye chakra, then his solar plexus chakra, then his hara chakra. I reached next for his root chakra, and realized that in my hands it had become a huge golden phallus, and as in the curious logic of dreams, there was only one obvious way to integrate that into myself—I mounted it, and at the same time, I reached up and removed the crown from his head, symbolic of his crown chakra, and placed it on my own head at the same moment as the phallus slid into me, and the universe exploded. It wasn't sex, it wasn't copulation, it was Union,

I was perfectly with and within him, and he was perfectly with and within me. It was Bliss, it was Light, it was Perfection. I heard his voice in my ear, saying, "You are She, in Whom all things are received; She in Whom all things are created; She in Whom all things are possible. All Life is Yes; all Love is Know. Know that You are She."

At about that moment, I heard your voice saying something about looking around for landmarks that would help me remember this place, and I laughed to myself that I wasn't likely to forget this. You said something else about bringing back a sign, or a key or talisman from this place, something to know and remember it by that would help me return, and I pulled back slightly from this Being with a wordless question, and his answer was to withdraw from me, and he ejaculated into my outstretched hands, a liquid golden light that turned into two glowing, golden diamond crystals that sank into my palms and disappeared as I watched.

Then your voice said it was time to return, and without another word or glance between us I was whisked up and away, coming back into awareness of my body with a nauseating thud, my head spinning, my heart pounding painfully. You started asking us questions about what we'd seen, where we'd been, and I was too nauseated and out of breath to answer, but was amazed to hear my classmates describing similar imagery, lotuses, columns, towers, pyramids, though no one else seemed to have experienced anything close to what had passed between me and that other Being—or at least, no one was admitting to it. I sat there in a haze, listening to them, thinking about my own experience, and waiting for my heart to quit pounding, my stomach to stop churning. I must have looked pretty stunned, because [my husband] asked me if I was OK, and all I could initially articulate to him as he looked over at me was, "What the f___ just happened to me?"

We broke for dinner at about that moment, and I realized my opportunity to share it with the class had passed. But I still wanted to tell you about it, and, of course, [my husband]. We had driven separate cars that day, so we met at the house before going to the restaurant, and there at home I told him. He stared at me while I told him about it, saying it was pretty amazing, but I'd better not say anything about it in front of the class as a whole, that it was way too personal to just lay out there that way. He suggested I call [my brother], that he'd be able to decode it for me and would definitely be interested. I agreed, but thought at the same time that I really should tell you, but wanted to do so in private.

We went to dinner and then to the meet and greet with the class, but I held back, there were always too many people around. Perhaps now, after reading my account, you understand my hesitancy. Because to be honest, I wasn't sure how to begin, I was still unsure of myself, unsure of how to confess to someone I had only just met that under his direction I had experienced a union that was way more than sexual with someone who was apparently a Being of Light, a resident of the angelic realms, and also not sure of what that said about me. But I knew who would know what it all meant, and so as soon as I got home on Sunday, I called my brother and told the whole story to him. He was jubilant, congratulatory, awestruck, and then he asked me, "Well, what did Lon say when you told him?" I had to admit that I hadn't been sure of what or how to communicate it, and had been further stymied by my husband's reaction to it. My brother was incredulous. How could I not have shared that vision with you, who of all people, would understand it and sympathize with my bewilderment at it? I should have told you everything, he insisted. I agreed and promised him I would write you. And so here we are.

My brother was curious to know which of the Aethyrs you had us reading from, and I couldn't remember; my husband thinks you said we were only going to push ourselves up a level, but my brother thinks I went farther than that and said you might recognize which one. There were things about the place that I recognized from dreams—it's a place I've dreamed of my whole life but never consciously remembered until now. I'm not unaccustomed to visions and vision quests, but this was unlike anything I've ever done before. My body's reaction to it was visceral; I crashed hard when I came back from it, and I continued to feel the physical aftereffects for several days (kind of like recovery from a bad acid trip). Today, Thursday, I'm finally feeling back up to steam. My brother said that's a normal reaction to astral projection; is that really what I did? I have my own theories about the imagery and symbolism. I'm a massage therapist and energy worker, a master of the Usui and Karuna systems of Reiki, and the student of a spirit guide who was a Native American shaman. The ejaculation of light that turned into crystals and sank into my palms resonates with me on several levels. I think one possible meaning is that it was a gift to use in my healing work. I can tell you that all this week, whenever I've "turned on" the Reiki or use one of the symbols, the chakras in my palms blaze with heat, my patients have actually commented on it! (In fact, they're heating up right now, just thinking about it.) [My brother] didn't exactly discount my idea about it, but he said there was a lot more mystical significance there than I realized, or than he should even talk to me about until I talked to you. Obviously, it's loaded with archetypal images, but I would love to know what you get from them, what level you sent me to, and if you recognize anything from my descriptions.

Thanks for your patience. This has turned from an email into a novella! I eagerly await your reply!

Brightest blessings!

Notes

1 Geoffrey James, *The Enochian Magick of Dr. John Dee*. (St. Paul, MN: Llewellyn Publications, 1994). Orignally published: *The Enochian Evocation of Dr. John Dee*. (Gillette, NJ: Heptangle Books, 1984) pp. 199–201.

2 Sometimes spelled "Kelley."

3 Meric Casaubon, ed. *A True & Faithful Relation of What Passed for Many Yeers Between Dr. John Dee and Some Spirits*. Ed. Clay Holden (orig. pub. London: Maxwell: 1659, rev. ed. New York: Magickal Childe Publications, 1992. A transcription of Dee's diaries from May 28, 1583 to April 2, 1587. The Magickal Child edition expands on the original and includes additional material by Clay Holden and Lon Milo DuQuette. Hereafter referred to as "*A True and Faithful Relation*."

4 Joseph H. Peterson, ed. *John Dee's Five Books of Mystery: Original Sourcebook of Enochian Magic*. (Boston: Weiser Books, 2003).

5 Jean-Claude Carrière, *The Mahabharata: A Play Based Upon the Indian Classic Epic*, trans. Peter Brook (New York: Harper & Row, 1987), 5.

6 Ibid.

7 Aleister Crowley, *Magick, Liber ABA: Book Four*, ed. Hymenaeus Beta, 2nd rev. ed. (York Beach, ME: Weiser Books, 1997), 126.

8 Francis Israel Regardie (1907–1985) was private secretary to Aleister Crowley in the 1920s. Regardie went on to publish the rituals of the Golden Dawn and a series of books that made him a venerated icon of the magical and hermetic movements of the late twentieth century.

9 Aleister Crowley, Israel Regardie, eds., *Gems from the Equinox* (St. Paul, MN: Llewellyn Publications, 1974; Scottsdale, AZ: New Falcon, 1992; San Francisco: Weiser Books, 2008).

10 Israel Regardie, ed. *The Golden Dawn: The Original Account of the Teachings, Rites & Ceremonies of the Hermetic Order*. (St. Paul, MN: Llewellyn Publications, 1969). There have been numerous revised editions to this book, the latest being issued in 2002.

11 These nearly illegible photocopies were printed from microfilm on primitive heat-sensitive paper that made your skin crawl whenever you touched it.

12 Sometimes spelled *Kelly*.

13 Aleister Crowley, Lon Milo DuQuette, and Christopher Hyatt, *The Enochian World of Aleister Crowley: Enochian Sex Magick* (Scottsdale, AZ: New Falcon, 1991).

14 Lon Milo DuQuette, *Tarot of Ceremonial Magick Deck: A Pictoral Synthesis of the Three Great Pillars of Magick* (Stamford, CT: U.S. Games Systems, 1995).

15 Lon Milo DuQuette, *Tarot of Ceremonial Magick* (York Beach, ME: Weiser Books, 1995).

16 There! That wasn't so hard. Thank you, O remover of obstacles. I do believe the evil spirit of writer's block has been banished.

17 Crowley, *Magick, Liber ABA: Book Four*, 193.

18 In magick, "invocation" usually refers to the *calling into* oneself the presence or the essence of Deity; "evocation" usually refers to *calling forth* a spiritual entity (angel, spirit, demon, etc.) into the magician's triangle of art, there to be constrained and charged to do the magician's bidding. Theoretically, once the magician has successfully invoked the divine presence within himself or herself, he or she then has the divine authority to evoke the spirits.

19 John Dee, *Mysteriorum*, and *John Dee's Five Books of Mystery*, p. 54: Sloane 3188.

20 Caitlin and John Matthews, *The Western Way: A Practical Guide to the Western Mystery Tradition* (London: Arkana/Penguin Books. 1986), 294.

21 The title *doctor* has for centuries been attached to John Dee, and certainly his academic and professorial stature among his counterparts was enormous. However, there are no records of him actually receiving a doctorate degree. We do know that he finished school in 1551 with a master of arts degree and subsequently given a modest pension from King Edward VI.

22 Peter French, *John Dee: The World of an Elizabethan Magus* (New York: Dorset Press, 1989).

23 John Aubrey, *The Natural History and Antiquities of the County of Surrey* (London: n.p., 1718), 82.

24 This tidbit of historical trivia did not escape the attention of former British intelligence officer Ian Fleming when he created his fictional superspy, James Bond. Dee's espionage exploits are featured at an exhibit at the International Spy Museum in Washington, D.C.

25 Sometimes spelled *skrying*.

26 *A True & Faithful Relation*, Magickal Childe edition, p. 174.

27 For good or ill, there will always be a few of these. Foolishness and naïveté are often the most valuable weapons in the magician's arsenal.

28 Ordo Templi Orientis.

29 Without which the magician "can do nothing."

30 Even though Dee and Kelley continued an on-and-off relationship until 1587, when one particularly significant Enochian magick-related operation occurred (see book III), for all intents and purposes their angelic operations ended on July 13, 1584.

31 Johann Wolfgang Goethe, *Faust*, trans. George Madison Priest (Franklin Center, PA: Franklin Library, 1979).

32 Lon Milo DuQuette, *The Chicken Qabalah of Rabbi Lamed Ben Clifford* (Boston: Weiser Books, 2001). 129.

33 *Mysteriorum Liber Primus*. Also *John Dee's Five Books of Mystery*, pp. 67–68.

34 What is likely Dee's own copy of *Aldaraia sive Soyga: Tractatus Astrologico magicus—the Book of Sogya* is found in the British Library's MS Sloane 8.

35 It is interesting to note that one row in the table Magistri of *The Book of Soyga* is not filled with letters.

36 I encourage readers who feel drawn to the mysteries of the tables to review the following brilliant cryptographic analysis of them: Jim Reeds, "John Dee and the Magic Tables in the Book of Soyga," in *John Dee: Interdisciplinary Essays in English Renaissance Thought*, Vol. 193, *International Archives of the History of Ideas/Archives internationales d'histoire des idées*, ed. Stephen Clucas (New York and Heidelberg: Springer, 2006).

37 Carl Sagan (1934–1996) was an American astronomer and popular-science writer. This quote is from his 1980 television series, *Cosmos*.

38 Aleister Crowley, *Magick, Liber ABA: Book Three: Magick in Theory and Practice*, 231.

39 Lon Milo DuQuette, *The Key to Solomon's Key: Secrets of Magic and Masonry* (San Francisco: CCC Publishing, 2006), 104.

40 I Kings 3:5. George M. Lamsa, trans., *The Holy Bible from Ancient Eastern Manuscripts* (Philadelphia: A. J. Holman Company, 1967).

41 Ibid., I Kings 3:9–12.

42 Just as no two people share the same history (karma), flaws, talents, or potential, each magician's career is entirely unique. Hence the Lord's comment to Solomon, "Lo, I have given you a wise and understanding heart, so that there has been none like you before you, neither shall any arise after you like you" (I Kings 3:12).

43 DuQuette, *The Key to Solomon's Key*, 105.

44 Dee, *Quinti Libri Mysteriorum*, Sloane 3188.

45 John Dee, *De Heptarchia Mystica*, Sloane 3191.

46 Dee and Kelley referred to their magical sessions as actions.

47 Dee, *Quinti Libri Mysteriorum: Liber Primus*, Sloane 3188.

48 My dear friend Glacier in Chicago fashioned both the Ring and Lamen for me from a plate of thin gold (see acknowledgements).

49 "From the year 1579 in approximately this manner, in Latin or English (and furthermore in another singular and particular manner around the year 1569, sometimes for Raphael and sometimes for Michael) it was most pleasing to me to pour forth prayers to God. May God grant his wonderful mercy to me. Amen." Dee, *Quinti Libri Mysteriorum: Liber Primus*, Sloane 3188.

50 Using the inconsistent spelling characteristic of the Elizabethan period, this phrase originally read, "Beware of wavering: Blot owte suspition of us; for we are gods Creatures that haue Raigned, do Raigne, and shall Raigne for eu^. All our Mysteries shalbe known unto you." Dee, *Quinti Libri Mysteriorum: Liber Primus*, Sloane 3188.

51 The letter *b* (or *Pa* in the angelic alphabet) is used liberally in Heptarchic and Enochian magick. The frequency of its appearance has prompted some modern scholars to speculate that it represents the number seven, the key or foundational number of Dee and Kelley's angelic magick.

52 The symbols of the planets are as follows: Saturn ♄, Jupiter ♃, Mars ♂, Sol ☉, Venus ♀, Mercury ☿, Luna ☽.

53 This prayer is not found as such in the original Dee and Kelley material. I composed it to reflect my understanding of the purpose of the Lamen as it relates to myself and the Holy Table.

54 Dee, *Quinti Libri Mysteriorum*: Appendix, Sloane 3188.

55 Most likely laurel wood.

56 It is estimated in Dee's day a cubit equaled approximately forty-four inches.

57 *A True & Faithful Relation* also includes excerpts from Dee's work with Bartholomew Hickman from March 20, 1607, to September 7, 1607.

58 Aleister Crowley, *The Equinox*, Vol. I, no. 7. Reprinted as *The Equinox: Volume I*, Soror Virakam, ed. (York Beach, ME: Weiser Books, 1999), 229.

59 Dee, *Quinti Libri Mysteriorum*: Appendix, Sloane 3188.

60 And just as we microcosmic human beings are said to be the reflection of macrocosmic Deity, the individual names of the kings and princes on the 12 x 7 table that create the Lamen (which are read from right to left) are the mirror image of the those found on the 12 x 7 table that create the Holy Table (which are read from left to right).

61 Dee, *Quinti Libri Mysteriorum: Liber Secundus*, Sloane 3188.

62 *Liber Juratis* (*The Sworne Booke of Honorius*) and Athanasius Kircher's *Eodipus Aegypticus*.

63 The Greek omega here is the only example of a non-Latin letter appearing on the Sigillum Dei Aemeth.

64 When new, the candles served to illuminate the altar during several years of Gnostic masses.

65 My thanks go to Enochian magician Michael Strader for these images, which he was kind enough to also fashion for our Monday night magick class in purified tin.

66 Casaubon, *A True & Faith Relation*, 209.

67 Dee and Kelley, *Liber Mysteriorum Quintus*, Sloane 3189.

68 Much of which can be found today in Sloane 3189.

69 Sloane 3188.

70 Peterson, *John Dee's Five Books of Mystery*, 32.

71 Dee, *Mysteriorum Liber Primus*, Sloane 3188.

72 Dee, *Liber Mysteriorum Quintus*. Sloane 3188.

73 For the full quote see Casaubon, *A True & Faithful Relation*, 174.

74 New volumes of *The Equinox* continue to be published today by Crowley's magical order, Ordo Templi Orientis.

75 The Ceremony of Preparation is found in chapter one and appendix I of this book.

76 Casaubon, *A True & Faithful Relation*, 74.

77 Ibid.

78 Ibid.

79 Ibid., 88.

80 The calls are also referred to as *cries* or *keys*.

81 In this fanciful vignette, Nalvage is reaching into the future to quote the venerable author of *The Chicken Qabalah of Rabbi Lamed Ben Clifford*.

82 Dee, Sloane 3191.

83 Some of the countries are difficult for us to pinpoint today. I am deeply indebted to Robin Cousins, who has done extensive research in this area and written a marvelous essay on the subject, which he has graciously allowed me to reprint in its entirety in appendix III.

84 Casaubon, *A True & Faithful Relation*, 170.

85 Ibid., 168.

86 The four cloths were colored: The one in the east was red; the south, white; the west, green; and the north, black.

87 Casaubon, *A True & Faithful Relation*, 170.

88 Casaubon, *A True & Faithful Relation*, 183.

89 The tribes were first identified by a number, one through twelve, and later identified by name.

90 David R. Jones, "The System of Enochian Magick, Part II: The Evolution of the Tablets," *Lion & Serpent* 4, no. 4 (2001). *Lion & Serpent* is a journal published by Sekhet-Maat Lodge, Ordo Templi Orientis.

91 Dee, *Cotton Appendix XLVI: Actio Tertia Trebonae Generalis.*

92 In particular, *Liber Scientae Auxilii et Vitoriae Terrestris* (Sloane 3191).

93 Casaubon, *A True & Faithful Relation*, 188.

94 Ibid., 168.

95 Ibid.

96 The Book of the Revelation 4:4: "Surrounding the throne were twenty-four other thrones, and seated on them were twenty-four elders. They were dressed in white and had crowns of gold on their heads."

97 INRI is an acronym of the Latin phrase *Iesvs Nazarenvs Rex Iudaeorvm*, "Jesus the Nazarene, King of the Jews." It appears in the Gospel of John (chapter 19, verse 19). The four letters also have profound esoteric meanings to Christian mystics and ceremonial magicians, who see in the letters a magical formula of creation and being.

98 In astrology it is the four fixed, or kerubic, signs of the zodiac that exemplify the purest elemental quality. For example, there are three zodiac signs that represent the element of Fire: Aries, Leo, and Sagittarius. Aries is the cardinal or initial aspect of Fire, Leo is the fixed (kerubic) or firmly defined aspect of Fire, and Sagittarius is the mutable and most easily influenced aspect of Fire.

The four fixed (kerubic) signs of the zodiac are: Aquarius (Air), Scorpio (Water), Taurus (Earth), and Leo (Fire). The classic symbols of the fixed signs (the angel of Aquarius, the eagle of Scorpio, the bull of Taurus, and the lion of Leo) are called the kerubic emblems and appear often in Christian iconography.

99 Casaubon, *A True & Faithful Relation*, 179.

100 Ibid.

101 Superficial, though not essential, transmutation.

102 Casaubon, *A True & Faithful Relation*, 183.

103 Ibid., 188.

104 Casaubon, *A True & Faithful Relation*, 196.

105 Ibid.

106 Ilemese is one of Sons of Sons of Light from the Sigillium Dei Aemeth. See chapter ten.

107 Casaubon, *A True & Faithful Relation*, 209.

108 Ibid., 209.

109 For the moment I will forego a discussion of the small cards of each suit. See appendix IV.

110 I don't fully understand why, but it is a consistent characteristic of Enochian magick to organize the four elements in this order: Air, Water, Earth, and Fire.

111 Charley D. and Milo, *Charley D. and Milo*, Epic Records, 1970.

112 The more the magician practices reciting the calls, the more sensitive he or she becomes to the shifts of consciousness each one produces.

113 Theoretically, each of the 156 lettered squares of an Elemental Tablet is an angel who can be contacted by continuing the hierarchical descent into the subangle. If you care to plunge this deeply into elemental work-ings, you are free to do so by discovering a further hierarchy of names and letters that seems most logical to you.

114 Donald Laycock, *The Complete Enochian Dictionary: A Dictionary of the Angelic Language As Revealed to Dr. John Dee and Edward Kelley* (York Beach, ME: Weiser Books, 1994).

115 DuQuette, *The Chicken Qabalah of Rabbi Lamed Ben Clifford*, 17.

116 The thirtieth Aire contains four parts.

117 Aleister Crowley, *The Vision & the Voice, With Commentary and Other Papers* (York Beach, ME: Weiser Books, 1998), 45.

118 Crowley, *The Vision & the Voice*, 8.

119 New edition of "The Physical Location of the Ninety-one Parts of the Earth Named by Man, as Detailed in the *Liber Scientiae Auxilii et Victoriae Terrestris* of John Dee," published in *Elizabethan Magic*, ed. Robert Turner (Shaftesbury, Dorset, UK: Element Books, 1989). 162.

120 Henry Cornelius Agrippa, *Occult Philosophy*, 1533.

121 Meric Casaubon. *A True & Faithful Relation of What passed for many Yeers Between Dr. John Dee and some Spirits*, London, 1659, p.153; and pp.153–159 for all quotations following.

122 Dee, like most of his contemporaries, believed the island of Friseland to exist. It was, in fact, a duplication of Iceland on an early map, an error which was repeated. When its coast was supposedly skirted, this was actually the coast of Cape Farewell, Southern Greenland. Note also that today Germania (Part 29) incorporates Poland. In Dee's time Poland was located further eastward and would have formed part of Sarmatia or Russia (Part 46).

123 The following is taken from chapter 20 of my book *My Life with the Spirits: The Adventures of a Modern Magician* (York Beach, ME: Weiser Books, 1999), 138–141.

124 Laycock, *The Complete Enochian Dictionary* (see footnote 115).

Bibliography

Casaubon, Meric, ed. *A True & Faithful Relation of What Passed for Many Yeers Between Dr. John Dee . . . and Some Spirits*. London: Maxwell, 1659. Reprinted with additional material by Clay Holden and Lon Milo DuQuette. New York: Magickal Childe Publications, 1992.

Clulee, Nicholas H. *John Dee's Natural Philosophy: Between Science and Religion*. Oxfordshire, UK: Routledge, 1988.

Crowley, Aleister. *Liber Chanokh*. St. Paul, MN: Llewellyn Publications, 1974; Scottsdale, AZ: New Falcon, 1992; York Beach, ME: Weiser Books, 2008. *Liber Chanokh* is a work by Crowley originally published in his periodical, *The Equinox* in 1912.

————. *Magick, Liber ABA: Book Four*. ed. Hymenaeus Beta, 2nd rev. ed. York Beach, ME: Weiser Books, 1997.

————. *The Symbolic Representation of the Universe: Being Derived by Doctor John Dee Through the Scrying of Sir Edward Kelly*. Found in *Gems from the Equinox*. Aleister Crowley and Israel Regardie, eds. St. Paul, MN: Llewellyn Publications, 1974; Scottsdale, AZ: New Falcon, 1992; San Francisco: Weiser Books, 2008.

Crowley, Aleister, Lon Milo DuQuette, and Christopher Hyatt. *The Enochian World of Aleister Crowley: Enochian Sex Magick*. Scottsdale, AZ: New Falcon, 1991.

DuQuette, Lon Milo. *Tarot of Ceremonial Magick*. York Beach, ME: Weiser Books, 1995.

French, Peter. *John Dee: The World of an Elizabethan Magus*. New York: Dorset Press, 1989.

James, Geoffrey. *The Enochian Magick of Dr John Dee: The Most Powerful System of Magick in Its Original, Unexpurgated Form*. St. Paul, MN: Llewellyn Worldwide, 1994.

Laycock, Donald C. *The Complete Enochian Dictionary: A Dictionary of the Angelic Language as Revealed to Dr. John Dee and Edward Kelley*. York Beach, ME: Weiser Books, 1994.

McLean, Adam. *A Treatise on Angel Magic*. York Beach, ME: Phanes Press, 1990.

Peterson, Joseph. *John Dee's Five Books of Mystery*. San Francisco: Red Wheel/Weiser, 2003.

Reeds, Jim. "John Dee and the Magic Tables in the Book of Soyga." In *John Dee: Interdisciplinary Essays in English Renaissance Thought Series*. Vol. 193 of *International Archives of the History of Ideas/Archives internationales d'histoire des idées*. Edited by Stephen Clucas. New York and Heidelberg: Springer, 2006.

Regardie, Israel. *Complete Golden Dawn System of Magick*. Scottsdale, AZ: New Falcon, 1995.

————. *The Golden Dawn: The Original Account of the Teachings, Rites & Ceremonies of the Hermetic Order*. St. Paul, MN: Llewellyn, 1969.

Suster, Gerald. *John Dee: Essential Readings*. Rochester, VT: Inner Traditions, 1987.

Tyson, Donald. *Enochian Magic for Beginners*. St. Paul, MN: Llewellyn Worldwide, 1997.

Zalewski, Pat. *Golden Dawn Enochian Magic*. St. Paul, MN: Llewellyn Worldwide, 1990.

And the electronic files of Sloane manuscripts numbers 2599, 3188, 3189, 3191, 3677, 3678, 3821, and 3824 and Cotton Appendix XLVI (including most of the source material for Casaubon's *A True & Faithful Relation*). These manuscript collections are housed in the British Library, London, and the Bodleian and Ashmolean collections are at Oxford.

Index

About the Author

Lon Milo DuQuette is a bestselling author and lecturer, whose books on Magick, Tarot, and the Western Mystery Traditions have been translated into ten languages. He is currently U.S. Deputy Grand Master of Ordo Templi Orentis and is on the faculty of the Omega Institute in Reinbeck, NY and the Maybe Logic Academy. Among his many books, he is the author of *My Life with the Spirits* (Weiser 1999), *Understanding Aleister Crowley's Thoth Tarot* (Weiser 2003), *The Magick of Aleister Crowley* (Weiser 2003), and *Tarot of Ceremonial Magick* (Weiser 1995). He lives in Costa Mesa, CA with his wife Constance. Visit him on the Web at: *www.lonmiloduquette.com*.